ON HINDUISM

ON HINDUISM
Reviews and Reflections

RAM SWARUP

FOREWORD BY
DAVID FRAWLEY
(Vamadeva Shastri)

VOICE OF INDIA
New Delhi

First published 2000
First reprint 2009
Reprint, 2024

ISBN 81-85990-62-X

Published by Voice of India, 2/18, Ansari Road, New Delhi–110 002.
Printed at Replika Press Pvt. Ltd.

Contents

	Foreword by David Frawley	vii
1.	Sanatana Dharma: *Anusmriti* and *Anudhyāyana*	1
2.	Cultural Self-Alienation Among the Hindus	37
3.	Buddhism vis-a-vis Hinduism	60
4.	Indo-European Encounter: An Indian Perspective	92
5.	Development in Huxley's Thought: Hindu-Buddhist Influences	124
6.	The Hindu View of Education	166
7.	Educational System During Pre-British Days	177
8.	India and Greece	196
	Index	207

Foreword

The Reawakening of Dharmic and Native Traditions

There are two major groups of religions in the world today. First are the conversion-based religions of Christianity and Islam. Each holds that it is the only true faith for humanity and solely represents God's plan and God's will. Both reflect an exclusivist ethos of One God, a single holy book, a final prophet or single savior, an historical revelation, salvation from sin, and heaven or hell as the ultimate resting-place for the soul. Christianity and Islam became the dominant religions of the Western world over the centuries through a long process of struggle and warfare, as they displaced, often cruelly, all other religions that came in their path. Both conversion-based religions are based on an older Jewish monotheistic tradition that was critical of the diverse Pagan cults around it. They turned this rejection, which for the Jews was meant to preserve their own culture, into an article of faith and a need to eradicate all other beliefs.

The second major group of world religions are the dharmic or meditation traditions of India — Hinduism, Buddhism and Jainism — of which Hinduism is the oldest and largest. Chinese Taoism and Japanese Shinto have an affinity with these and can easily be placed among them. Dharmic traditions reflect a spiritual ethos of natural law (dharma), karma and rebirth, yogic practices, and a pursuit of direct experience of truth and self-realization through meditation. They became the dominant religions of the Eastern world, not through any process of intimidation, but by growing up organically with the cultures of these lands. Dharmic traditions define the Divine more as an impersonal and timeless consciousness than the personal Creator of Biblical traditions. They are tolerant and pluralistic and can accept other spiritual paths as valid and have no need to displace them.

In addition there are various indigenous traditions and native creeds like those of the pre-Christian Europeans, the ancient Egyptians and Babylonians, and the many Native American, Asian, Pacific Islander and African groups. These appear more like the dharmic traditions of the East than the conversion-based religions of the West, which disdainfully call them pagans, heathens, kafirs or barbarians — the same terms that they use to characterize dharmic approaches. Like dharmic traditions these native ways have an experiential spirituality, ritual worship, use of images, multiplistic ideas of divinity, connection to the Earth and nature, and the recognition of a Great Spirit, though perhaps not as clearly defined as in dharmic paths.

As the world has now moved out of colonial domination by monotheistic creeds, a new respect for Eastern dharmic traditions is arising everywhere. The impersonal consciousness of Indic traditions has much more in common with the universe as perceived by modern science than does the jealous God of the Bible and the Koran. Karma and rebirth make more sense to people than do heaven and hell for explaining the fruit of our actions. Yoga and meditation done on a personal level have become more meaningful spiritual activities than attending churches or getting involved in missionary efforts. Overall, a new era is dawning in which organized religion and institutionalized belief — the characteristics of conversion-based creeds — is being set aside in favor of diverse spiritual and cultural approaches that characterize the paths of dharma.

As part of this process, a new awakening is happening in native traditions from a Celtic revival in Europe to a resurgence in the native religions of Africa. Even Anglo-Americans are looking to the Native American religion and its sweat lodges and vision quests — which their forefathers denigrated as the base superstitions of the Red Man — for a connection to life and nature that Christianity has failed to bring them. Many people see the need for religion to be connected to the land, to a people and to a culture, that is not a mere belief but a way of life, emphasizing spiritual practice. Slowly but inevitably, Eastern dharmic traditions and native traditions are finding a common cause and creating a new alliance to this end.

At the same time, there is an awakening among non-Western peoples to their oppression not only by colonial armies but also by the missionary cults that blessed their aggression. They are now recognizing how their own more spiritual native traditions were denigrated and destroyed by less tolerant beliefs employing violence and deception to further their conversion aims. Conversion-based creeds are being revealed as unethical and inhumane, dividing up humanity into the believers and the non-believers and allowing the believers to oppress the non-believers with a vengeance justified from on high. The righteous zeal of the missionaries is being unveiled as a form of bigotry and prejudice, not a means of salvation.

This awakening has led to some apologies by Christians for their excesses, particularly for their history of racism and enslavement of the Blacks. However, so far it has not led to any Christian rejection of its exclusive claim to salvation or an honoring of such native religions as the Black Africans as valid in their own right.

Dharmic traditions are also beginning to speak out against the ongoing missionary aggression against them, though missionary beliefs have done little to respond to their legitimate questions. Hindus are beginning to face their history in which their temples were destroyed, their libraries burned and their priests killed by Islamic votaries of the One God. They are uncovering the bloody history of the Portuguese Inquisition in India that employed torture to bring Christianity to the Hindus. They are recognizing the intolerance behind the continuing need of Christians and Muslims to convert them. Hindus and Buddhists are uniting and trying to create a common front against the missionary efforts that continue blindly today.

The Importance of Hindu Dharma

Hinduism remains the largest of these dharmic and native religions and the most representative of pluralistic and non-conversion-based beliefs. Therefore, a study of it is essential for understanding the spiritual urges of humanity, for discovering the religion of the future as well as the past as the hold of monotheism over the minds of people gradually fades.

Hinduism has given rise to profound philosophies like Vedanta that project a Supreme Self (Atman) and Absolute (Brahman) of Being-Consciousness-Bliss (*Sacchidānanda*) behind the magical universe in which we live. It has spiritual and meditational practices like the many types of yoga (*jñāna*, *bhakti*, *karma* and *rāja*), which show systematically how to develop a higher consciousness from a non-dogmatic approach.

Yoga and Vedanta are now popular and respected all over the world. Many Hindu gurus travel the globe and have disciples in all countries. Books and classes on Yoga and meditation from an Eastern perspective are available everywhere. Sanskrit terms like guru, mantra and shakti have entered into common parlance even in the Western media. Yet there is still much confusion about what Hinduism really is. People approach Hinduism more through a particular guru or sect and often fail to recognize, much less understand the greater tradition behind it.

Hinduism views religion as a way of Self-realization and God-realization. It sees religion as a science or way of knowledge, *vidyā*, to discover eternal truth. It can accept modern science into its worldview that has always acknowledged the value of such disciplines as mathematics, astronomy and medicine for understanding the external world. Hinduism does not have the religion/science dichotomy such as characterizes Biblical beliefs. It is a tradition of knowledge, not faith that helps us uncover the truth of ourselves and of the unbounded universe in which we live, which are both pervaded by a common spirit.

Hinduism is also a culture that contains art, music, dance and literature. It sees the universe as a manifestation of Divine bliss/love energy (*ānanda*) and creation as a play of *rasas* or moods of Divine delight. It does not separate art and imagery from the spiritual life, as Biblical traditions tend to so violently to do. Though Hinduism has a clear set of social principles as revealed in its many Dharma-Shastras it treats these only as general guidelines to be adjusted on an individual basis and attuned to the needs of every age. It is not tied to any system of religious law, like the Sharia of Islam, and can easily adapt itself to different social orders and the demands of new ways of living.

Hinduism has perhaps the largest and most ancient literature of all religions with its many Vedas, Upanishads, Puranas, Tantras and Yoga Shastras. Its literature defies any stereotype and has an encyclopedic view of culture and the universe that is detailed and inclusive of all nature and of the occult worlds as well. Yet most of this literature is unstudied and misunderstood, particularly in academic institutions of the West which, dominated by an outer looking intellect, have failed to really come face to face with the enlightened mind of the East.

Hinduism is like life. Hinduism is the very religion of life and accepts all life into itself. It works through the spirit of life, not through some sterile, artificial or purist creed. Hinduism is a religion of nature and the Earth, finding holy places in every mountain, stream, valley or shore. Its roots are organic. It arises out of the soul and out of the land, like other Pagan and native traditions. It is universal but encourages local variations, being able to embrace native cultures and customs without denigrating or subverting them.

Hinduism is not a proselytizing cult. It sees no need for all people to have the same religious label any more than it regards it necessary for all people to eat the same food or wear the same clothes. For it religion is an internal practice of self-development, not an external battle to conquer the world. It holds that the world and all creatures are inherently saved or one with God. All that is necessary is to dispel the ignorance that prevents us from seeing this inherent divinity and leading a truly divine life.

Hinduism has endured throughout the centuries, as other countries, cultures and religions have come and gone. It has withstood the onslaughts of Islam, Christianity and Communism, which other great countries of Asia fell to. It has preserved many of the oldest and highest spiritual urges of humanity. It invents itself anew in every generation, looking to modern teachers and gurus over old books and set rules.

Distortions of Hinduism

Unfortunately, Hinduism is without doubt the most denigrated and misunderstood of the major world religions, if it is recognized as a world religion at all. It is common to look down on Hinduism as primitive and those who call themselves Hindus as backward or obsolete. Instead of looking at Hinduism in terms of its profound philosophies and deep mysticism, it is associated with idolatry, caste and various social evils, as if there were nothing more to it.

Those used to more monotone religions claim that Hinduism with its organic pluralism is not a religion at all, but only a group of cults or sects with little in common. Such people are so jaded by the monotheistic code they cannot appreciate the broader and deeper spiritual urges that are as varied as the types of creatures on this planet. Many of them complain about the primitive idol worship in Hindu religion.

After all, Hindu gods like Hanuman and Ganesha have animal faces and forms. Such people are offended to see an animal face on God, though they eat animals, and their God with his wrath often has traits that would be regarded as tyrannical or egoistic in a person.

Others complain that Hinduism, particularly Vedanta, with its concept of the Absolute and liberation from the cycle of rebirth lacks compassion and a sense of caring for the world. They compare this with the compassion of the monotheistic concept that wants to save everyone and is concerned about the poor and the sick (though conversion-based religions have commonly destroyed peoples and cultures, and only offer help where there is a chance of conversion). That seeing the Self in all beings and all beings in Self, which is the Vedantic vision, is the very essence of Divine love and compassion escapes them.

This denigration has occurred largely because Hinduism has borne the brunt of missionary propaganda, perhaps unparalleled by any religion in the world. After all, Hinduism is a religion that includes an extensive set of images or idol worship, such as the Biblical prophets, the Christian fathers and the Muslim prophets criticized not only as unholy, but often as positively evil. Everything associated with Paganism in the Biblical mind has a clear manifestation in Hinduism with its many gods and goddesses, its gurus and godmen, its understanding of the occult and its practice of yoga.

Hinduism represents the survival of the very type of traditions that the conversion-based religions have tried so hard and so long to stamp out. While the Egyptians, Babylonians, Greeks and Pagan Arabs have all long fallen to the missionary assault, Hinduism has survived remarkably the onslaughts of both missionary religions for a period of over a thousand years! And to their dismay in the modern world, Hindu teachings are spreading again and getting revitalized.

Hinduism has also been under siege by Marxist thinkers, who have been strong in India for some decades, because it represents a spiritual tradition that obstructs their road to power and challenges their materialistic worldview. The other dharmic traditions of Asia have been under the same type of attack. Buddhism in China was marginalized by the Communists that have also nearly succeeded in destroying Tibetan Buddhism in its own homeland. While Indian Marxists have not wielded such power, they have worked hard to harm Hinduism through their influence in the media and academic realms in India, which has been significant.

Indian Marxists have even formed a common front with the missionaries to eliminate Hinduism, their common enemy. Now that Marxism is dying in the world, Indian Marxists are becoming more strident, trying to hold on to their last bastions of power in the intellectual realm, which only makes their anti-Hindu propaganda more shrill and more irrational.

While dharmic traditions are gaining respect in the West, the assault on them by conversion-based creeds is increasing in Asia. Christian missionaries, for example, are very active in Mongolia, where the Tibetan religion has one of its last strongholds. Islamic fundamentalism, fueled by petrodollars, continues its assaults, particularly in India where they can use the Islamic minority as a means of expanding their influence, building mosques and encouraging separatism.

Christian missionary groups, leaning on the great wealth of the West, have targeted India and China for conversion with massive millennial evangelization plans using the weapons of the modern media. They have made headway in smaller Asian countries like South Korea, which has been largely Christianized, and hope to do the same in larger Asian countries.

The Catholic Church has spread its tentacles into India, hoping like what it did to ancient Greece to subvert the profound philosophies of the region into tools of the Christian faith, reformulating the Hindu Upanishads like the Aristotelian philosophy of the Greeks into a form of Christian theology. Its priests are dressing up like swamis, its rituals and symbols are getting Hinduized, not out of respect for Hindu traditions, but to aid in conversion in the post-colonial world by convincing Hindus that Christianity is not really an alien or foreign cult.

Evangelical Christians in America like the Southern Baptists, the largest Protestant sect in America, are targeting India with their cruder but more forceful and vitalistic creed, preaching of hell, fire, damnation and the impending end of the world. Part of this is a counterattack against the influence of Hinduism in America, which Christian fundamentalists see behind the New Age movement that so disturbs them. The New Age movement, combining alternative medicine, eastern spirituality and new life-styles, has now become a major cultural force, influencing a significant percentage of the American population and challenging the intolerant Christian mind in its own backyard. One Christian fundamentalist in America noted that there are only two religions in the world, Christianity which excludes everything and Hinduism which includes everything. Clearly they see Hinduism as the perennial Pagan enemy of the children of God.

In America, Evangelical Christians like to bring Hindu women who have converted to Christianity onto their programs to denigrate firsthand the "terrible" religion that they came from. Such groups have gone so far as to publicly describe Hinduism as a religion of the Devil, Satan, darkness, superstition and evil. They associate all of India's social problems with its polytheistic religion of idolatry that is an affront to God and Jesus. While one may ridicule these groups — which even in America are perceived as backward — one should not underestimate their resolve in achieving their aim, whatever disruption it requires. It is amazing that such groups still think of themselves as enlightened and don't see how much out of touch they really are with the modern world and any global perspective. Unfortunately, though a minority in America, they can still marshal extensive resources for their overseas missionary activity, through the great wealth of America today that they hold part of.

Such conversion efforts are bound to fail in the long run but they can do much damage along the way. Asia is still recovering from Marxism and colonialism, which makes the poor and uneducated, who are basically looking for social upliftment, vulnerable to missionary work which promises that as a by-product of conversion. Asians tend to uncritically embrace the West for its economic and technical advancement, and think that Western religions, which are really fossils from the Middle Ages, are necessary parts of modernization. They don't realize that Evangelical Christianity with its rejection of the theory of evolution, which they want removed from the schools, represents one of the most regressive trends in American culture and is largely a religion of the farm belt ridiculed in the universities.

Even Catholicism has become primarily a religion of backward countries of South and Central America and is only nominally followed in North America and Europe. The most devout Catholics in the world are the poor and uneducated Catholics of the Third World, not the scientific or intellectual elite of the West that is largely agnostic. Christianity is not a politically or educationally advanced religion of the modern West but the shadow of the very forces that have for centuries resisted modernization. Asian countries that accept Catholicism are more likely to end up poor like the Philippines, the main Catholic country in Asia, not developed like Japan which did not accept Christianity as a part of modernization but relied on its own warrior spirit instead.

Unfortunately, many of the Western followers and well-wishers to dharmic traditions do not understand the degree and danger of this new missionary assault in Asia and are doing little to deal with it. This is because Christianity has become so marginalized in the West that they don't see its danger elsewhere in the world. Their interest in dharmic traditions is more personal and often lacks any sense of social responsibility. People in post-independence India are also failing to notice the missionary threat because its effort is aimed mainly at poor and rural Hindus that they really don't want to take care of anyway. It is this scenario that makes the work of Ram Swarup so important. He, perhaps most poignantly and directly of modern thinkers, has understood the current world situation, the dangers to Hinduism, the value of Hinduism for the future of humanity, and a practical way to both overcome the dangers and promote the opportunities for the good of all.

Ram Swarup

Many people today think that Hinduism is not an intellectual religion and does not have, in spite of its many great spiritual philosophies, any real modern intelligentsia to represent it. They look on Hinduism as a religion of an uncritical, if not naïve faith in various gods and gurus. Or if Hinduism has an intellectual side they see it only as a transcendent Vedanta that offers no real critique of other religions, no plan for society, and does not make itself relevant to current problems or pressing human needs.

Ram Swarup shows that this is not at all true. He reveals the Hindu mind in action as a creative and spiritual force to change both the individual and the society for both the inner and the outer good. He outlines a Hindu approach to the problems of the world that offers deep and lasting solutions that go beyond the limitations of Western religions or Western science, following the development of consciousness as the real thrust in civilization.

One of the problems with Hindu thinkers is that they seldom express themselves well in an English idiom, which has now become the global language of communication. However insightful their ideas their impact, therefore, becomes limited in the global forum. Ram Swarup is a thinker who can use the English language with forcefulness, wit, logic and irony that can serve as a powerful conduit for Hindu ideas into the collective psyche and reach the English-trained audience all over the world. He can communicate ideas in English that have traditionally required the precision of Sanskrit to get across.

The global Hindu magazine *Hinduism Today* has described Ram Swarup as "perhaps Hinduism's most cogent analyst." The Prime Minister of India, Atal Behari Vajpayee, spoke of him as "a representative of India's rishi tradition in the modern age." Ram Swarup had a unique ability to go to the essence of a problem and, with profound simplicity, form a clear understanding of it and practical line of response to correct it. He was a Hindu thinker of the first order, comparable to the many great Hindu thinkers of previous centuries. He approaches all issues not from a merely intellectual or academic side, but from a deeper spiritual and yogic vision that characterizes the Hindu mind. He sees Hinduism as a living tradition and is in contact with its most vital currents, not only in the outer world but also and more importantly in the cosmic mind.

Ram Swarup has thoroughly and critically studied the religions of the world, and Marxism, the secular or materialistic religion, as well. He can speak of these systems with an in-depth knowledge and ability to quote and mirror what they really think, which even their dedicated followers seldom possess. He was perhaps India's foremost critic of Marxism and exposed its danger to the country decades ago when it was fashionable for every intellectual and every journalist to uncritically follow it. He preserved Hindu intellectualism during its Marxist Dark Age and has initiated its revival in the post-Marxist era.

I was fortunate enough to contact Ram Swarup personally and known him over the last ten years. He was a helpful guide and provided a steady inspiration to my own work relative to India, Hinduism, and the Vedas. Ram Swarup was a notably cheerful and loving person, with a great respect for each individual. He was considerate and soft spoken and a good listener. He never tried to aggrandize himself, build a following around him, gain donations or create institutions. He seemed unaware of material needs and compulsions. Though not officially a sadhu he lived like one. There was nothing extreme, abrasive or fanatical about his life or his expression. Though he was aware of critical global problems he also realized the transience of all human affairs. Though he spoke eloquently he realized that the real truth is beyond words. Though he made sure to take a stand on important issues, he also realized that whatever he did was small in the greater scheme of things and just a vehicle for the workings of a higher power. He did not make too much of himself for all that he knew.

The Present Book

Ram Swarup has left an important legacy of many works on a broad range of topics including religion and philosophy, yoga, mysticism and social issues. His *Hindu View of Christianity and Islam* is a classic in the field of comparative religion, for the first time perhaps introducing a yogic view of altered states of consciousness to understand the powerful and sometimes dangerous workings of religious experience. The present volume consists of various essays on Hinduism, including several important essays never published before. It covers a wide spectrum of ideas. The overall theme is Hinduism and its articulation in the present world context. It begins with a new model of Hinduism, discusses how and why Hindus view themselves in a distorted light, and then focuses on the relationship between Hindu and Western thought.

Hinduism has many teachings on dharma that explain right living on all levels, personally and collectively, socially and spiritually. It has different *darśanas* or philosophies that allow us to understand ourselves and the universe at the deepest level of the mind. It has many manuals of *sādhanā* or spiritual practice that deal with all religious practices from prayer and ritual, to sophisticated meditation techniques. But it lacks a systematic and overall presentation of its essence to the modern mind. We might say that approaching Hinduism is a question of missing the forest because of the trees. Ram Swarup, probably better than any other modern thinker, puts Hinduism into its proper perspective so that we can understand its foundation and its motivation.

On Hinduism shows how to revive and revitalize the tradition in a practical way and to present it in the modern forum with clarity, conviction and universality. It is a manual of Hindu resurgence, not simply a commentary or set of personal observations. The first chapter on "Sanatana Dharma: *Anusmriti* and *Anudhyāyana*" is a masterpiece in this regard. It sets forth a new explication of Hinduism and its principles that is perhaps the best primer on the religion — concise, succinct and deep. While many great spiritual teachers have come out of India in modern times, perhaps no one has formulated the tradition in such a relevant manner.

An important issue is how different dharmic traditions should relate, given the common missionary assault upon them, particularly Hinduism and Buddhism, the two largest such traditions and the main forces of enlightenment in the world. Unfortunately, many Hindus want to turn Buddhism into another form of Hinduism without really looking into its unique tenets and practices. Ram Swarup's study of Hinduism and Buddhism is one of the best of its kind, pointing out both the similarities and differences between these kindred paths and their need for a common agenda in the modern scene. He shows how both can be united in a common dharma, in which Buddhists can return to a broader Hindu ethos once they understand Hinduism in a more genuine way. The missionary distortions of Hinduism have even prevented other dharmic traditions from understanding it. Ram Swarup dispels these illusions in this chapter. He also helps Hindus understand how Buddhism works and how Buddhist ideas can be relevant to them.

A similar important issue is the relationship between India, the fountainhead of Asian culture, and Greece, the fountainhead of European culture. We tend to think of both types of culture as different and as constituting a dichotomy of East versus West, orient versus occident. But if we really look at ancient Greeks and Hindus we discover much in common. We find similar idealistic philosophies from Parmenides, Plato and Plotinus to the Upanishads and the Gita. We find similar elaborate mythologies with the many Greek and Hindu Gods, Goddesses and heroes. We find similar religions of temple worship, the use of rituals and images, and honoring sacred places in nature. Even the names of deities like Zeus and Dyaus are cognate. A yogic type mysticism and belief in rebirth can be found in the Greek mystery religions as well. We find a similar concern for science and mathematics and early experiments with republics in ancient India as well as in Greece. Ram Swarup draws such a connection to enable us to reintegrate these two great sources of world culture.

The dialogue between India and Europe is another vital concern. Over the last century it has been more of a non-dialogue with the West ignoring India and Indian thinkers slavishly imitating the West. The eighteenth and nineteenth centuries in Europe saw either a romanticism about India that was almost naïve, or a colonialism that was generally ugly. The same trends continue today in a New Age romanticism of India that is seldom deep, and a disdain for India in the intellectual establishments of the West that is at best condescending.

So far there has been little mature interaction between the thinkers of India and Europe, either intellectually or spiritually, owing to deficiencies in both camps. Ram Swarup addresses this issue with great acumen, using the work of Wilhelm Halbfass, one of the few Westerners with real insight into India, as the basis for discussion. Much of the spiritual potential of the West lies hidden in its older and ongoing connections to India. Ram Swarup opens the ground for such a mature interaction. He follows this with an important essay on Aldous Huxley, one of the few Western thinkers who had a real understanding of India and its spiritual systems. Huxley provides a good foundation to launch such an East-West dialogue that unfortunately was not followed by other Western thinkers. Ram Swarup sets this process in motion again.

Two of his essays address the issue of education. Modern India has followed a British model of education that it has modified in a Marxist direction. That such an approach would fail to awaken the country or bring about a real understanding of its older traditions is hardly surprising. He shows how the current illiteracy in India is not the product of traditional educational systems — which the British dismantled in the nineteenth century — but of the damage to that traditional system which began with them. Old India had a high rate of literacy, particularly because of its educational system, its Sanskrit and its *gurukulams*. Ram Swarup also shows how Hindu models of education remain relevant in the modern world, where we need to reintroduce spiritual values and models of consciousness to prevent the moral decay and decline in intelligence that we see rapidly increasing in the affluent West. America today imports a large number of its scientists from Asia, including India, because its own system of education, falling under the lassitude of a culture of self-indulgence, is failing to produce them.

The Challenge of Ram Swarup's Work

Ram Swarup's work has already influenced a number of important groups in the world, from the Swamis of *Hinduism Today* to some of Pagan Europe's most profound thinkers. His influence has reached far, not by the power of big organizations, a sophisticated media, or by any proselytizing effort but by the sheer force and inevitability of his ideas. The question is how will people respond to the challenges set forth by his present volume?

How will the missionary beliefs respond to his critique of their motivations as springing from an undeveloped spiritual consciousness? Clearly an enlightened yogi does not need to convert the world to his belief, nor will he formulate the Divine as an exclusive or jealous God with a chosen people and day of judgement. Probably such groups will ignore or condemn Ram Swarup as another unsaved and unregenerate Pagan.

How will Western intellectuals respond to an intellectually resurgent Hinduism such as Ram Swarup indicates? They may also want to ignore or belittle it, as the intellect tends to have its own arrogance and the West has tried to hold a monopoly in the global thought field for some time. But they will soon have to hear its voice and deal with its logic. They will have to accept a deeper spiritual truth beyond their personal, rationalistic or aesthetic approaches. They will have to recognize a higher state of the *buddhi* or intellect that reflects dharmic truth, rather than mere human theories. While many Western intellectuals are examining Buddhism in a more sensitive light, they cannot leave its sister religion of Hinduism far behind, though it has been more tainted with missionary and Marxist stereotypes so that it is harder for them to appreciate than Buddhism's more rational and humanistic creed.

Above all, how will modern Hindus, who are often lazy thinkers and lack a global or historical perspective, respond? They passively accept Marxist, missionary or colonial denigrations of their traditions, and may be surprised with Ram Swarup's deeper and more thorough presentation. They may feel initially disturbed to be woken up from their slumber, even though it has only given them bad dreams. But Ram Swarup's ideas can revitalize them not in a narrow or fundamentalist way but to real creative action. His writings can serve as a lightning flash to break the veil of ignorance and show a way beyond the darkness of intellectual servitude and sloth that is perhaps even more weakening to the soul than political bondage.

The future of India hangs in the balance of the intellectual and spiritual challenge posed by Ram Swarup's work, with important ramifications for the entire world. While most groups may not want to listen to this voice, they can no longer pretend that it does not exist.

Hindus need their own voice and their own intellectual self-determination. They should no longer accept their definition by less evolved missionary religions or by unspiritual materialistic creeds. It is time for them to question Eurocentric interpretations of their history and culture that are based on colonial prejudices or cultural arrogance. In this regard Ram Swarup is a great pioneer pointing out the way out of this wilderness.

With Ram Swarup the Hindu voice has spoken clearly to the modern world. The voice of the oldest and largest spiritual tradition of India or the world, and its ancient rishi heritage, has sounded its clarion call to the minds and hearts of people today. It has taken the challenge of the modern and scientific age to present a truth that is global and universal. It has used reason but also brought in a higher yogic perception — a truth of consciousness and self-realization not merely material prosperity or monotheistic salvation as the ultimate goal of life.

Many Hindu modern teachers have been too accommodating in their definition of Hinduism and left it devoid of any real critical voice. They say that you can find God by following faithfully whatever religion you like —whether Hinduism, Christianity, Islam or Buddhism — as if the differences of religious doctrine and practice had no meaning at all. They give the impression that anything called a religion should be accepted and the results can only be good. They have left behind the great Hindu tradition of debate and turned the religion into a blind acceptance of all creeds, including a whitewash of their history, however bloody, and however anti-Hindu.

Part of this has been a sincere effort to be tolerant of other faiths, and we should be open to what other people say and honor different creeds. But perhaps a greater part of it has arisen from a lack of self-confidence. Those under foreign rule tend to praise or flatter their rulers out of fear. Those who have been told that their religion is that of heathens or kafirs first respond by saying that their religion is equal to any other, before taking a critical view of the religions so rudely denigrating them.

Ram Swarup questions such politically comfortable statements of religious accommodation and appeasement. Hinduism is a pluralistic path that accepts One truth and many ways to it. It holds that all individuals should be free to find the truth according to their nature and temperament. However, like all things in human life religion is a varied phenomenon and contains both the good and the bad, the high and the low. That there are many paths does not mean that all paths can only be good or that all must lead to the highest goal. A religion that does not recognize liberation as the goal of life, that does not have a path to Self-realization, that has no living yoga tradition cannot take you to that Divine Self whatever you may do with it. This is not a statement of intolerance or religious bigotry but the plain and honest truth that cannot be ignored. You can't climb a mountain by digging a hole into the ground, however well you can dig!

Hinduism is a religion with a strong sense of dharma. It cannot accept anything or everything that calls itself a religion as true. From its point of view religion should be a *moksha*-dharma and a yoga-*pantha*, a teaching that gives inner liberation and projects a path to achieve it. Its purpose is not to make one subservient to a particular God, prophet, guru, savior, holy book, church or institution but to free us from all external bondage. Religions which do this are not true *moksha*-dharmas or spiritual paths but just additional forms of conditioning that keep us trapped in the worldly mind and its egoistic motives.

Conclusion

Most people, including Hindus, have never looked into what Hinduism really is. If you ask people about Hinduism, most Westerners will have quick answers about its polytheism, idolatry or castism, but if you ask them about the Upanishads or the Gita, about Atman and Brahman, they will have little to say. Most Western textbooks define Hinduism as a conglomeration, an ethnic religion, a castist creed, or a worship of many gods. Such people need to read Ram Swarup to really know what they are dealing with in what is called Hinduism. He will not let them get away with such a sloppy and superficial approach to what is perhaps humanity's oldest heritage of spiritual knowledge.

Hinduism, perhaps more so than any religion, has always formulated itself as a Sanatana Dharma, an eternal and universal tradition of truth and natural law. While its formulation may be imperfect and worn by time, it is hardly dead or out of date. It is like a great Banyan tree, with many roots and branches, growing into the air as well as into the earth, accommodating a great variety of creatures and reducible to no pattern or conclusion.

Out of its background in the twentieth century have come such great saints and sages as Ramakrishna, Vivekananda, Sri Aurobindo, Ramana Maharshi, and Anandamayi Ma to mention but a few. These great souls were not conscious of themselves as sectarian Hindus opposed to other religious beliefs but as part of Sanatana Dharma and its great lineages and approaches. Ram Swarup unfolds this Sanatana Dharma with both a panoramic vision and a pinpoint accuracy so that it comes alive to the reader as an internal force of consciousness and light.

For those who really want to understand the heart and soul of Hindu Dharma, the work of Ram Swarup is perhaps the best place to start. His expression is lucid, modern and concise, but firmly rooted in ancient traditions and a yogic understanding. He is aware of the many misconceptions and systematically works to remove them to arrive at the underlying truth that is helpful to all.

For those who want to understand the Hindu religion as a whole, Ram Swarup's work is perhaps the best available guide. He is not speaking in terms of any particular guru or *sampradāya* but about the essence of the entire tradition, which pervades all of its multifarious manifestations. He is going back to an older, perhaps more rigorous but more honest presentation of this greater tradition which is beyond time and person, and which stands fearless in itself, not bowing down to any inferior creeds.

Let us hope that the message of Ram Swarup travels far and wide — that people take the time and care to really listen to what he is saying and contemplate it deeply. College students, particularly, need to hear his views in order to remove the confusion caused by all the misinformation about this venerable religion. Hindu teachers, who often find themselves groping for words to explain their traditions to a modern audience, should ponder over it thoroughly. Non-Hindus as well should look into these writings that explore the essence of all religion and philosophy. Though it may challenge worn patterns of thought, if not stir up deep-seated prejudices, for those who accept his message, it will ennoble their minds and hearts, and sharpen their discrimination to reach a real understanding of our true nature and purpose in life.

May the Divine Mother, whose words are the Vedas and whose global embodiment is India, again smile upon us!

DAVID FRAWLEY
(Vamadeva Shastri)

April 4, 2000
(Chaitra Shukla Pratipad,
beginning of the year Vikrama or Victory)

For those who want to understand the Hindu religion as a whole, Ram Swarup's work is perhaps the best available guide. He is not speaking in terms of any particular path or *sampradāya* but about the essence of the entire tradition, which pervades all of its multifarious manifestations. He is giving basic overall order, perhaps more rigorous but more honest presentation of the greater tradition which is beyond time and person, and which stands fearless in itself, not bowing down to any alien dogmas.

It is hoped that the message of Ram Swarup travels far and wide and that people take the time and care to really listen to what he is saying and contemplate it deeply. College students particularly need to hear his views in order to remove the confusion caused by all the misinformation about this venerable religion. Hindu teachers, who often find themselves groping for words to explain their traditions to a modern audience, should pond over it thoroughly. Non-Hindus as well should look into these insights that explore the essence of all religion and philosophy. Though it may challenge many patterns of thought, if not stir up deep seated prejudices, for those who accept the message, it will enrich their minds and hearts, and sharpen their discrimination to reach a clear understanding of our true nature and purpose in life.

May the Divine Mother, whose words are the Vedas and whose global embodiment is India, again smile upon us!

David Frawley
(Vāmadeva Śāstrī)

April 4, 2000
(Chaitra Śukla Pratipad,
Beginning of the Year Vikrama or Yugādi)

Chapter 1

Sanatana Dharma: *Anusmriti* and *Anudhyāyana*

Repeated and Cherished Recollection and Meditation on Sanatana Dharma

1. I take refuge in the great Sanatana dharma, the mother of many religions.

Spiritual Teachings: *Ātma and Anātma*

2. The ancient sages studied man and for that they started with themselves; they turned their gaze inward and found there a vast internal life. Going still deeper, they discovered, beyond their more external being, another life or principle which takes another language to describe it; they found it self-existent, bodiless, pure, luminous and conscious; they found that it is in some way unborn and undying; that it does not come along with the body nor does it die with it; that it is beyond sorrow and decay; that it shines from within and it knows itself as self-evident. They found that it is their very essence, their true Self; they called it *ātman*, which is pure, immortal, and untouched by evil.

3. They found that this innermost truth of their being is also the truth of all beings, that it is inside as well as outside, that it pervades all; that the *ātman* is also *brahman*, that the immanent divine principle is also the transcendental principle and divine ground of all.

4. By the same token, they saw in man the other side of the coin, the principle of *anātma*. They saw how man gives himself deceptive identities, how he confuses himself with

various physico-mental constructs (*nāma-rūpa*); how there is nothing in him which is abiding, which he can own or call his own; that everything is a concatenation, a link in a chain; that nescience (*avidyā*) and ego reign everywhere; that they have deep roots in man; that they are not only in our attachments and hatreds — in the more *tāmasika* and *rājasika* part of our nature — but they inform our *sāttvika* nature too, our good intentions and high principles, which become worse when they pretend to be better than they are. Think of all the make-believe, ego and even dishonesty of much that goes under the name of our charities, our high-minded ideals, missions and theologies. So, to much the seers had to say that This too is *anātma*, that This too is not I, that This too is not That — the *neti neti* (Not this, Not this) of the Upanishads.

5. The two views, looking at the same thing from two angles, found their eloquent expression in two traditions known as Brahmanic and Shramanic, or, to put it differently, Rishi and Muni traditions. Both studied man in his more internal and metaphysical being and the two views were complementary. The two together gave us a great science of man, a veritable spiritual anthropology, which is different from the anthropology that we know today, the one based on the lower, psycho-physical definition of man.

6. Concentrating on the Ātmic truth, the Vedic seers found that though it resides in all, it is also beyond them all; that its truth is beyond all that a man has seen or heard, beyond his speech and mind, beyond his power to describe, imagine or conceive, and certainly beyond expounding (*avyākrita*), for there could be no simple Yes or No to various queries.

7. They taught that though this truth is beyond number, gender, definitions, descriptions and indications, yet it is a man's most intimate reality. It is the eye of his eyes, and ear of his ears, and in fact he is *It* and *It* is also all this. They taught that this reality is realized in the "cave" of one's heart, and they also described it as *sat*, *chit*, *ānanda*..

8. They taught that though this truth is Unmanifest, the

Nameless and Formless (*nirākāra* and *nirguṇa*), it supports all manifestations, names and forms. They saw in the world a great moral and spiritual order (*rita*), which knows no transgression, which sets up from within forces of self-correction and redress when violated. Sanatana dharma believes that truth triumphs, and that which is true never lacks true being.

9. Sanatana dharma teaches a passage from the unreal to the real, from darkness to light, from death to immortality. It holds that the world is supported by *abhayam*, *ritam*, *yajñam*, austerity.

Gods

10. A deepened spiritual anthropology or rather anthroposophy (*ātma-vāda*) gave a lofty theology (*deva-vāda*). Indeed no great thinking about Gods is possible without deep thinking about man. Religious ideologies which are poor in *ātma-vāda* are also poor in *deva-vāda*. Their gods lack both immanence as well as true transcendence. Sanatana dharma saw Gods within; and the more it saw them within, the more it saw them outside and also beyond; it saw them filling the world, *īśāvāsyam idam*; it also saw that its fullness, *pūrṇam idam*, derives from the fullness of that, *pūrṇam adah*. True spiritual transcendence like true spiritual immanence, both are attributes that properly belong only to Yogic Gods.

11. As it saw in the Self all Godly attributes, it saw in Gods the truth and powers of the Self; indeed, it taught that one who worships a God as other than himself becomes his sacrificial animal, his draught-animal. He is driven and ridden by him.

12. Sanatana dharma worshipped God under many symbols and celebrated each Name with a thousand Names. The Names represented attributes of Gods as well as the attributes of the soul, one representing and echoing the other. It found the loftiness of Gods in the depths of the soul. It celebrated soul's yearning for God — its pangs of separation and its delights of union — in a thousand songs all over India. It

taught love of God who has no form; it also taught that he takes on the form in which he is worshipped; it also made God incarnate on earth for the sake his devotees. [It is a lawful spiritual and psychic process and has little to do with those theologies which arbitrarily proclaim a man of mere historical interest a God or saviour or intercessor.]

13. Sanatana dharma teaches us that true Gods are met when man goes beyond his sensuous mind, beyond his ordinary desires and hankerings; he sees them by himself becoming, in some sense, God-like.

14. There are a thousand places where man could make contact with his deity. Sanatana dharma teaches worship of him in his various pre-eminent manifestations (*vibhūtis*).

15. It also gives us "visible Gods" (*pratyaksha devatā*) to worship. The sky, the Sun, Ganga and Kavery, father, mother and teachers are visible Gods and they are to be regarded as such.

Worship, "Forms" of God

16. Though Nameless, this reality is also the source of all names and attributes. Sanatana dharma teaches worship of him under various names and attributes. He is worshipped as the Path, the Abode, the great Shelter, the Witness, the Foundation, etc.

17. Sanatana dharma teaches that God is without form though he upholds many forms. All forms proclaim him. Sanatana dharma gives us Gods of many spiritual and transcendental forms. He is *tapas-svarūpa*, *satya-svarūpa*, *vijñāna-svarūpa*. He is *vijñāna-ghana* (concentrated consciousness); he is the embodiment of delight (*ānandamaya*); he is *śānta*, *śiva*, *advaita*. Religions which lack interiority and Yoga have only a vague idea of these transcendental forms.

18. In Sanatana dharma, man is conceived in the image of Gods, while some religious ideologies conceive their God in the image of human passions and preferences. No wonder,

such a God has chosen people, preferred spokesmen and habitually indulges in acts of wrath and vengeance.

19. To give human form to a God for purposes of worship presents no great problem. In fact, it may even help spiritually in focussing the mind. But to give him unregenerate human passions and worship him is the real hurdle on the spiritual path. Images on the altar are no problem; but idols in the mind and heart are the great enemies.

20. No wonder that while the followers of this god could not claim better morals than their neighbours, they found their religion best fulfilled in destroying the shrines of the latter.

21. Not only under many symbols, but the deity is also worshiped in many ways, Sanatana dharma tells us. There are many paths that lead to him, and one's path is often defined by one's own special endowment, his *svadharma*, his nature *svabhāva*, his aptitude (*charit*). He is worshipped through Yoga, through austerities, through disinterested service, through devotion and wisdom. Some may worship him through many costly sacrifices, but he is as easily pleased with a leaf, a flower, a fruit, or water offered to him with devotion.

Exclusive Gods

22. In Sanatana dharma Gods are conceived in various ways: as single, as multiple, and as one in all and beyond all.

23. The Gods thus conceived take no particular pride in being single or singular and do not object to being multiple, for they know that they are both.

24. A God of this conception does not deter partners for he does not become less by having them.

25. A God of the conception of Sanatana dharma says: "Those who worship other Gods also worship me," but a God conceived in exclusive ideologies says: "Thou shalt have no other Gods before me." The Gods of Sanatana dharma are not "jealous"; they live in friendliness; they represent each other; in each one can see all. A God of this conception does not

abhor "other" or "strange" Gods, for there are no "others" and no "strangers" here; He is in all and all are in Him.

26. In Sanatana dharma one does not love one god by hating another; nor does he need to hate the gods of others for loving his own. It teaches that Jehovah can be loved without hating Jupiter and Allah loved without hating Al-lat and Al-uzza.

27. Sanatana dharma teaches *advaita*; it says God alone is. But this teaching is different from the teaching of "only one god". The concept of "god alone" is not the same thing as the concept of "the only god." The latter is particularistic, negative and pretentious. Its motive is to deny "other" gods, or more exactly the gods of others.

28. But as Sanatana dharma denies no legitimate spiritual expressions, it fully admits national deities and ancestral Gods (*kula-devatā*). It has no difficulty in admitting the God of one's "fathers", the "God of Abraham, and of Isaac, and of Jacob."

Prophets and Saviours

29. Cults of exclusive gods have often given birth to cults of exclusive prophets. A god of this kind says to his chosen people: "I shall be your God and you shall be my people; I shall raise amongst you a prophet and I shall speak to him and he will tell you what I intend you to do. If you do not obey him I shall punish you."

30. Sanatana dharma rejects this approach and these categories. It preaches neither exclusive gods, nor exclusive prophets. Sanatana dharma accepts the fact of gifted God-men but rejects exclusive communicants. The truths it teaches are experiential and open to all. 'Come and See for yourself' is its call. It rejects the doctrine of the *only prophet* (put forth under the guise of *the last prophet*) or the *only saviour*.

31. By this token, Sanatana dharma cannot be a proxy religion. It teaches that one cannot live on truths seen by others. It teaches you direct and personal perception of truth.

The voices and visions of one man cannot become standard or authority for all.

The Revelation

32. Sanatana dharma teaches that different parts of man's mind and being project their own "revelations" and "truths", and they share the qualities of their source. An impure source gives impure revelations; it gives boastful and self-regarding gods, and self-proclaimed saviours and intermediaries; it gives birth to *dvesha* and *moha* dharmas, to ideologies of hate and delusion which launch you on fierce and aggressive deeds. Sanatana dharma teaches that mind has to be purified through *sīla* and *samādhi* before it can receive higher truths without distortion; it teaches that even Yogic *dhyāna-bhūmis* require constant purification and uplifting for contact with higher spiritual truths.

33. So according to Sanatana dharma the source of higher truth is not an agitated mind under excitement of some special idea or mission, but a purified and illumined *buddhi* or *dhī*.

34. Not without reason, the representative figure of Sanatana dharma is a seer, a sage not a missionary or a crusader, a martyr or *shahid*. Similarly, in Sanatana dharma only those who are good and are men of knowledge and wisdom are regarded as 'saints'; in prophetic ideologies, saints are knight of the church or *ummah*, its sappers and miners, and even its storm-troopers.

Denial of God

35. According to Sanatana dharma God is dishonoured and denied in many ways: He is denied when he is made in the image of man and personifies his unregenerate passions and preferences; when he is made to seek sole communicants; when he is made to "abhor" other Gods; when he is denied in his "manyness" and in his various manifestations; or when he is denied in the Gods of one's neighbours and consequently in the neighbours themselves — denying the Gods of one's

neighbours is often a prelude to denying those neighbours themselves, prelude to attacking them, enslaving and subjugating them in the name of one's own special God. Bad and undeveloped theologies have been a great source of imperialist wars, domination and oppression.

36. God is denied when he is made into an all-time male and denied in women and denied female expression. Theologies which have lacked Goddesses have also been great oppressors of women. Historically, they have also been great persecutors of "infidels".

Moral Code

37. Different available moral codes have derived from what men have thought of their deity, of themselves and of their neighbour. If divinity and even morality are external to man, then his moral code too is external. It is made up of Commandments, and compliance with them is secured by threats of hell-fire and promises of a paradise.

38. Sanatana dharma however believes that man is spiritual and moral in his essence; that compassion, truthfulness, disinterestedness reside in his soul, therefore it expresses these luminous and divine qualities in his action too; that if man is depraved and sinful by nature, he neither needs nor is he capable of a developed moral action. What does a sinner need morality for? His moral code has to be rudimentary and it is good enough for a man of this definition. In any case, such a man is looking for a saviour and even an underwriter, not for sinlessness — a state which is impossible for him by definition.

39. Similarly, a limited physical-vital view of man does not need much ethics. If a man live only for himself and for a day, he owes little to others and to tomorrow. Only a higher vision of man gives and can sustain a higher system of ethics.

40. An ordinary man's moral code is prudential in intention. He refrains from doing many things unto others lest they also do them unto him; he also sometimes does good unto them

expecting they would do the same unto him. But Sanatana dharma teaches that one should be good and do good for its own sake. One does good because it is one's nature. However, it also knows that the law has its limitations. Forgiveness and patient bearing (*kshmā*) under all circumstances cannot be laws of ethical behaviour for all, while mutuality and reciprocity are. Sanatana dharma also holds *daṇḍa-nīti*, the science of administering justice, in high esteem; it teaches punishment where it is due though it does not forget the divine in those it has to punish and its penal code has been humane and based on deep understanding. It also teaches that the *ātatāyins*, aggressors and invaders of various grades, are to be opposed with resolve and force. Are we not aware of ideologies and forces that are aggressive in their very creed and premises, which treat others harshly in the name of one principle while they expect to be treated indulgently in the name of another principle?

41. Broadly speaking, Sanatana dharma has spoken of four aims of man's pursuit (*purushārtha*). The first two, physical well-being and acquisition of wealth, even for their fulfilment, have to accept the guidance of the third, the ethical law, the *dharma*. Dharma in turn is rooted in the fourth, *moksha*, the principle of liberation in man from the pull of his lower nature. There can be no lasting ethical behaviour without cultivating dispassion and a taste for higher life. A Hindu sannyasin takes the vow of fearlessness; he takes no offence and offers no injury to anyone.

Neighbour

42. An ethical code defines a man's behavior, his duties and obligations towards his neighbour. But who is a neighbour? According to prophetic religions, a man belongs to a body of believers, and he has no other existence. They do not have a concept of man as such and their definition of a neighbour excludes non-believers. In this view, a believer owes nothing

to them. In fact, he is taught to deny them, to deny their Gods and their God-men, and it is his special obligation to destroy their temples and their groves. In this he fulfils his God's most favorite command.

43. But Sanatana dharma's definition of a neighbour is very inclusive. It includes all men, in fact, all living beings, and even all elements; it includes Gods and angels; it includes beings who have gone before and those who are yet to come; beings on all planes and in all modes of existence. Sanatana dharma teaches, that man owes duties towards them all, that he is indebted to them. It preaches that he pays his debts to them. Therefore he is asked to make daily "sacrifices" to them, to offer his daily oblations to Gods, to ancestors, teachers and rishis of old, to men; in fact to all orders of beings including Gandharvas, Nāgas, Yakshas and Rākshasas, and to all elements (*bhūtāni*) including oceans, rivers, mountains and heavenly bodies. Therefore, when a Hindu eats his food, he mentally offers and invokes all beings on different planes living in different modes (*ābrahma-stamba-paryantam*). He eats the "remains" of this food. He eats sinfully who eats for himself.

Animals

44. Our sister animal creation has failed to receive sympathetic recognition at the hands of man. It has been under the curse of the Biblical God. He put the fear and dread of his followers upon every beast of the earth, and upon every fowl of the air and told them that every thing that moveth was their food and under their domination. Modern European thought carries forward that tradition. And though it derives man from the animals, it has not led to the teaching that animals may be treated like men but on the other hand to the opposite teaching that men may be treated like animals.

45. While modern secular thought sees animals in man, Sanatana dharma saw Gods and the power and presence of Gods in animals. It saw Agni in goats, Varuṇa in rams and

sheep, Sūrya in horses, and Soma in cows and calves. It taught kindly treatment of animals; it taught *jīva-dayā*.

46. Widespread vegetarianism in Hinduism is a practical expression of this *jīva-dayā*, of the sense of larger unity.

Ecological Ethics

47. Modern materialist thinking which is linear and which holds that everything is for man's use and manipulation is losing credit. Man is being forced to define his attitude towards elements like the earth, the waters, the air, the sky, the rivers. Are they dead? Or, living? Are they strangers? Or, close relatives — father, mother, brothers, sisters, and friends? Are the oceans, the atmosphere merely great sinks, huge waste-dumps? Are the minerals, the plants, the great animal sister-creation there just for human exploitation? Have they no life and rights of their own. Sanatana dharma takes the view that they have their own rights and we have duties towards them. It says that we should cherish them and live in togetherness. If we violate this law and continue to injure them, we create karmas that will strike back in ways we can hardly imagine.

48. The ethical thinking of Sanatana dharma derives from this larger conception of man. Man belongs to a great community and many forces, mostly invisible. He is a meeting-point of many influences; he derives his sustenance and even his being from many planes, many sources. He belongs to a whole universe of interconnections; he is part of a common and larger bio-sphere, and beyond that of a larger psycho-sphere, a larger cosmic moral and spiritual order (*rita*). Man is more than ecologic; he is cosmic in his being.

49. Sanatana dharma teaches that there is an interchange going on between Gods and men, between heaven and earth, between men and men, between the past, the present, the future, and they each owe one to the other. It thinks of life as a *yajña*, an interchange, between different forms and modes, and transformation.

50. Sanatana dharma teaches that only such a large view of

man and his ethics can provide the basis of a truly great and compassionate culture.

Dharma

51. Sanatana dharma believes that man is capable of higher moral action only when he grows into the qualities and powers of the Spirit: that he grows morally when he grows spiritually; therefore it teaches an ethics of personal spiritual growth. It teaches the ten-fold laws and qualities of dharma: contentment (*dhriti*), forgiveness (*kshamā*), self-control (*dama*), purification (*śaucha*), sense-control (*indriya-nigraha*), wisdom (*dhī*), knowledge (*vidyā*), truthfulness (*satya*), and abstention from anger (*akrodha*).

52. Therefore, Sanatana dharma seeks "rebirth", a new life in *daivī sampad*; it teaches you to cultivate your hidden powers, new powers of the soul, like *śraddhā*, *vīrya*, *smriti*, *samādhi* and *prajñā*. It teaches an upward and inward look.

53. Sanatana dharma teaches man to embrace the Vast, the plenum (*bhūman*) and reject the Small (*alpa*).

54. Sanatana dharma regards God as the inner-controller, and moral action as spontaneous and natural. In being moral, a man is being true to himself.

According to one's Readiness

55. While teaching highest *ātma-dharma*, Sanatana dharma makes allowance for different capacities, different talents, different starting-points, and different needs. A man starts from where he is, and he moves along his *svadharma*, his bent of mind, his capacity of the moment. Thus his starting-point, his route are his own, and he reaches his destination in his own way.

56. Besides the principle of *ādhāra-bheda*, there is also the principle of *ishṭa*. Here one chooses one's deity too. The seeker starts according to his spiritual readiness, and he thinks of God in the form most dear to him and most in affinity with his inner nature.

57. By its very nature such teaching cannot be put in a creed or *Kalmah* or formula; it cannot be exported and sold by vendors of religion; it cannot be had at the stalls of missionaries, nor can it belong to the kitbag of invading armies. One has to grow into it. That is true conversion. All other conversions are political and military and they have no spiritual significance.

58. By the same token these truths cannot be borrowed or stolen; one cannot make them one's own by stealing or robbing, or by cunning adapting and adopting. For learning them, one has to go fuel in hand (*samid-pāṇi*) in humble seeking and supplication. These truths are for the seekers; Vedas cannot be stolen.

59. It also follows that creeds of undeveloped spiritual vision can neither have nor do they need a developed ethical code.

Many Lives, Many Planes, *Moksha*

60. All these teachings have a meaning when the background and the foundation is a vast (*brihat*) and even an undying life. Sanatana dharma teaches that there are many lives, many births, many incarnations; it tells us how a soul drops one body and puts on another; it tells us how when a man apparently dies, he draws unto itself all that he has done and thought and desired, in short, all the "impressions" and "proclivities" of this life and restarts on another journey in another body.

61. Sanatana dharma teaches not only many lives but also many "modes" of life on many planes or *lokas*, and many kinds of beings on different *lokas* with different powers and possibilities. It tells us that life on some of these planes is grossly physical while on others it is more mental, psychic and spiritual. It tells us of the worlds of Fathers, Gandharvas, Prajāpati, Gods, Brahmā. It teaches that man is also born on these planes and among their denizens.

62. Though Sanatana dharma has spoken extensively of

these *lokas* and birth in these planes, we need not go into them here. For the principle of all these births and *lokas* is that man becomes what he thinks, desires, acts, aspires to; that man is *śraddhāmaya* and that he is shaped according to the faith, desires and aspirations of his heart; it says that the doer of good becomes good and the doer of evil becomes evil.

63. It further says that on this journey of self-formation, there is no discontinuity, no moral or spiritual break. One makes his start, and the *sādhanā* of this life is taken up in the next. On this path there is no loss of effort, nor any transgression, where goodness and virtue are one's protectors in this as well as future life. Dharma is undying and even a bit of it protects a man from great fear.

64. Sanatana dharma also teaches *moksha*. It says that at one time or the other, some more contemplative types realize that all this coming and going is no part of their true self and adds nothing to it. They reject all that is *not-self* (*an-ātma*). They become aware of forces which stain the natural purity of the soul, which keep man bound to lower forms of life, the lower pull (*kleśas*, *āsravas*, *saṁyojanas*, *lesyas*). They develop *nirveda*, a distaste for this world, or rather for worldliness. Hindu spiritual teachers have spoken a good deal of this *nirveda*. They say that without this great turning away, one cannot develop longing for emancipation. They have seen that the forces that keep men in bondage are powerful. They have seen everything — one's eyes, one's ears, one's mind, etc. — on fire, burning (*ādīpta*) with attachment, with aversion, with delusion; and blinded (*andha-bhūta*) by them. They say that a man should work with zeal for his emancipation (*apavarga*), get out of this cycle and become a non-returner, *nivritta*, *anāgāmin*. Renunciation has an honoured place in man's spiritual growth.

65. A man who has broken his fetters and cut the knots of his heart develops another vision: that a man in his soul already holds all his lives, past and future, terrestrial and celestial; that he is already in touch with all the *lokas* and their

beings, that nothing is too distant for him and that no one is a stranger, that Gods, angels and ancestors are kith and kin, that there is *sādriśya* and *ekātmatā* between them all; that he is all, knows all, belongs to all.

66. Sanatana dharma has done a lot of thinking on life and death, on what is a noble life and a noble death, on rebirth and the law of karma, on what might be called *pāra* or post-mortal states, on the two paths of light and darkness (*archi mārga* and *dhūma mārga*), on *mārga-yāna* and *deva-yāna*, on birth in celestial realms, on *moksha* and *nirvāṇa*. These are important questions and intimately related to man's being. Cultures which don't raise these questions are spiritually poor.

One Life, One Judgement, Hell, Heaven

67. The perspective of certain religious ideologies has been different. According to them, there is nothing to account for a man's present birth. He begins suddenly and his end is as "sudden" as his beginning. He dies and is dormant till a particular day when he is raised more or less as he was in his body as well as in his mind or in his affections and appetites and desires, and is judged once for all and condemned or rewarded for an eternal punishment or reward. In this view, a man's life is at best merely an interlude between two blanks. He came from nothing; there were no inputs from a past life, nor does he leave any traces or proclivities of a future life. No past shaped his present life and he is shaping no future life for him. There is a single life, a single judgement and an eternal punishment, but in cases where man belonged to a right religious *ummah* eternal reward. But in Sanatana dharma, as we have seen, the perspective is very different. There are more than one life and, of course, there is no single judgment. In fact, there is no judgment at all as such, for the idea is to help and not to judge and condemn. The inner dynamics of incarnation is not reward or punishment but self-improvement, and ultimately self-discovery and self-recovery, *moksha*.

68. In these ideologies, there are no "other" worlds properly

speaking. The first place to which a man goes after his death is the purgatory, a sort of detention-camp and a place of torment for the expiation of sins not sufficiently paid for here in this world. Here men wait in torment until the day of Judgement when they are judged for all time and most of them condemned and go to hell and a small minority saved and sent to heaven.

69. In these ideologies the reward itself is conceived in most sensuous terms. There is no concept of a higher life, concept of a man released from its lower nature. Their paradise reproduces the present in all its unregenerate aspects and hardly adds any new dimension; it gives widest scope for fulfilling a man's worst passions, his appetites, concupiscence, his revenge. It provides pleasures dreamt here but often denied; it is one of the greatest pleasures of the heaven of prophetic religions that, from its balcony, the believer can watch his enemies, the pagans, the unbelievers, the heretics roasting in hell.

70. Another *piece de resistance* is their hell. Its tortures have been described with such great fervour and flourish that for centuries it has held believers in great fear. It gave birth to an ideology of "religious terrorism," as it has been aptly described. Indulgences were and are still sold and bought. Poor men do everything and submit to everything to procure some relief from the tortures of future life for themselves and their dear ones.

71. It also encouraged the cult of Saviours and Mediators. The hotter the fire of the hell, the greater the demand for a Saviour or Mediator.

Modern Western Thought

72. Sanatana dharma and modern European thought disagree in many things, in their method, approach as well as conclusions. But they agree in one most important thing: they are not dogmatic and they do not punish dissent and both allow reason freedom to question and inquire. [In India where

this freedom was never under question, we do not even see the importance of the problem. But in the West, this right was won the hard way. There the Church claimed that it had all the knowledge, spiritual as well as secular; it knew who is God and whom He has begotten; it knew when the world began and when it was to end; it knew that the earth was flat and the sun and the moon were set in the firmament to give light upon the earth. These were dogmas and to question them was dangerous and invited burning at the stake.]

73. But here the agreement ends and both have followed their own characteristic methods of inquiry. One has looked inside, the other outside; one has wanted to know that by knowing which all this is known; it thought that by knowing oneself, one would know all. The other studied the outside world and thought that in this way man would also know himself. There was also another difference in their method: one method was discursive and analytical, the other concentrative and intuitive.

74. The two also disagree in their conclusions and approach and temper. One derives the higher from the lower while the other sees even in the lower the play of the higher. As a result, one derives man from animals, the other derives him from Gods and says that man's roots are above (*ūrdhva-mūla*), and that he is a soul that has come down into an earthly body and has lost the memory of his true home. Similarly, one school is reductionist in approach while the other allows different levels and multiple dimensions. Sanatana dharma has found out a transcendental dimension; modern secular thought denies it altogether; the former takes into account man's spiritual nature and gives it a high place, the latter treats him mainly as a body, though sometimes grudgingly as a mind too regarding it as the body's appendage.

75. In conformity with its basic approach, modern thought explains the world mainly in physical terms. This view is not new and as a school of thought is quite old and found in all cultures wherever any philosophical thinking was done. What

is new is the intellectual prestige the view has acquired in scientific circles as a result of certain marvellous achievements in the field of technology by following its quantitative approach. The view has also the support of our senses and empirical mind and therefore has a universality of its own. In India too this school of thought has existed from very ancient days though it did not belong to the mainstream.

76. The physical view of the universe went along with a physiological and biological view of man, and also supported a particular ethical theory of man's conduct. It said that the highest aim of man is to fulfil his desires and those desires are mainly of his body. This view holds, to put it in the language of the Gita, that the world is without moral basis, without spiritual governance, without Gods, and that its motive force is lust and greed. Modern philosophical thought works on these premises and accepts these views of the world, of man and his ethics.

77. Sanatana dharma rejects these views. It rejects the view which identifies man with his body alone or even with his mind. It accepts man's physical and physiological being but it regards it as only the first definition of man. Beyond this man, *annamaya purusha*, the sages found other dimensions which constitute man's deeper being.

78. They therefore also rejected the ethics based on this identification. They denied that the highest aim of man is merely to fulfil the desires of this body, "to make it happy and wait upon it." They called it an asuric doctrine.

79. They in fact rejected all such views of the world, man and his conduct which deny worlds other than the world of the senses and pragmatic mind, which deny the hereafter, which deny sowing and reaping, which deny law of karma and the path of dharma, which deny higher motivation and larger life. India has known its Chārvāks and Jābālis, but has found their definition of man, and consequently their ethical thinking too, as inadequate and unacceptable.

80. Sanatana dharma teaches that materialism and hedonism

in their exclusive demands are very unsatisfactory, that cultures based on a purely psycho-physical definition of man are neurotic, that they cannot provide the basis of a truly stable society. These cultures lack vision and sympathy; they are violent. Think of all their meat industries and their slaughter-houses and even their laboratories and experiments. See how they kill whole species for food, for entertainment, for commercial profits. Think of all the tears and sighs involved. They must be leaving karmas behind, must be setting up forces of nemesis somewhere. These cultures are also wasteful and self-destructive. Think of their poisoned food, poisoned soil, poisoned waters and air; how they mine away their soil, how they exploit whole continents and peoples, how they use away in a decade nature's assets accumulated over thousands of years — to feed the ever-hungry Market, the new Moloch-God. And behind and supporting all this wastefulness and cruelty, one can also see the *mindlessness* of the whole prevailing system, its forgetfulness (*vismriti*) of any higher dimension. Think of its sensation-seeking, its entertainments, its education, its health systems based on a narrow definition of man.

81. Sanatana dharma also rejects the stupendous ego-centricity of modern Europe which regards all human past as "primitive", all Asia as "outmoded", and believes that it has been the centre and secret meaning of all human endeavour and that man's history by an inner law has been leading up to it and it has now reached its finale!

82. Time and space of Hindu thinking were vast. It is only recently that modern Europe attained those scales — though it still regards them too physically and has no idea of psychic time and space. However, the old Biblical chronology of creation it had inherited from Christianity is still active. It has come by the backdoor and it is now applied to the history of civilization giving it five or six thousand years, the same it once gave to creation. This view suits Europe's ego, but Sanatana dharma rejects it. It believes that man's history is

long and he has seen and known many civilizations which have come and gone and reappeared more than once. It believes in cycles, in patterns, in repetition. It also believes that civilizations had more than one centre and that fortune smiled on different peoples and regions and they created great civilizations at different times. But in this matter too, the West was moved by its Biblical bias. It concentrated its archaeological labours in the Palestinian land and its neighbourhood, believed to be the place where the Garden of Eden was and where lived Adam and Eve. In this way the first site of creation also became the first and foremost site of civilization.

Universality

83. Sanatana dharma is a soul religion, therefore it is universal. Wherever there is sincere seeking, it comes into play. Therefore though it found its most profound and continuous expression in India, it belongs to all whose spiritual quest is sincere.

84. Its truths have been confirmed in every age, but one has to work for them in order to make them one's own. These truths are closed to the sensuous mind, but they are revealed to a *sāttvika buddhi*; they are closed to the foolish, but they are revealed to the pure (*śuchivāna*) and the wise (*vijña*).

85. By its very nature, Sanatana dharma cannot be a religion of a chosen people or a favourite church or *ummah*. It expresses man's secret seeking for truth, therefore it belongs to all seekers. It rejects the approach which divides humanity into believers and infidels or heathens, and regards this division spiritually untenable.

86. Its sympathy is not limited to humanity; its compassion reaches out to all beings, all creatures. It teaches compassion for all beings on all planes, those who are living, and those who have gone and those who are yet to come.

87. Sanatana dharma believes that a tribal god belonging to a particular *ummah* trying to become the god of all through conquest has no universality. A true universal God is met in

the interiority of one's soul where what is intimately individual is also truly universal. Similarly, a god who owns and rules the world but has lost his soul or inwardness is no true god.

Repository of Many Religions: Religious Renewal of the World

88. Last centuries have been dominated by ideologies, religious as well as secular, which were based on denial and exclusion. They denied truths they did not know; they denied peoples and continents they did not control; they denied their neighbours' Gods; they denied and maligned mankind's whole religious past; they dismissed it as "age of ignorance"; they described their human ancestors as "benighted", or as is the fashion of modern anthropology — a development of Christian theology — "primitive". They saw nothing good in anyone before them or beside them or after them. Modern Europe's social sciences, philosophies and ideologies — its sociology, anthropology, its Darwinism and Marxism — all are merely carrying forward the old bias of its narrow, self-centered Christian theology. They are blackening with a big brush man's whole heritage, in fact, the whole of past humanity itself and quite a part of present humanity as well. But now this thinking is facing difficulties and there is a growing realization among the more perceptive thinkers that this view of mankind and its past is inadequate. Hinduism which views human history in great time cycle can help this process of rethinking.

89. Sanatana dharma teaches that one's world is relative to one's consciousness, the world of a predominantly physical mind is physical; it is dead and inert and lacks inner movement. But there is another mind which views things differently; its world is animate, conscious; it is also made up of "things", but those things are powers, personalities; they have mana in them; they are internally linked and one could stand and signify another. However, during the last millennium, the physical mind has been dominant. It has given

rise to ideologies which see the world that way, dead, inert, and passive. Under their auspices, we have learnt to deny many cultures, continents and peoples as "animists", or as "ancestor worshippers". Hinduism rejects this approach; it accepts the world-view of these cultures as valid and believes that something of it is needed by the modern man for his own self-renewal, that man must relearn that world-view of great spiritual truth, and that he needs these ancient views to cure his own deadness and rootlessness.

90. Sanatana dharma was known in many lands under different names. But at one stage or the other, it came under the attack of monolatrous creeds which lacked internality but were moved by a fanatic idea. Many countries lost all memory of it but India has been able to preserve it though in a form badly damaged. Thus India has come to preserve spiritual traditions which many ancient cultures and countries have lost. Today Hinduism represents not only India but the ancient wisdom of humanity and therefore in a most vital way that humanity itself. In Hinduism many ancient countries can still rediscover their religious past, their old Gods and their old spiritual traditions.

91. And while it reveals their past, it is also a pointer to their future; while linking them up with their roots, it tells them that they can best develop by following their own inner light. No borrowed gods, saviour and prophets would do.

92. Hindu dharma is the dharma by knowing which many ancient religions become known; it is the illuminator, interpreter (*bodhaka*, *prakāśaka* and *vāchaka*) of many a religion of the world, both past and present. It also fulfils man's deeper religious seeking at any point of time.

The Great Refuge

93. I offer my obeisance to Sanatana dharma of the Vedas and the Upanishads, the Purāṇas, the Epics and many Āgamas.

94. I take refuge unto this dharma which has been nourished from generation to generation by great sages and teachers.

95. I take refuge in Sanatana dharma, whose precepts and practices are pure, which is auspicious in its beginning, auspicious in the middle, and auspicious in the end; whose roots are deep, whose fruits are sweet.

96. I take refuge in Sanatana dharma whose teaching is pure, whose desires, aspirations and works are pure.

97. I pay my obeisance to Sanatana dharma which gives us a vision of a higher life, a great and immortal life, a life renewed by a higher truth, a life which goes beyond its present limitations.

98. May I be a sharer in its truth! May I be a worthy sharer in its heritage! May it be given to me to serve it with all my heart and mind.

99. God grant me that I make its truth my own. Make me a participant in its truth. May I become worthy of it. Expand me and deepen me. Take the veil off from thy face and reveal thy face and thy inner truth.

100. I pay my obeisance to Sanatana dharma which teaches oneness of men and Gods, oneness of all life. May I be one with Gods! May I be one with our ancestors! May I be one with those who have gone before me! May I be one with those who have yet to come. May I serve those who are immediately around me, and also those who are hid from my sight. May I serve all beings on all the planes!

101. I pay obeisance to Sanatana dharma which has power to heal and reconcile, power to awaken, and re-form. May this dharma restore my people and my country! May it bless all humanity and all beings! May all be auspicious towards each other.

102. Sanatana dharma protects those who protect it. Therefore protect and serve it in order to deserve and claim its protection.

103. Sanatana dharma is as wide and profound as its subject. Like its Gods, it has a thousand names and facets, but only some of them have been indicated here.

Hindu Dharma, Hindus, India

104. India was the place where Sanatana dharma flourished. Its people were called Hindus and their religion came to be known as Hindu dharma. Hindu dharma went abroad from time to time and vitally influenced the cultures and religions of many lands and regions of the globe, but India remained its home par excellence, and it never tried to set up a foreign Empire. Its influence was purely spiritual, cultural and intellectual.

105. Hindu Dharma raised fundamental questions and made profound answers. It discussed Gods and the discussion was most intimate and profound and we find nothing like it anywhere. It also discussed man — a most important question but altogether neglected in many religious ideologies, particularly prophetic ones — and asked many questions about him. Is he one or multiple? Is the visible man the only one, or has he also an invisible dimension? And after great investigation, the answer it gave was that man is made up of many sheaths (*koshas*), one inside the other; that he comes from higher sources; that much of him, his form, his beginning and end and his resting-place are indiscernible. Similarly, it raised questions about living, dying and immortality; it raised questions about the quality of life, about suffering and death, and about the way to overcome them; it discussed the law of karma and found that its working was inscrutable. It discussed man's own internal enemies, and friends, the forces that bound man and those which liberated him.

106. It raised other similar questions centering on the same theme. It raised the question about *purusha* and *prakriti*; it raised questions about *bhakti* and *mukti*, about *karma* and *dharma*, about *saṁsāra* and *nirvāṇa*, about *pravritti* and *nivritti*, about what is action and what is inaction, what is *yajña* (sacrifice) and what is worship, about *śīla*, *samādhi* and *prajñā*, about *yama* and *niyama*, about *tapasyā*; it spoke of the

two lives, one that is worthy, righteous and good and the other which is merely pleasant (*śreyas* and *preyas*); it showed how life could be uplifted, how man could develop an upward and inward look. It spoke about *vyakta* and *avyakta*; it asked questions about Gods, about ancestors, about different spheres and planes (*lokas*), about the "invisible" worlds corresponding to the "invisible" man and vice versa. In the same vein, it asked questions about the four *purushārthas*, about the four *varṇas* and *āśramas*.

107. The truths that Hindu dharma taught were profound and recondite, but they were made available to the least of its members. It was done through epics and the Puranas, through songs and psalms, through stories and parables. What the village minstrel sang in direct and simple language was what the Upanishads taught in cryptic and terse language. The same truths were conveyed both through Sanskrit as well the more ordinary medium of discourse. No antagonism was ever felt between Sanskrit and Prakrit, or any other local language in use. The source was the same, the inspiration was the same, the message was the same.

Reason and Religion

108. Hindu dharma was a great reconciler. It reconciled various viewpoints, various doctrines. It knew how to look at things from various angles and viewpoints. It knew no conflict between science and religion, between rationalism and spiritualism. It was so because it was not dogmatic either in its reason or its religion. Its spirituality did not deny reason, nor its reason denied spirituality. And why should they? Both are great truths of man's being and both are needed and they reinforce each other. But where one or the other or both lack in depth, conflict is inevitable. In cultures where spirituality and philosophy were undeveloped or underdeveloped, the two have been either in conflict or they have lived in uneasy co-existence.

Varṇa-āśrama Dharma: Social System

109. Hindu dharma has also been described as *varṇa-āśrama dharma* which represents an important facet of ancient Hindu thinking. The old sages saw that men are broadly divided into four psychological types (*chaturvarṇa*), a very different thing from the castes-system with which it is often confused. They found that these psychological differences were natural and their variety matched the variety of man's needs. Similarly, they thought of man passing through four stage: as a student when he should be acquiring knowledge both vocational and liberal; then as a householder when he enters life, marries, earns and creates wealth for himself and for others and supports all other activities of the society; and at the end he retires from these activities and in the last two stages becomes an intense seeker of truth and spends his time in self-reflection. All these stages or *āśramas* were important but in a certain context the householder was declared superior to all for he supported and protected the rest. This ordering involved no iniquity for each man was also all others at different times.

All this thinking and ordering derives from what these sages thought of man. They found that each man is a multiple being: he is physical, mental and spiritual and that all these parts should find fulfilment. From this also came the celebrated four aims (*purushārthas*) of Hindu conception we have already mentioned. Man should work for his physical and economic well-being; he should hand down the torch of life from one generation to another; he should also earn and create wealth; he must also search and follow values and discover the meaning of life. Man was both spirit and body, though he was more of the one at one stage than of the other. The sages followed this natural law and made their recommendations accordingly. The four *āśramas* and the four orders were conceived to fulfil the fourfold nature of man and the four aims of life.

The society had the same needs as its individuals: physical, mental and spiritual. Similarly, its members were endowed with different talents and the results were best when their work, talents and training went together. The *varṇa-āśrama dharma* was meant to serve this end as best as it could. The society needed creators of wealth and in the Indian scheme they also owned the best part of it; it also needed its warriors, defenders and protectors and also its thinkers, teachers and priests. For what is a society without them? — an easy prey and a bountiful reward for various aggressive forces around. [It is also the class which accustomed invaders and practised imperialists most hate and would like to destroy and discredit — they only care for hewers of wood and drawers of water who are leaderless and whose resistance has been broken.]

In all this ordering of the society, there was no iniquity. Dharma set limit and informed all relations. Its inherent justice can be seen from the fact when we remember that Hindu social order neither knew slavery nor serfdom as a system. It did not live on Imperialist and feudal occupation of other peoples' lands, nor on forced tributes, or the "holy fifth," or *jazia*. The society produced its wealth by its own members living in self-governing communities. Only that wealth was praise-worthy which was honestly earned and shared (*śuddha-sudhana*).

Now the *āśrama* system hardly exists, and only its memory remains. *Varṇas* were never castes which followed their own laws. But even castes too have lost their old vocational and cultural relevance; they exist, and sometimes even too insistently, mainly politically and they have grown their own vested interests. They are a hot subject and need more mention.

Castes and Communities

110. No society is a mass; it has always a social configuration. Any developed human society follows the law of differentiation. So did the Hindu society. For better self-articulation, it divided itself in many segments; but in all its

diverse expressions, it remained one in spirit. In its caste and community organizations, we see pluralist Hinduism in action. Various people had various talents, various aptitudes and were variously endowed and they all served social needs which were also various. They had also special vocations and special rules and usages (*niyam*), but they all shared deeper truths taught by Hindu dharma. Rules of ethical conduct (*śīla*) like harmlessness (*ahiṁsā*), truthfulness (*satya*), non stealing (*asteya*), hospitality (*ātithya*), and inner disciplines of the spirit like *śaucha* (internal and external purity), *yama* and *indriya-nigrah* (self-control) were shared truths of all. So were yoga and various other modes of worship. They had shared deities and shared incarnations, and even when they went to different temples, the Gods on the altar were the same. They all remembered their ancestors and performed *śrāddha-karma*. They all offered *tarpaṇa* for Bhishma, the adopted great-great ancestor of all. They all reverenced and worshipped the mother Earth, the rivers, the Sun and the sky. All this constitutes oneness and unity at a deep, psychic level. But deep things are difficult to see and show and we have learnt to be satisfied with the externals. As a result caste has now become Hinduism's badge and flag, its defining mark. It owes to the fact that during its lean years Hinduism lost its right to self-definition. That right passed on to our rulers and they have been defining it for us. There was a time when Hinduism was described in terms of its spiritual wisdom, its Yogas, its philosophy and practices of self-transcendence and self-exceeding, its law of karma and dharma, its mighty and manifold creations; but now it is presented as a system of idolatry, polytheism and castes. For example, once Hinduism was known for its *brahma-vāda*, now its detractors present it as a doctrine of *brāhmaṇa-vāda* and we have lapped up such definitions.

111. To an external eye, different castes in their more outer circumstances might have looked different, but in their inner attitude and approach, they shared a common life, a common

spirit shaped by Hindu spirituality and ethical system. High or low, they all followed as best as they could different attributes of Hindu dharma — often ten have been named by law-givers. Thus in the midst of a great variety of conditions, one could easily see deeper Hindu shaping influences at work. These influences were so deep that they left an impress behind even on those who were converted; they remained closer to their older brothers than to the those whose fold they had to join.

112. The contribution of Hindu thought in the social field was great indeed. It taught us how to create a society of more or less self-governing communities; it gave us "communitarian democracy," the foundation of a true democracy. In this society, no one was rootless, no body belonged to an anonymous mass; everyone had a niche, a place where he was not a stranger; as a member of a great community, no one could be pushed around and he had the protection of the community. And yet no community was a law unto itself. Each followed the guidance of dharma. Never was there a society so free from coercive state apparatus. Every one belonged, everyone had security, dignity, a vocation. The world needs this system or something like it — and much advanced thinking is veering round to this view — in order to overcome the rootlessness and the atomization that is becoming man's lot under new forces at work.

113. Hindu dharma taught respect for all classes. It cherished its *tapasvins* and intelligentia, it cherished its soldiers and administrators, it cherished its producers, traders and artisans and workers. A Vedic verse prays for lustre and light (*rucha*) to reside "in our Brahmanas, Kshatriyas, Vaishyas and Shudras." Everyone was honoured. In the old system, caste represented the principle of security and continuity — one was employed as soon as one was born; it represented the principle of vocation, of training, of excellence, of pride, of dedication; it represented the principle of co-operation, conciliation, culture, and dignity; it was also a great centre of national

power and national expression. It is very much later that caste acquired negative characteristics. It is only a recent phenomenon when under a different ideological conditioning one caste is maligned in the name of another, and caste is being used by powerful vested interests for the fragmentation of the society. Old India had castes but no casteists; new India has casteists but no worthwhile castes. In old India, all people and castes united in defending their society, in defending temples, Brahmins and cows — still worthy objects of protection by a great and compassionate people and civilization.

114. The caste in India was different from the class or estate in the West. Caste was not economic in concept or organization; it was social and cultural. Different castes produced poets, saints and God-men highly honoured by all. Castes were not also as a rule economically or politically disadvantaged. They had often their own rich; they had their Rajas and chiefs and some of them produced at different times great rulers for the whole country. Traditionally the Brahmins were the poorest (and as a class they remain so even at present) for their philosophy was self-abnegation — anyone who lived a mental life, whether a student, a scholar or a sannyasin, was expected to live in voluntary poverty.

115. There was a time when the caste system was not static and castes often rose and fell in social status. It was also the time when no caste was "depressed" though there were social differences. Castes became static and depressed during the period of a protracted foreign rule. The old Hindu social system raised the lowest and treated even the Sudras like the Brahmins; the foreign rulers lowered the highest and treated even the Brahmins like the Shudras. Under foreign domination the status of every community became depressed and those on the margin or those who offered persistent resistance became even more depressed. Under these pressures, entirely new classes arose. The sweeper class with its present funcions is phenomenon of this period. Among them and the tribals, one finds many Rajput gotras.

116. Thus the caste that old India knew was different from what is said about it. The caste of modern persuasion and understanding is a Western-Christian *construct* of the last few centuries. It was conceived as an aid to foreign rule. But the old stereotype continues to dominate and we have even made it our own. It continues to serve old interests while it has created quite some new ones of its own. Old Imperialist forces trying to stage a comeback are doing their best to keep political casteism alive.

Women

117. Hindu dharma reverenced women; therefore, it had no difficulty in conceiving Goddesses. Hindus also learnt to give their women the honour they gave to their deities. Hindu law-givers taught that women must be honoured by their fathers, brothers, husbands and brothers-in-law, who desire their own welfare; that Gods are pleased where women are honoured, but where they are not honoured sacred rites yield no rewards.

Hindus

118. Once Hindus were rich in crops and flocks; their baskets and stores were full; their fields yielded abundantly; they were great organizers, great merchants and entrepreneurs; they were truthful and honest in their dealings; they were noble and generous in character; they were brave and chivalrous — they neither oppressed nor suffered oppression; they were wise and valorous; they avoided fault-finding, and only saw and encouraged what was good in others. They worshipped light and followed its lead — *jyotiragrāḥ*.

119. They were also versed in many fields of knowledge and sciences; they were masters of many arts and crafts; they knew much, they were curious, inventive and dexterous, they were great ship-builders and navigators and explorers.

120. While Hindu dharma flourished, India was also great and happy and creative. It was the mother of many religions; it was the land of many chants, *stavans*, *bhajans* and *kīrtans*,

and night-vigils; the land of many philosophies, austerities, *tapasyās*, reflections; the land of purity and spiritual discrimination; the land where Gods were sung and invoked under various names; the land of much *dāna*, *dakshiṇā* and service. It was the land where the incomparable Mahabharata and the Ramayana were written, works of awakened souls writing about similar souls, depicting dharma in action, showing human characters shaped in the truths of the spirit and embodying higher powers, showing Gods and men in constant interchange, showing them coming down and going back, giving the spiritual history of the nation which belongs as much to the past as to the future. It was the land where women, the elders and the wise were honoured and children cherished. It excelled not only in spiritual sciences and religious, philosophical and ethical domain, but in every field of human endeavour. Its creations in astronomy, mathematics, logic, grammar, linguistics, education, agriculture, music, law, medicine, health and hygiene, tank-digging, method of resource-conservation, architecture, social and political thought and organizations, handicrafts, textile and steel were equally outstanding.

Self-Alienation

121. The causes that govern the fall and rise of nations and cultures are difficult to comprehend. Perhaps they have their appointed destiny. A time came when Hinduism also went down. Its very virtues became its weakness. It became too pacific; it neglected its weaponary; it failed to take into account the new rules of warfare its enemies practised; it neglected to study its neighbours now under a very different ideological orientation. During the last several centuries, it came under the attack, both physical and ideological, of monolatrous creeds. Under this attack, it lost its self-confidence; it became apologetic. A demoralized Hinduism accepted the superiority of the invaders and became their admirer; it accepted their standards, their criterion, their judgment.

Hinduism itself became a dirty word, a word of reproach and shame and dishonour; Hindus became a song of others, and even fell down in their own esteem. They lost pride in their heritage, and they became self-alienated. Many of their sons and daughters even learnt to deny themselves in various ways. May we learn to look at ourselves with pride again!

122. A country cannot be defeated politically unless it is defeated culturally. Our alien rulers knew that they could not conquer India without conquering Hinduism — cultural India's name at its deepest and highest, and the principle of its identity, continuity and reawakening. Therefore Hinduism became an object of their special attack. Physical attack was supplemented by ideological attack. They began to interpret for us our history, our religion, our culture and ourselves. We learnt to look at us through their eyes. From them we picked up views and slogans that served them. During these years, they set for us our intellectual agenda. Under their auspices, we learnt to distrust "brahmanism", the pride of our culture. Thus a whole class of self-alienated people grew up to carry the tradition of the old conquerors. The old order continues under native auspices and has therefore become even more powerful. May we again learn to use our eyes to look at us — and also at others!

123. The long period created an atmosphere of mental slavery and imitation. It created a class of people Hindu in their names and by birth but anti-Hindu in orientation, sympathy and loyalty. They knew all the bad things and nothing good about Hinduism. Hindu dharma is now being subverted from within. Anti-Hindu Hindus are very important today; they rule the roost; they write our histories, they define our nation; they control the media, the academia, the politics, the higher administration and higher courts. They are now working as clients of those forces who are planning to revive their old Imperialism. Once Hinduism identified and defined India; now they are busy denying and destroying that identity and definition.

124. During this period our minds became soft. We became escapists; we wanted to avoid conflict at any cost, even conflict and controversy of ideas, even when this controversy was necessary. We developed an escape-route. We called it "synthesis". We said all religions, all scriptures, all prophets preach the same things. It was intellectual surrender, and our enemies saw it that way; they concluded that we are amenable to anything, that we would clutch at any false hope or idea to avoid a struggle, and that we would do nothing to defend ourselves. Therefore, they have become even more aggressive. It also shows that we have lost spiritual discrimination (*viveka*), and would entertain any falsehood; this is *prajñā-dosha*, *drishṭi-dosha*, and it cannot be good for our survival in the long run. People first fall into delusion before they fall into misfortune.

125. During these years millions of its sons and daughters were enslaved and sold in foreign lands. In the country itself, they were reduced to the status of second-grade citizenship; under those pressures, invaders were the head and Hindus the tail. Under various pressures, many of its sons and daughters were forced to leave their ancestral fold. But in the days when we are free again, we have done nothing to reclaim them. May the Hindu society become decided and strong enough to receive them again!

126. There was a time when boundaries of cultural India extended far beyond its physical borders. But even physical India has been contracting for centuries. We have now got used to thinking of India without Afghanistan, without Punjab and Sindh, and lately without Kashmir too. We have got used to the idea of its enemies planning its dismemberment, subvert it from within and threaten it from outside. We have become used to the idea of a shrinking and shrunken India. May the old concept of Bharatavarsha with its ancient dimensions return!

127. Even today, the old iniquity pursues us. India is subjected to large-scale infiltration, organized subversion,

planned terror and blasts; Hindus are subjected to systematic proselytizing, political blackmail and electoral manipulation. Hindus have become refugees in their own country and they remain second-grade citizens. Let Hindus learn to assert themselves and let the concept of India as a land of the Hindus be restored!

128. Finding Hindus soft, forces traditionally hostile to them have again become active. They are making use of all divisive forces, and aiding and organizing terroristic organizations. They are mobilizing local fifth-columns, anti-Hindu Hindus, casteists and opportunists, elements for a war of subversion from within while they work in perfect safety from abroad. Old forces of bigotry and Imperialism are trying to stage a come-back. They use the language of human rights, radicalism and equity to achieve reactionary ends. No doubt they will be defeated.

129. I offer my obeisance to Hindu dharma which has suffered much, overlooked much, excused much, but when necessary also fought with great valour. I invoke that unconquerable (*durdamya*) spirit, that *kshātra* dharma which knows no defeat and which when roused must prevail.

Civilizational Principle

130. Hinduism enunciated truths of the spirit; it taught the art and philosophy of higher life, of deeper self-culture, of self-exceeding; it was never an ideology of self-aggrandizement; it spoke of man and the human family and knew not itself as anything apart; it even gave itself no name, no separate designation. It knew no *ummah* principle and it gave itself no role as a vanguard of an ideology, religious or secular. Hindu society was organized for peaceable and harmonious ends, not for continued confrontation with the rest of the world in the shape of pagans and unbelievers. But at one stage when it found itself faced with narrow ideologies — aggressive, embattled and organized on the principle of a militant church or *ummah* — it too, in self-protection, had to imbibe a minimum

"national" identity. But it still fully retains its humanist and universalist core and remains rooted in its old vision of human and cosmic unity. Hindus need an identity not merely to cope with narrow ideologies, they also need it in order to serve humanity. And humanity itself needs a Hindu society with a recognizable face for its own spiritual rediscovery.

131. Hinduism once represented a great civilization, but now its revival is being treated as *communalism*, not only by its enemies but even by its many self-alienated sons and daughters. Let Hindu dharma recover its self-confidence, its self-identity (*ātma-smriti*), its unique civilizational principle (*prajñā*). May it rise again and make its contribution to the world! Its revival and message are needed by religious humanity for its own self-revival.

Initiation into a particular *sampradāya*

132. Hinduism in its great fecundity and profundity has given rise to many *sampradāyas* (orders). It is how it should be. A great truth with many facets is lived like that in all its plurality. A *sampradāya* makes necessary adaptation possible. But sometimes, it has also led to unhappy results. The new *sampradāya* forgets its larger identity. It begins to make unwarranted claims. In the process, it itself becomes rootless and begins to play a negative role. Therefore, when a Hindu joins a particular *sampradāya*, the following could be the part of his vow.

133. Hindu dharma has many facets; it is inexhaustible; it is a great ocean. One drop from it is enough to for me.

134. The Sanatana dharma has been well explained (*svākhyāta*) by a succession of great sages and teachers. It has been confirmed by them in their lives.

135. I belong in the first instance to this great unbroken tradition. Now I join this *sampradāya* in order to live some of its truths more intensely.

Chapter 2

Cultural Self-Alienation Among the Hindus[1]

When two cultures meet on unequal military terms — as the Hindu culture met the West and earlier met Islam — it gives rise to grave problems of self-identity for the defeated party. When India finally realized that she had lost in the military and diplomatic contest and that the British were supreme, she was overwhelmed and filled with a deep sense of inferiority. Under such circumstances, as it usually happens, other non-military forces came into play. Different people sought psychological rehabilitation in different ways. Some retired into their shell and became apathetic; a majority met the situation by self-repudiation and wholesale imitation. They disowned their nationhood and their culture and adopted the ways and attitudes of the victors whom they regarded as their superiors. They saved their self-respect through self-alienation.

This self-alienation was an important component of the intellectual ferment that followed the British conquest of India. It was very pervasive and attacked all strata of the society, particularly the intellectual elites. Even people who eventually came to fight the British politically surrendered to them culturally. This surrender gave rise to what may be called the politics of self-alienation and, fed by many sources, it became increasingly more powerful. Today it seems to dominate.

---

[1] An edited version of an article that appeared in three instalments in *The Times of India*, July 2-4, 1987.

Reawakening

But when the initial shock was over, and the military presence became less obtrusive though not less real, and some kind of civic life returned, and we also became more familiar with the victor, a maturer reaction and strategy emerged. A military-political inferiority was accepted but reassertion took place at the religious-spiritual level.

This reassertion was the beginning of greater things in future. It was to sustain us even in our political struggle.[2] Leaders like Dayananda, Vivekananda, Aurobindo and Gandhi went deeper into the truths of their spirituality and felt renewed by it. They saw in Hinduism an incomparable truth, or, at least, a truth by which alone India could rise.

For them, India's struggle was more than political; for them, it had a rich spiritual content and had a deeper intent. India was fighting for *svarājya*, for *svadharma*, for self-recovery. To many it was sufficient if the British political control was withdrawn and replaced by a Government controlled by the Indians themselves. But to these leaders, this was not sufficient. They wanted the country to realize its full potential, to wake up to its soul-life. Aurobindo thought that India was rising for the *Sanatana Dharma*. Gandhi said that he would not like to live in an India which had ceased to be Hindu.

In this concept there was no parochialism and there was no rejection of any truth the West had to offer. In fact, the West could not be wished away and it had to be fully taken into account. What they opposed was mechanical imitation. In the place of this imitation, Aurobindo, taught what he called "assimilative appropriation" (*ātmasāt-karaṇa*). We borrow whatever is necessary but what we can assimilate and transform in the light of our own *svadharma*. This keeps out

[2]It had happened earlier also. During the medieval ages, religious revival preceded military revival (or defence). Kabir, Nanka, Tulsi, Chaitanya, Ramdas gave birth to Shivaji and Govind Singh. Saints paved the way for heroes.

bastardisation of the culture. Let it be made clear that this view is not syncretic which says that we should create a new entity by borrowing and combining what is good anywhere, and for anyone. Cultures like individuals are organisms and do not behave that way.

Though these people presided over India's national struggle, their spirit was universal in the highest degree. Even Sri Aurobindo who saw in India the very image of the Divine Mother said at the peak-time of the struggle that "we do not recognize the nation as the highest synthesis." A nation is the highest synthesis in the European thought, but in the Indian thought, as he said, there is a still higher synthesis, *humanity*. Beyond this lies another synthesis, the synthesis of the living, suffering and aspiring world of creatures, the "synthesis of Buddhism", as Aurobindo called it. He yet recognized another synthesis, the "highest" one, "the Hindu Synthesis", the synthesis of Vedanta.[3]

Thus nationalism to these leaders of the nation was only a temporary phase. "We must live as a nation before we can live in humanity," said Sri Aurobindo. In traditional Hindu spirituality, it was all God, compassion and humanity, and the truth of its own self-identity was neglected. The new leaders came and provided a corrective. And thus was born Indian nationalism. It was carved out of a larger truth and it retained the impress of its original source; it remained rooted in the Hindu vision of human and cosmic unity.

It is obvious that in such a conception of Indian nationalism, there could be no place for rancour against the British, nor any

---

[3]Semitic religions have no concept of man or humanity. They divide humanity into *believers* and *non-believers*, the faithful and the infidels. No wonder these religions also lack the concept of *jīva-dayā*, compassion for all living beings, a conception which is such a living part of all Indian traditions, Buddhist, Jain and Vaishnava. Vedānta goes still further. It teaches us to see God in the visage of all, to regard them as our own *ātman*, to serve them as the manifestation of Vāsudeva. It teaches us not to be put off by human suffering but to accept it too with a glad heart and see in it the *līlā* or play of Nārāyana.

unthinking rejection of the West. India's struggle for freedom was rooted in Hindu spirituality which has a universality of its own. This universality of course has nothing to do with the universality of the multi-nationals or with the universality of hedonistic consumerism; nor with crusading and proselytizing religions trying to become universal through wars of conquest and organized falsehood; nor has it to do with the vague internationalism under Marxist auspices made popular by Pandit Jawaharlal Nehru. Indian world-view is not economic or political or ecclesiastical. India's message, to itself as well as to the world, as propagated by its leaders, ancient and recent, was that of their spiritual self-recovery and self-discovery.

II
Hindus Learn to Look at Themselves through Borrowed Eyes

The two approaches — the approach of self-discovery and creative response and the approach of self-alienation and imitation — both were inherited from the immediate history of the freedom struggle though they derive their strength from the deeper sources in the psyche. The two views are basic and their impact can be seen all along the line. They inform our thinking, our way of regarding ourselves and others. One ideology regards the society culturally, the other economically; one regards it as a community and as a habitat, the other as a guild and a mart; for one the problem is of helping the society to find its roots, for the other to remake it in the image of a chosen pattern; the one serves, the other manipulates.

Illustrating the difference between the two approaches, when Gandhi toured the country, he saw in the lives of our villagers a hidden nobility and dignity; but when Chandra Shekhar did his *padayātrā*, he saw in the same people nothing but illiteracy, poverty and depravity. Aurobindo illustrates the same difference. He did no *padayātrā* but in the inmates of his jail, most of them poor and illiterate, he saw the visage of

Narayana, putting to shame by their humility and simplicity his own intellectual achievements.

Once the approach of Aurobindo and Gandhi formed a powerful current and the freedom struggle was waged under its auspices. But increasingly its hold became weak and in our own times it seems to have lost altogether. The earlier revolutionaries were inspired by the Gita: the gospel of the latter-day would-be revolutionaries was the Manifesto of Karl Marx. Some see in this change a triumph of Nehru over Gandhi. They, of course, do not mean Nehru as a person for Nehru was merely a symbol and he represented, in his own way, a typical response, the response of a defeated nation trying to restore its self-respect and self-confidence through self-repudiation and identification with the ways of the victors. The approach was not altogether unjustified at one time. It had its compulsions and it had also a survival value for us. But its increasing influence can mean no good to us.

We, however, believe that deeper Indian nationalism, which is also in harmony with deeper internationalism, may be weak just now, but it has the seed-power and it is bound to come up again under propitious circumstances. Meanwhile, let us try to understand the forces which give strength and sustain the politics of self-alienation.

Satellite Ideology

A dominant ruling people or race also creates a dominant ideology. It gives birth not only to economic and political compradores but also to intellectual compradores. In India, too, we developed a local satellite ideology derived from the dominant imperialist ideology. It believed what it had been taught, namely, that India was not a nation but only a name for a geographical region occupied by successive waves of invaders, that its past was dark, its religion degraded and superstitious, and that its social system was a tyranny of castes and creeds.

This Western-Missionary view of India was increasingly

adopted by a growing intelligentsia and became a veritable part of its intellectual equipage. The intellectual and cultural conquest of the West has proved more spectacular and durable than its military conquest.

Started by the British, this intellectual programming received powerful reinforcement from Marxism, a new ideology arising in the West. In fact, it was old imperialism establishing itself under new slogans. It was a new name for old facts. In the new dress, it became even more effective; it remained about the same in its larger aims, yet it acquired a radical look into the bargain.

Little do we realize how completely European is the orientation of Marx and Engels. In *Das Capital* of Marx or the *Selected Works* of Marx and Engels, the great civilization of China is not mentioned even once though one might say that China is lucky in this indifference. India appears only as an appendage of the British Empire. Taking his cue from die-hard imperialist writers, Marx tells us that India is no nation and it has no history. She is "the predestined prey of conquest", he says. "Indian society has no history at all, at least no known history. What we call its history, is but the history of successive intruders," he adds. Here we have Macaulay, Mill and Bishop Heber in their most uninhibited form.

With this kind of understanding, the next step was inevitable. To Marx, the British conquest of India was a blessing. The question, as he puts it, "is not whether the English had a right to conquer India, but whether we are to prefer India conquered by the Turk, by the Persian, by the Russian, to India conquered by the Briton".

The Indian Marxists have borrowed this thesis wholesale except that while Marx preferred a British conquest, his Indian disciples prefer a Turkish conquest. This is part of the compulsion of their secular conscience — a conscience which accepts no other compulsion. Read M.N. Roy and other Marxist historians (they dominate our universities) who tell us how Islamic conquest brought a new message of brotherhood and equality to a degraded Hindu India, and how it completed the work begun by Buddhism.[4] Here anything can be anything and imperialism is a beautiful thing if the victim is Hinduism.

Here we find a complete convergence of Imperialism and Marxism. We should keep it in mind. Today, Marxism represents the most systematic and sustained attack on deeper India, on the India of Gandhi, Vivekananda and Aurobindo.

III
Politics of Self-alienation

Some present political analysts divide Hindu intellectuals into two categories: liberal and communal. But this division is falsely flattering to one and unfair to the other. For if we closely examine the names that sail under the two categories, we find that many of the so-called "liberal" Hindu intellectuals are plain Hindu-baiters while many of the so-called "communal" Hindu intellectuals are plain patriots.

Nor is this categorization exhaustive. It does not take into account even the more important shades. For example, where will we place in this *schema* persons like Dayananda, Vivekananda, Aurobindo and Gandhi who, though they led the movements of the day for national awakening, yet spoke for the whole humanity and its future? They were more than "liberal"; they were seers.

---

[4]Marxist writers are not "indiscriminately" anti-imperialist. They are selective in their anti-imperialism. They have their favoured imperialism about which they can be very lyrical. M.N. Roy calls the "Arab Empire", a "magnificent monuments to the memory of Mohammad". According to him, Islam had already "played out its progressive role before it penetrated India". Here its flag was planted on the "banks of the Indus and the Ganges not by revolutionary Saracen hereoes, but by Persians demoralised by luxury and the barbarians of Central Asia who had embraced Islam". But, for M.N. Roy, even this corrupted Islamic imperialism was good enough for degraded India, for he tells us that "it was welcomed as a message of hope and freedom by the multitudinous victims of the Brahmanical reaction which had overthrown the Buddhist revolution and had consequently thrown the Indian society into chasos" (*The Historical Role of Islam*, Delhi Reprint, 1981, pp.88-89).

And where will we place Nehru, the "only nationalist Muslim" of Sardar Patel's description? he will have to belong to the category of liberal Hindus — we owe it to his importance and position. But where will we place the prolific crowd of P.N. Haksars, Mulk Raj Anands, Nikhil Chakravartys, Romila Thapars, Inder Gujrals, Rajni Kotharis, Kuldip Nayars, etc., a class by themselves waiting to be named, a class of Hindus by accident of birth but anti-Hindu by their freely chosen role? (The role may not be as freely chosen as it looks at first though, for it may be the result of an equally accidental Marxist or secularist conditioning. But it is there.)

We also come across a further and related distinction between two types of Hindu communalism — negative and positive. Negative communalism, we are told, consists in being merely anti-Muslim in varying degrees, while positive Hindu communalism consists in appealing in the name of a positive Hindu identity. But since the positive Hindu identity is extremely shadowy due to lack of internal homogeneity among Hindus, positive Hindu communalism is not viable. Therefore, as an inescapable conclusion, for a viable communalism, the Hindus are left only with the negative kind; this however is not desirable.

In this way of thinking, not only positive Hindu communalism, however free from anti-Muslim bias, but even Indian nationalism which has any Hindu orientation is *a priori* condemned to failure; for, it is argued, Indian nationalism makes "contradictory demands." In order to mobilize the people in a Hindu land, it need to invoke Hindu symbols. But that is "bound to further alienate the Muslims."

Under the circumstances, it has been seriously propagated that Hindus should give up their symbols and even Hinduism itself in order to placate the Muslims. In fact, many Hindu elites go about condemning Hinduism in order to prove their Indian nationalism and make it more convincing to the Muslims and to themselves. Thus we have another variety of nationalism — the super-positive nationalism of those Hindu who hate Hinduism for and on behalf of Muslims as well.

But there were others like Gandhi and Aurobindo who saw and acted differently. They did not feel that their Hinduism contradicted their nationalism. In fact, it gave them strength to be great nationalists and great humanists.

Sri Aurobindo was a trenchant exponent of both Hinduism and Indian nationalism. He invoked Hindu symbols, comparing India with Mother Goddess. There is no evidence that he was ill-disposed towards the Muslims, but he refused to give up his Hinduism simply because it might make the Muslims feel crossed. Nor was there any question of his ignoring the Muslims, but there was also no intention on his part of giving them a veto either. His position on the Muslim question was clear. "We do not shun, we desire the awakening of Islam in India even if its first crude efforts are misdirected against ourselves; for all strength, all energy, all action is grist to the mill of the nation-builder. In that faith we are ready, when the time comes for us to meet in the political field, to exchange with the Musalman, just as he chooses, the firm clasp of the brother or the resolute grip of the wrestler," he had said.

Aurobindo had probably another reason for his stand on Islam. He believed that Islam's role in the deeper destiny of India was peripheral. In this sense, he had a vision of India very different from the one that holds the field today. He believed that Sanatana dharma represents the soul of India and that India was rising for the sake of the Sanatana dharma. Vivekananda held a similar view and had expressed his belief that India means Hindus and Hindu means India. Such a vision of or role for India is now unmentionable.

Homogeneity

It has been observed that Hindus are not a homogeneous community in the same sense in which the Muslims are. It is probably true. It is not that the Muslims do not have their internal conflicts — in fact they are quite cut-throat; but they do have a keener sense of belonging to a Muslim brotherhood.

On the contrary, a Hindu, generally speaking, belongs to a caste before he belongs to the Hindu community. This places him at a disadvantage vis-a-vis societies which have a keener sense of fraternity.

The difference arose because Hindus were organised on different principles. Hinduism was organised for peaceable and harmonious internal co-existence, not for continued confrontation with external enemies in the shape of unbelievers. It is no accident of history that though Hinduism knew internal feuds like any social polity, it never crossed its borders to wage wars against people simply because they worshipped different Gods. By its very philosophy and organising principles, the Hindu society was not conceived as a Church Militant or as an *Ummah* on the march in the service of Jehovah or Allah. In fact, its very conception of deity is fundamentally different — but that is a question we need not discuss here.

Organised on such non-military principles, there is no wonder that Hinduism did not even have a name for itself. This agreed with its nature and genius. In this sense, it was like many "pagan" societies which are taught to live their spirituality, good or bad, unconsciously.

While leaving Goa for farther East, Francis Xavier said: "I want to be where there are no Moslems or Jews. Give me out-and-out pagans."[1] Here, Francis Xavier was formulating his experience that Pagan societies without self-conscious identities are an easy prey of crusading and proselytizing fraternities with their divinely conceived roles. This realization is being forced on the Hindus. They are realizing that they are at a disadvantage vis-a-vis those fraternities which have self-conscious identities. Therefore, the Hindus too are now in the process of acquiring as much self-conscious identity as is necessary for their survival. Whether they will succeed is another matter. But this has already made the opposed parties with vested interest in a weak Hinduism cry, *Hindu Backlash*. Marxist and secularist writers, whose work is convergent with Muslim politics and designs, are full of this cry.

Unassimilable Identities

The lack of homogeneity in the Hindu society may be admitted and it is a sorry lack in the present context. But this lack is not, however, the main problem. Indian society allows a unity in which the principle of diversity finds full place. In Indian society, different communities followed their own customs and usages. True, there were certain dominant ideas and values but there was no forced conformity. In Indian society, the problem has never been of diverse communities and diverse customs. But after the advent of Islam, the problem has been and is of unassimilable elements.

We are often told that the Muslims in India are "a self-conscious minority" and that they are convinced that "they have a religious-cultural-linguistic heritage which is worth defending whatever the price". But is this all that this Muslim "self-consciousness" amounts to — just defence of its religious-cultural-linguistic identity? If we believe this, we are fooling ourselves. This Muslim "self-consciousness" has already led to one partition of the country, and it is preparing for another. This "self-consciousness" has greater aims and convictions and greater historical dynamism. It is supported by a deeper and far-reaching ideology, it has at its back the whole theology of *dar'l-harb* and *dar'l-Islam*. Its unfolding takes time but its aim is fixed. To think of "Indian" Muslims without taking into account the Islamic theology and ideology, without taking into account Arabia and Pakistan, is like thinking of "Indian" Communists without taking into account the Communist ideology and the Leninist-Stalinist tactics and the "vanguard role" of Soviet Russia. Refusing to see the problem in its larger perspective is to deceive ourselves, in which lies great peril for the future of the nation.

Some Problems Hinduism Faces and Some Remedial Measures[5]

1. Hinduism[6] faces some grave problems that need serious attention:

(a) it lacks ideological cohesiveness;

(b) it lack leadership. Its elites are becoming illiterate about their spiritual heritage and history and indifferent about their future destiny;

(c) it is weak organizationally. Its has no recognized centres where it could take stock of its sorry situation and think of remedial measures;

(d) it is poor financially. Great poverty has overtaken its religious institutions. Most of its temples are in a state of near-destitution. Its religious priests and *ārchāryas* (scholars) have hardly any prestige left and they are badly neglected;

(e) Hindu society is badly divided into castes and denominations. Once when Hinduism was spiritually vibrant and politically strong, these divisions expressed natural, and healthy diversity; but now in its present weak state, they are used by its enemies for its disintegration. Election politics is being utilized for the dismemberment of the great Hindu society;

(f) Hinduism is ceasing to be a practising religion. Awareness of a larger God-life is becoming dim; worship, studies, *sādhanā*, *japa*, spiritual meditation and reflection are fast declining.

---

[5]A paper circulated among concerned friends in September (1st), 1981.

[6]*Hinduism* is a comparatively recent but now popular name for ancient *Sanatana Dharma*. In its comprehensiveness, it includes many spiritual traditions, disciplines and denominations; it includes what the Gita calls the two *nishṭhās* of Sāṁkhya and Yoga, both equally ancient and both taught by the same divine teacher; it includes what the Buddhist and Jain sacred literature so repeatedly and lovingly mentions — the two traditions of *śramaṇa* and *brāhmaṇa*; it includes Śaivaism, Śāktaism, Vaishnavism (which includes Sikhism of Guru Nanak), and many other paths, *pantha* and *sampradāya*.

In short, it is a situation painful for the lovers of Hinduism and pleasing for its enemies.

2. There are many great Hindus (like Vinoba) who accept and cherish Hindu scriptures, the Gita and the Upanishads, but they have little use for its history, its national and corporate life. They forget that this side too is important and needs nourishing. Upanishads repeatedly speak of the physical and mental vehicle or abode of a spiritual truth, the *adhishṭhāna* that holds that truth. How can the Hindus contribute anything to the world, if they lose their national life and identity?

3. The problems of Hinduism are internal as well as external. The attack comes both from inside and outside. While the forces of self-alienation are increasing within the society, external enemies have intensified their attack. The two forces interact and reinforce each other. All unfriendly elements like Communism, Islam, Christianity have powerful international links, ideological, financial and organizational. The entry of Arab money on a large scale in the last few years spells a most ominous development — it spells the return of Medieval days.

II

1. India has been held together by Hinduism. But now this bond is under great ideological attack and is weakening. As a result, the social fabric of the nation is falling apart and fissiparous forces are on the increase. The moral quality of the nation is also deteriorating. Ashramas, religious orders, temples, *kīrtans*, *kathās*, pilgrimages are still doing useful work. They generate spiritual life at the grass-roots. But these institutions are losing their *elan*, inwardness and vision. A general rootlessness is growing, and these institutions are not drawing the new generation. This puts into jeopardy the very future of Hindu society.

2. The Hindu philosophy and *sādhanā* are individual. Hindu mode of worship helps an individual ethically and spiritually,

but it does not raise his collective consciousness. For example, one could go to all the temples of the land, listen to *kīrtans* and *bhajans*, read all the scriptures without ever hearing the word 'Hindu'. But it is different with religions like Islam and Christianity which are organized round the idea of a tribe, a church, an *ummah*. They may help one very little ethically and spiritually, but they do give him a sense of communal solidarity. Their social organization is also aggressive, in keeping with their aggressive philosophy. This puts deep and universal but passive religions like Hinduism, Buddhism and Taosim at a disadvantage vis-a-vis those ideologies which are aggressive in their philosophy and tribal in their social organisation.

3. But with all its lapses and shortcomings, Hinduism is the only adequate religion of the Spirit. In contrast, Islam and Christianity are not religions; they are *ideologies* and, in their true essence, political creeds. They are not based on any deep truth of the Spirit but are built on a passionate and fanatic idea. If Hinduism awakens to its own truth, it can defeat these irrational and unspiritual forces. But while Hindus sleep the thieves are on the prowl.

III

1. While a Hindu has a truly cosmic sense, his neglect of the social dimension and corporate life is stupendous. Hindus do not have a sense of belonging to a larger whole. The Communist movement is frankly world-wide. There is a strong ecumenical movement among the Christians. Whatever may be their differences in Europe, they work with real co-operative zeal in the lands of the heathens. If there is any competition, it is in the interest of selling the same product. Similarly, there is a powerful pan-Islamic movement among the Muslims. And in spite of their mutual cut-throat conflicts sanctioned by their history, there is a real ideological appeal; they readily rally against infidel countries, particularly if those countries are weak. Islam teaches its adherents to hate *kafirs*

and to keep exerting against them (*jihād*), collectively and individually and under all circumstances.

2. All these ideologies have their World-Centres. Communists[7] have their Comintern working overtly or covertly; the Catholics have their Vatican, a much older centre, having much expertise in and long tradition of subverting non-Catholic societies. The Protestants with about similar aims and strategies in the Third World are also united in their World Council of Churches. The Muslim Caliphate was abolished after the First World War and the Muslim powers have been in bad shape for over a century. But a very active and aggressive pan-Islamic movement is emerging. An Islamic International, a kind of Muslim Vatican, *R'abitah al-'alam al-Islāmiya*, is in the offing. It is oiled by petro-dollars. Because of its present military weakness and dependence, it cannot do much mischief yet in Europe and America, but its immediate targets are the poor and weak countries of Africa and Asia. All these totalitarian ideologies are a threat to pacific and tolerant religions, and pluralist and democratic societies.

Hindus, however, have no centre, no common platform where they could meet together, take stock of the situation and take untied counsel. Hinduism is just a sprawling body without a head. How long could it hope to continue to exist in that way under the new threats that are maturing?

3. These international forces work through local agencies. Decisions taken at their World-Centres are converted into local plans and programmes. They sponsor "liberation fronts", demands for separate "homelands". They work in the name of civil rights, human rights, minority rights, democracy and freedom. They float political parties and maintain an extensive agit-prop apparatus. They create entrenched interests, and privileged enclaves. They bribe, buy and blackmail. They train and finance local propagandists, ideologues and terrorists.

---

[7]This was written before the breakdown of the Soviet Union as the World-Centre of Communism.

They infiltrate the universities and the media. In India, they already control our academic and intellectual life; they define for us our national ideology and write our history. Thanks to their work and their eminent position, Hinduism has already become a dirty word and the Hindu elites have learnt to be apologetic and ashamed of their identity.

IV

1. Communists run many Schools, in India and abroad, where they train their followers in their philosophy and ideational framework. Christians maintain hundreds of Seminaries where they teach Christian "apologetics"; they also maintain Missionary Seminaries where they train their recruits specifically for missionary work in native lands. Muslims have their al-Azhar and their Deoband; many new Madrasas are also coming up and a lot of *tablighi* work is going on.

2. Hindus, however, do not have even a single centre like this. Let them fill up this lacuna. Let them have at least one good and well-endowed Study-Centre or Seminary for self-training, for studying and projecting Hindu ideation and Hindu values and to defend them against the onslaught of inimical forces. At this centre, let them study themselves and study others. Let this centre identify problems facing Hinduism; let it draw the attention of different Hindu leaders, monks, scholars, and teachers to these problems. This centre should initiate, activate, energize and coordinate; in short, it should work as a gadfly and play the role of an vanguard.

It should discuss the dangers that Hinduism faces and suggest remedial measures. It should engage in the task of meeting such dangers as are posed by such ideologies as Communism, Islam and Christianity. It should aim at developing what Sri Aurobindo calls an "aggressive defence."

3. The scope of work of the proposed Centre or Seminary could be as wide and various as the problems that Hinduism faces.

V

Let us, here, name some of the more empirical problems for illustrative purpose without any claim to completeness.

1. Temples

(a) Hindus temples have been under unprecedented attack for a thousand years. They suffered desecration, destruction, confiscation of their property and iniquitous taxation under the Muslim rulers. Under the British, the more physical methods ceased but fiscal methods were adopted for undermining "heathenism". A large part of the land and properties of the temples were taken away under all kinds of pretexts.

(b) After independence, the temples have fared no better. Their properties have not been restored to them and they continue to exist in deepening poverty. In the South where there are still many noble structures left, the temples are under the control of a Government which takes pride in being "secular", and whose secularity is thoroughly anti-Hindu in orientation.

(c) Hindus should study the problem of the temples in all its ramifications. They should run their religious institutions themselves. They should build temples once destroyed, and build new temples where they are needed. They should rejuvenate the temple life and they should take all measures to put the temple institution on a sound financial footing.

(d) Temples should become more active in the teaching of the culture which upholds them. They should become more than mere places of formal worship. They should become centres for promoting Hindu *dharma*.

(e) Wherever possible, the temples should have more open space, more halls for such religious activities as *kīrtanas* and *kathās* and religious discourses. Such activities make a religion more living.

(f) With these activities is connected the institution of

wandering monks bards and *bhajan-maṇḍalīs*. Once this was a very living institution but like other religious institutions of the Hindus it is also declining now. Let us do our best to revive it too.

2. Priests

Inevitably the priests too have suffered along with the temples. They have become indigent and illiterate. Thanks to their indigence and illiteracy, they have suffered in prestige too. It is a great national loss. Effort should be made to rehabilitate them and raise them educationally and financially.

3. Other Functionaries: Hindu *saṁskāras*

What is happening to priests in the temples is happening all along the line to all the priestly functionaries connected with such events as birth, wedding, death, *śrāddha*, etc. Illiteracy and poverty have overtaken them. Many times these functionaries are not available at all. They are dying out fast as a class. Hindu leaders must give their attention to this problem too.

Hindu *saṁskāras* are profound and deeply significant. They teach one to see the infinite and the eternal in the finite and the perishable. They widen the vision and they are deeply integrative. Their profound significance should be explained and every effort should be made to make the Hindus familiar with them, reflect on them and perform them.

The performance of Hindu *saṁskāras* need not be costly at all for they can be performed "internally" as well. But their outer performance is also important, particularly of reeducative and social purpose. Therefore, means should be found whereby not even the poorest have to go without having to perform them for lack of even small funds.

4. Foreign Funds

(a) While we have said that the Hindus should re-build their temples and look after their priests, we know it is easier said than done. There are sharp limitations. Here we come up face to face with a political question. While Hindus have no Government of their own, they have to compete with the so-called "minorities" who have scores of Governments and rich nations at their back. As a result, while even many of the most renowned temples remain in a dilapidated condition and cry for most urgent repairs, it is possible for hundreds of thousands of mosques all over India to get a face-lift almost simultaneously. Similarly, while most of the temples go without proper daily *pūjā*, it is possible for a million mosques to acquire a public address system from one corner of India to another, literally in one morning. Common sense will tell us that some great planning is at work and simple arithmetic should show that huge funds are involved.[8]

(b) Hindus suffer a similar disadvantage vis-a-vis Christian missionaries. According to Government figures, 4,340 million rupees came openly last year (1980) alone for subverting Hindu culture and the country's political set-up. The missionaries have already monopolized several important spheres of national life. And since money begets money, a lot of property is passing into the hands of Christian institutions.

(c) Hinduism in India is a target of a cold-war. The aggressor is well-equipped. Hindus have hardly any defence. They do not have even a Government of their own. They should raise the question of "foreign funds" and even the question of the nature of the Indian Government in a big way.

5. Social Evils

(a) They are galore; here we mention only a few of them. Vulgarity is creeping in the celebration of our festivals like Deepawali, Holi, Ramaleela, Durga Puja. These have become occasions for gambling, drinking, vulgar film music.

---

[8]One million mosques (only a portion of the total number of mosques) multiplied by Rs.5000 (cost of a public address system on the lower side) gives us the figure of five hundred crores.

Vulgarity is also creeping in celebrations connected with wedding.

(b) Cinemas are becoming great moral and social pollutants. They teach crime and cynicism. New literature and journalism wallow in obscenity. There is great vulgarity in advertisements.

(c) Our women are not receiving due respect. The old are being neglected. The spirit of cherishing and reverence are on the wane. Faith and fidelity are going out of relations. The sense of meaninglessness is on the increase. The spirit of excellence, vocation and *sādhanā* is yielding place to commercialism, cynicism and nihilism.

The spiritual leaders of the society have to meet these problems as best as they can.

6. Beautification of our Land

The spiritual values Hinduism teaches are comprehensive. They include in their ambit social and ecological values too. Hinduism teaches simplicity and *śuchi*; it teaches us reverence for the elements, for animals and plants. We have been taught to see life in rivers and woods; taught to see even divine figures behind the Himalayas, the Ganga, the Yamuna, the Godavari, the Kavery. Let us accept them as symbols and start a movement for keeping them clean. Let us start reforestation; let us see that our mountains are not denuded.

7. Ideational, Cultural and Educational Work

(a) A great spiritual culture also throws up a great system of ideas. A great spiritual truth also seeks an ideational vehicle. When the ideational work is neglected, spiritual truths also become weak.

Hitherto Muslims, Christians and Communists have been writing for us our history, philosophy and religion — and increasingly we are accepting their version. Let us, for a change, look at Islam, Christianity and Communism from the Hindu angle. It is a great task, a necessary task. Let us look at their scriptures, their revelations, their concepts of God and Prophetism from the vantage point of the Yoga. We should not accept them at their words. Let us look at them a little more critically.

(b) Since we have neglected the role of ideation, hostile ideas have taken possession of our intellectuals. Therefore, there is great need for more intellectual understanding of ourselves and of our opponents. Deeper and more sustained ideological and spiritual work alone could meet the challenge of hostile ideas.

The absence of self-understanding and self-articulation is doing havoc. For example, our history was once written from the British-Christian view-point; now it is bring written from a "secular" viewpoint, adding another source of distortion. Similarly, galore of books are coming on "Hindu" castes as if Hinduism has nothing else and as if Christians and Muslims have no castes of their own. But to promote this view of Hinduism is part of a larger mischievous plan.

8. Vanavasis and Harijans

Mischievous elements are active amongst them. Christians were already active in the field. Now Muslims, armed with Arab money, have also joined the game. We must give our best thought to the problem. More work is needed amongst them.

9. Islam, Christianity and Communism

(a) All of them pose a danger. They have their own quarrels, but they all unite in subverting India. Islam has already taken away a big chunk of the Indian land and population; it is now coveting the remaining part too. Muslims are fanning our differences; they are buying up our politicians and intellectuals.

(b) Throughout 800 years of Muslim domination, we *fought Muslims*, many times bravely; *but we never fought Islam. We never studied it. And yet it is not Muslims but Islam that is our problem.* And it is a continuing problem. We must look at it more closely. We must study its origin, its history, its inspiration, its founder, its scriptures more critically.

(c) We should understand the Muslim society, it castes and creeds, its *ashrāfs* and its *arzāls*. We should find out who came from outside as invaders and who became converts under compulsion from the great Hindu society. While isolating the foreign elements, we should help the local converts to come back to their ancestral fold and accord them a warm welcome, as Gandhiji desired.

(d) Muslims love to talk of their grievances. Let us for a change also talk of ours. Let us make a directory of the temple they have destroyed; let us prepare an account of the nations they have enslaved and exploited and millions of men and women they have slayed; let us tell them about their predatory imperialism.

(e) For ourselves we must also realize that these facts of their history are not incidental, but they are related to the basic tenets of their religion; they are the natural expression of an undeveloped and distorted spirituality.

(f) Let us also become aware of what is happening in the far-away corners, in Assam, Arunachal, Meghalaya, Ladakh; what silent nibbling is going on there; the large-scale conversion and infiltration.

(g) We must show determination in stopping large-scale infiltration of men and women numbering into millions from Bangladesh. It is a planned invasion — there is no doubt about it.

10. Conclusion

These are some examples of the kind of problems that demand our attention. It is obvious that these problems are not temporary but they have a deeper source. It is also obvious that they need more than agitational approach. No *ad-hocism* or temporizing will do. The situation demands not sentimentalizing but realistic appraisal. It demands deep-sighted and far-looking work. It demands vision, faith and perseverance. It requires a mind which is not seeking quick results and push-button solutions, but can work for distant aims. It demands work at a deeper level; it demands spiritual and ideational preparation.

Chapter 3

Buddhism vis-a-vis Hinduism[1]

Buddhism is returning home to India after a long exile of a thousand years and, like the proverbial prodigal son, is being received with open arms. Religious tolerance of the average Hindu partly explains the warm reception. But a very important reason is the fact that Buddha and Buddhism form an intimate part of Hindu consciousness. Buddha was a Hindu. Buddhism is Hindu in its origin and development, in its art and architecture, iconography, language, beliefs, psychology, names, nomenclature, religious vows and spiritual discipline. Though living in distant lands for so long, it remains essentially Hindu, at least, in the expression of its religious ideals

[1][This essay was first written and published in July, 1958. It subsequently saw two more editions published with minor changes here and there. It is being included in this volume too with small changes and addition of a few footnotes placed in brackets. It was read by Sri C. Rajagopalachari. We reproduce his comments from *Swarajya*, dated May 21, 1966: "I read with great interest Sri Ram Swarup's scholarly paper on the intimate connection, amounting almost to identity, between Buddhistic philosophy, and the Vedanta of the Upanishads. Hindu conformism sensed the danger lurking in a close identity with a school of thought which may well be misunderstood to be a denial of God and soul. Consequently Hinduism kept Buddhism rigidly out of the pale. Sri Ram Swarup's paper explains how Hinduism saved itself from the dangers of its own philosophical dialectics through the cult of Bhakti and surrender. The concluding passage from Sri Ram Swarup's paper takes us to out own time:

> "New India looks upon her spiritual inheritance as a reactionary and undesirable burden. The class that now controls the political, cultural and intellectual life of the country proudly and openly proclaims atheistic beliefs and positivistic values. Today India prides herself in being a 'secular' State, a secularity which is more anti-spiritual than anti-communal in its temper.
>
> "There is a beautiful dialogue of Lord Buddha with a disciple monk who was dissatisfied with the Buddha's non-discussion of the nature of God and the Soul... then is reproduced the long dialogue with Venerable Malunkyaputta given in this essay."]

and spiritual experience at the highest level. Hinduism is not all Buddhism, but Buddhism forms part of the ethos which is essentially Hindu.

Though that is the general reaction of an average Hindu who carries within him the memories of a distant past, academic scholarship, dealing in views and schools of thought as self-sufficient entities and discussing religious systems of thought divorced from the living tradition of religion, has reached quite a different conclusion. According to these scholars and translators, Buddhism was a revolt against Hinduism, not only against certain prevalent sacrificial cults and certain rigidities in caste organization, but also against the whole spiritual tradition and premises of the age.

In fact, certain intellectuals and groups of materialist-secularist persuasion are extending a warm welcome to Buddhism because in it they see a timely corrective to the "supernatural prejudices" of Hinduism regarding God and Soul, "superstitions which weaken a nation". According to them, Buddha was rather a clever student of logical positivism, a thorough-going rationalist and empiricist. Endowed with healthy scepticism, he saw through the so-called established truths of religion, but being also discreet he refrained from expressing his *real* opinions on religious questions too fully and openly. Thus observing tactical silence over religious questions he taught people a *rational morality* called his three *śīlas*, in this way lopping off by means of an Occam's razor the whole mystical superstructure.

Thus Buddhism is being recommended as a school of rationality and social morality without the superfluous adjuncts of religion: morality without God or Soul.[2]

[2]Even Dr. Radhakrishnan, no foreigner to religious thought, has made statements which strengthen this positivistic interpretation of Buddhism. He says of Buddha that "he is a rationalist, since he wished to study reality or experience without any reference to supernatural revelation. He wished to lead men by mere force of logic to his views... He wanted to establish a religion within the bounds of pure reason. He is a dialectician, arguing with his opponents to lead them to liberation." On another occasion, he turns Buddha into a modern agnostic. He declares: "Suspended judgment was Buddha's attitude."

A deeper study does not support these evaluations of Buddhism. True, Buddha was a great mind whose eyes pierced through the show of things to their core, but he was no rationalist in the modern sense of the term. Instead, he had a healthy contempt for intellectual systems and theories so popular with rationalists of all ages. On more than one occasion (in Aggi-vacchagotta sutta, Majjhima Nikāya, for example), he called these theories "a net of sophistry (*diṭṭhi-jāla*), a web of tangle (*diṭṭhi-ganthi*), a jungle (*diṭṭhi-gahana*), a wilderness (*diṭṭhi-kāntāra*), a thorn or puppet-show (*diṭṭhi-visūka*), a writhing (*diṭṭhi-vipphandita*), a fetter (*diṭṭhi-saṁyojana*), and an intoxicant (*diṭṭhi-āsava*)... coupled with misery, ruin, despair and agony (*dukkha*, *vighāta*, *daur-manasya*, *upayāsa*)". For arriving at truth, he did not adopt the method of classification, comparison, verification, deduction, experimentation which is what rational approach means, but the method of moral purification, meditation, intuition, passive waiting combined with alert watchfulness, steady and sustained aspiration, all leading to transcendental illumination, progressive or sudden — the method of going beyond discursive mind for the light of the Truth.

Nor do we agree with the other view which equates Buddhism with a moral discipline alone. Buddha himself rejected this view of his teachings in no uncertain terms. He affirmed that his teachings on moral conduct were "not significant" and were only of "secondary, importance." He declared that his teachings regarding meditation (*samādhi*) and transcendental knowledge (*prajñā*) were the most important. Those who admired him for his moral teachings alone were, according to him, "witlings", men of ordinary intelligence (*puthujjana*).[3]

So Buddha's rationality and morality had a transcendental base above. This transcendence is the highlight and essence of

---

[3]We have refrained from mentioning here a third rendering of Buddhism which is existentialist. "Being trapped", "nothingness", "emptiness", "meaninglessness", the usuals Sartrian fare, constitute, according to this rendering, the basic motifs of Buddhism.

Buddha's teachings, the justification of his claim to be a great world teacher and guide.

Similarly, Buddha's compassion was not merely secular or even humanistic; rather it was a deep and living concern of the "Enlightened One" for worldly creatures caught in the wheel of existence, birth, disease, decay, old age, death. The peace he taught was Upanishadic "peace beyond understanding", not merely civic and political truce amongst men and nations. The joy he taught was not just a physical release of tension or a physical sense of well-being or even some psychological euphoria; on the other hand, it was the joy of emancipation from the web of repeated births.

After this brief digression, we come back to the point from where we started, namely, the relationship of Buddhism with Hinduism.

A discussion of this relationship is important for various reasons. Firstly, because it will help us to understand the deeper ideas and ideals of half the world which owes allegiance to the two religions. Secondly, because it will be interesting and instructive to see how the world's two most ancient, most mystical, most abiding, most creative religions have expressed their intuition of the Transcendent. Thirdly, because, it may help all spiritual seekers in their inner exploration, illumine their paths and give voice to their own experiences. To understand the two religions is to understand some of the deepest questions relating to spiritual theology, a whole gamut of yogic practices and spiritual disciplines.

Buddha's Silence

The nature of relationship between Hinduism and Buddhism is clouded and misunderstood and its intimacy minimized for two reasons.

One reason is Buddha's silence over such fundamental questions as *Brahma*, God and soul, questions which occupy the centre of interest in the Upanishadic literature. The other reason is Buddha's individual nuances and emphases. These nuances are not lacking in the Upanishads; but there they form only a part of a larger whole, and, therefore, do not create the same one-sided impression of escapism and painfulness of existence.

First, we shall discuss Buddha's silence. The reasons why he refrained from discussions relating to God and soul are two. He refused to answer all questions that did not lead to an individual's practical spiritual benefit. Spirituality tends to be very practical. It avoids all idle preoccupation with intellectual systems.

It was eminently necessary in the days of Buddha. From the Buddhist accounts of those days one finds that the country was reeking with innumerable soul-losing systems of thought, a bewildering maze of opinions in which the mind was irretrievably lost. There prevailed 62 systems of philosophy, 18 theories regarding the origin of the world, 44 theories regarding its end. There were 23 methods of penance in food, 12 in clothing. There were interminable discussions regarding the state of the soul after death. There were *akriyāvādins*, *daivavādins*, *jaḍavādins*, *akritavādins*, *aniśchitavādins*, dialecticians and intellectuals of all varieties. There were big halls in every city where intellectuals foregathered and discussed theories regarding God, soul, time and space. No wonder the soul got lost in these intellectual exercises. Mentation became a perfect substitute for God-seeking. For a spiritualist, this atmosphere is truly uninviting. Right effort is more important than idle cerebration. No wonder Buddha refused to entertain these questions. Clever people would come to him and put the same question in several forms (mostly in the form of the quadrilemma), but Buddha responded to them with silence.

That the interests of Buddha were fully practical is very well brought out by a dialogue the Blessed One had with a monk named Venerable Māluṅkyaputta. The monk said to himself: "These theories which the Blessed One has left unelucidated, has set aside and rejected — that the world is eternal, that the world is not eternal, that the world is finite, that the world is infinite, that the soul and the body are identical, that the soul is one thing and the body another, that the saint exists after death, that the saint does not exist after death, that the saint neither exists nor does not exist after death — these the Blessed One does not elucidate to me." He therefore decided that if the Blessed One did not do that he would abandon religious discipleship.

The Blessed One called him dull and silly (*mogha-purusha*) and answered his doubts with the help of an inimitable illustration. He began by saying: "It is as if, Māluṅkyaputta, a man had been wounded by an arrow thickly smeared with poison, and his friends and companions, his relatives and kinsfolk, were to procure for him a physician or surgeon; and the sick man was to say, 'I will not have this arrow taken out until I have learnt whether the man who wounded me belonged to the warrior caste, or to the Brahmin caste, or to the agricultural caste, or to the menial caste; learnt his name and the clan he belonged to; learnt whether he was tall, short, or of the middle height; was black, dusky or of a yellow skin; was from this or that village or town or city; whether the bow which wounded me was a *chāpa* or a *kodaṇḍa*; whether the bowstring was made from swallow-wort or bamboo or sinew or *mārava* or from wilk-weed; whether the shaft was a *kaccha* or a *repima*; whether it was feathered from the wings of a vulture, a heron, a falcon, a peacock, or a *sithilahanu*; whether it was wound round with the sinews of an ox, a buffalo, a *ruru* dear or of a monkey; whether it was an ordinary arrow, or a claw-headed arrow, or a *vekaṇḍa*, or an iron arrow, or a calf-tooth arrow, or a *karavīrapaṭṭa*'. That man would die Māluṅkyaputta, without ever having learnt this."

"In exactly the same way," Lord Buddha added, "Māluṅkyaputta, any one who should say, 'I will not lead the religious life under the Blessed Once until the Blessed One shall elucidate to me either that the world is eternal, or that the world is not eternal...or that the saint neither exists nor does not exist after death;' — that person would die, Mālunkyaputta, before the Tathāgata had ever elucidated to him."

The teacher further concluded: "The religious life, Mālunkyaputta, does not depend on the dogma that the world is eternal, infinite or finite, that the soul and the body are identical or different, or the dogma that the saint exists or does not exist after death." The elucidation of these points is bootless. It "profits not, nor has it to do with the fundamentals of religion, nor tends to aversion, absence of passion, cessation, quiescence, the supernatural faculties, supreme wisdom, and Nirvāna." (Chulla-Mālunkya-sutta, Majjhima Nikāya 2.2.3)

Ineffability of Transcendental Experience

There was another reason why Buddha refused to discuss metaphysical questions. It was not only the futility of these questions, but the impossibility of answering them in a language intelligible to the mind. The *Kena Upanishad* says: "There the eye goes not; speech goes not, nor the mind. We know not, we understand not. How one would teach it?" Buddha found himself in the same predicament. Things which according to all spiritual literature lie beyond mind cannot be rendered into mental concepts. Any answer made to these questions therefore "does not fit the case", as Buddha emphasized repeatedly.

Buddha illustrated this point with the help of a very apt analogy which, incidentally, also indicated his view of the question of the real status of a liberated soul. If a fire were to burn in front of you, you would be aware of this fact. You would also be aware of the fact that the fire depended on fuel of grass and wood for its burning. Further, if this fire were to become extinct, you would also be aware of this fact. "But, Vaccha [a mendicant of *vats gotra*], if some one were to ask you, 'In which direction has that fire gone, — east, or west or south?' — what would you say, O Vaccha?" asked the great teacher.

"The question would not fit the case, Gautama. For the fire which depended on fuel of grass and wood, when that fuel has all gone, and it can get no other, being thus without nutriment, is said to be extinct," Vaccha replied.

Buddha concluded: "In exactly the same way, Vaccha, all form, all consciousness by which one could predicate the existence of the saint, when that form and consciousness have been abandoned, uprooted, pulled out of the ground like a palmyra-tree, and become non-existent and not liable to spring up again in the future. The saint, O Vaccha, who has been released from what is styled as form and consciousness is deep, immeasurable, unfathomable (*gambhīra, appameyya, duppariyogaho*) like the mighty ocean. To say that he is reborn would not fit the case. To say that he is not reborn would not fit the case. To say that he is both reborn and not reborn would not fit the case. To say that he is neither reborn nor yet reborn would not fit the case." (Agg-vaccha sutta, Majjhima Nikāya 2.3.2).

In a parallel passage, the *Muṇḍaka Upanishad* says:

As the flowing rivers in the ocean
Disappear, quitting name and form,
So the Knower, being liberated from name and form,
Goes unto the Heavenly Person, higher than the high.

Indeed, what could be said about the status of the freed Soul or Self? Can it be called individual, or universal, or transcendental? Can this state be described or measured? Can it be called existence, or non-existence in our sense of the terms? The state is deep, immeasurable, unfathomable.

The Vedānta has not given a different answer. True, its language has been more positive, but the answer has not been dissimilar. According to the *Māṇḍūkya Upanishad* the transcendental reality is *a-drișṭa* (unseen), *a-grāhya* (ungraspable), *a-cintya* (non-thinkable), *a-lakshaṇa* (non-distinctional), *a-vyapadeśya* (undesignable).

When the soul or self is enthralled in matter, in the relativity of things, in names and forms, what "one" knows (or rather what is known) is change, flux, pain, bondage, a cluster of sensation-groups which one regards as one's self. But when the knot of existence has been loosened, when the world of names and forms dissolves, vanishes, the saint or the freed soul enters into a state which is "deep, immeasurable, unfathomable like a mighty ocean" and which is, as we shall see, characterized by the attributes of freedom, peace, bliss and consciousness.

The Nature of Buddha's Experience of Nirvāṇa

There are two methods of dealing with a problem: practical and theoretical; psychological and metaphysical. For example, the Sāṁkhya discusses *tattvas*, principles; the Yoga assuming those principles, discusses methodology, the processes. Similarly, while the Vedānta discusses principles, the nature of the Supreme Reality, Buddhism discusses methods, the moral and meditational disciplines leading to supernatural experiences whose nature Buddha refused to describe. True, Buddha also speaks of *prajñā*, the four noble truths, but these too are offered in the first instance for practical purposes, for the purpose of fixing one's mind on them, for creating a state of *vairāgya* in the aspirant, for turning him away from the world of names and forms. Their full transcendental meaning is revealed only at the end. And when that happens, that is Buddhahood, Enlightenment, Nirvāṇa whose nature he refused to discuss.

But can we guess, in the face of Buddha's silence, the meaning of what he meant? By guessing, I do not mean arriving at and knowing the truths as he knew them. That is not given to intellect at all. By guessing, I mean, can we place him in the spiritual tradition? That is — was Buddha just a freak in the sense that what happened to him happened to none else before and to none else after him except of course to some of his bright disciples? Or was he a mighty representative, a leader of a well-authenticated spiritual tradition such as is so highly developed in the Upanishads and confirmed by great teachers and seers of ancient times ? In short, did he belong to a spiritual tradition which is timeless; or was he a freak, an accident in the spiritual tradition of his country?

I believe that posed thus the question is not difficult to answer. His spiritual experience could not be a freak, arbitrary and personal. It must have been of a character universal and necessary. There is reason to believe that his spiritual experience was wholly in the Vedantic tradition. This conclusion is inescapable as one studies Buddha's teachings. Buddha himself claims no more. He only claims to have "seen an ancient way, an ancient road followed by the wholly awakened ones of olden times". In Buddhism as in the Vedānta, self-abnegation was to precede a transcendental experience. One has to discover the voidness of the seeming full before one can discover the fullness of the seeming void. "Not by speech, not by mind, not by sight can He be apprehended." Desire has to go. All mental constructions, imagination and fancy have to go. "When cease the five sense knowledge, together with the mind and the intellect stirs not," "When are cut all the knots of the heart on earth," then begins the dawn of the spiritual knowledge and freedom. Buddha confirms the Upanishadic truth above. He says, "The Tathāgata, O Vaccha, is free from all theories; but this, Vaccha, does the Tathāgata know, — the nature of form (*rūpa*), and how form arises, and how form perishes; the nature of sensation (*vedanā*), and how sensation arises, and how sensation perishes; the nature of perception (*saṁjñā*), and how perception arises, and how perception perishes; the nature of the predispositions (*saṁskāra*), and how the predispositions arise, and how the predispositions finish; the nature of consciousness (*vijñāna*), and how consciousness arises, and how consciousness perishes. Therefore say I that the Tathāgata has attained deliverance and is free from attachment, in as much as all imaginings, or agitations, or false notions concerning an Ego or anything pertaining to an Ego, have perished, have faded away, have been given up and relinquished." The seeming self, the vital as well as the mental, which is mistaken for the permanent and the eternal has to fall silent.

Not only in the self-noughting of the phenomenal but also in the characterization of the transcendental, Buddha follows the Upanishads. The nihilistic rendering by which Buddhism is known today is caused by some of his future followers but there is nothing in the teachings of the Master himself to support this negativism.[4] "The Deathless has been found by me," declared Buddha after his enlightenment. Nirvāṇa was described as a state "in which there is neither old age, nor fear, nor disease, nor birth, nor death, nor anxiety". In Udāna (Suttapiṭaka), it is called *abhūta*, *ajāta*, *akaṭa*, *asaṅkhata* (unbecome, unborn, unmade, uncompound). This is almost the language of the Vedānta, the THAT of the Upanishads, declared to be imperishable, deathless, free, unborn, self-existent (*svayambhū*), uncompassing (*paribhū*) by *Īśa Upanishad*; resplendent (*divya*), formless (*a-mūrta*), pure (*śubhra*) by *Muṇḍaka Upanishad*; timeless (*a-kāla*), without parts (*a-kala*), great glory (*mahad yaśas*) by *Śvetāśvatara Upanishad*. In this state which is called Nirvanic by Buddha and Brahmic by the Vedānta, there is a complete cessation of diminution or development; it is the state of *prapañcho-paśama* as the *Māṇḍūkya Upanishad* declares. It is *self-same eternally* and "deep, immeasurable and unfathomable".

The interesting account of Buddha's spiritual experience of enlightenment confirms and closely agrees with the Upanishadic teaching regarding the nature of the Ultimate Reality.

"At that time The Buddha, The Blessed One, was dwelling at Uruvela at the foot of the Bo-tree on the banks of the river Nerañjarā, having just attained the Buddhaship. Then the Blessed one sat cross-legged for seven days together at the foot of the Bo-tree experiencing the bliss of emancipation...

---

[4]According to Edward Conze, a great scholar of Buddhism, the term *Empty* (*śūnya*) though known to the Abhidharmists, occurs only on a few occasions in the Pali Canon, the earliest Buddhist literature.

Then the Blessed One after the lapse of seven days, arose from that state of exalted calm, and leaving the foot of the Bo-tree...sat cross-legged at the foot of the Ajapāla banyan tree for seven days together, experiencing the bliss of emancipation."

Thus he kept enjoying this supernatural calm and bliss for 49 days at a stretch moving from tree to tree every seven days.

Here the experience of Nirvāṇa is not couched in the language of "nothingness", "emptiness", but is constituted of "exalted calm, bliss, emancipation, bodhihood". It is just as the Upanishads speak, *śānti*, peace that passeth understanding, *sat*, *chit*, *ānanda*, knowledge, freedom, light.[5] In the spiritual tradition this state has been called both *void* as well as *all* and *full.*

Nothingness of the Phenomenal World

So, at the time of enlightenment, Gautama not only entered a state which was "deep, immeasurable, unfathomable", not only saw a reality full of "calm", "bliss," "liberation" and quite indescribable as the Upanishads assert, but was also vouchsafed the vision of the true status of the phenomenal world. This vision was not different from the Vedantic characterization of this world. Buddha saw in a moment the entire process which constitutes this *saṁsāra*, this world-cycle, this fleeting stream of life. He saw that which causes births and rebirths without end, which frames the edifice of repeated births, decay, dissolution and death. He saw the mighty Law of Karma, the Law of Dependent Origination (*pratītya samutpāda*): he saw the twelve links in the chain that

[5][In most ancient Buddhistic literature, the Nirvanic state has been described in most positive terms and it has taken on almost the same epithets as the Brahmic state in the Upanishads and the Puranas. Rhys Davids tells us that Nirvāṇa has been called "the harbour of refuge, the cool cave, the island amidst the floods, the place of bliss, emancipation, liberation, safety, the supreme, the transcendental, the uncreated, the transquil, the home of ease, the calm, the end of suffering, the medicine for all evil, the unshaken, the ambrosia, the immaterial, the imperishable, the abiding, the further shore, the unending, the bliss of effort, the supreme joy, the ineffable, the detachment, the holy city, and many others" (*Early Buddhism*).]

constitutes the "wheel of life". He saw that the root of all existence is *avidyā* (nescience, ignorance); from this arises *saṁskāra* (predispositions, or unshakable volitions or *chetanā*, the compelling *kamma* which produces rebirth); from this comes *vijñāna* (the rebirth or relink consciousness); it is the basic consciousness with which one is born; in it reside all the past impressions, characteristics and tendencies of the individual life. Corresponding to this consciousness arises a psycho-physical individuality called *nāma-rūpa*. Suitable to this individuality follow the six organs of sense and their six-fold spheres, *shaḍāyatana*. Then follows *sparśa* (contact of the subjective with the objective world); then come successively *vedanā* (feeling, sensation), *trishṇā* (craving, or thirst for life), *upādāna* (grasping and clinging to life; it gives birth to a false notion of "I" and "mine"); *bhava* (renewed existence, or those active and passive psychological forces which condition future birth); *jāti* (rebirth), followed by *jarā-maraṇa* (old age and death), *śoka-parideva*, *daurmanasya-upayāsa* (tribulation, grief, sorrow, distress and despair). Round and round. The doctrine is deep and the meanings of the terms describing the process have to be fixed internally through *sādhanā*.

Buddha saw the law forward and backward. He saw how it gave rise to the entire aggregate of misery. He also saw how on the complete fading out and cessation of the last term or link, the whole chain snaps and the entire aggregation of misery ceases. And as he saw the law of the phenomenal world, he was also released from its bondage. He sang:

> O builder! I have discovered thee!
> This fabric thou shalt never rebuild!
> Thy rafters are all broken now,
> And pointed roof demolished lies!
> The mind has demolition reached,
> And seen the last of all desire!

What Buddha experienced was the vision, celebrated in the Upanishads, that the world of man divorced from Brahma, the phenomenal world conceived independently of the transcendental principle is nothing, is less than nothing. Conceived as such it is an illusion, *māyā*, an imposition, a house of cards, a castle of sand, mere saw-dust, dry-rot, a sagging, sinking, stinking garbage-heap. They build in vain who build without *That*.

This "builder" who weaves the fabric of existence is everywhere. Its power is found to be so flimsy when the true knowledge comes, but before that it is so nightsmarishly real. Having no support anywhere *in essence*, it is yet so ubiquitous in its external expression. It surrounds one on all sides. It seeps through every pore. It is laid thick layer upon layer. It is gross as well as subtle. Its empire is vast. Its sovereignty is everywhere. It lives not only in the grosser acts and thoughts of men, it lives in their righteousness, ideals and good too. No wonder sages who have seen its universal sway have tried to describe it by different images and names. They call it *līlā*, *māyā*, *avidyā*, Inconscience. This power is the author of the whole realm of names and forms, good as well as bad. So *māyā* or *avidyā* is not just like wrong perception or an error of judgement; it is a basic category which imposes itself at the very source of all phenomenal perceptions and judgements, enters into the very constitution and fibre of our empirical knowledge, effort and will.

Though so compelling and powerful, yet when the transcendental light dawns, it is either completely transfigured or it completely disappears like mist before the sun. Men and women of a deeper seeking have found the phenomenal world joyless and unfulfilling, and they have sought release from its insufficiency, and yearned with all their heart to be granted refuge at the feet of the Divine. There are beautiful poems by Kabir, Surdas, Ramaprasad and Mira on the subject which echo the cry of the human soul in bondage and exile for freedom and re-union in and with the Divine from whom they came.

The dying-to-self, inner purification, transcendence from the world of mind and desires are normal things that happen to any saint of stature, but the process is generally silent. It is rare that the knowledge of the origin and the dissolution of the whole world of all names and forms is revealed so powerfully and intimately as it was to Buddha. Again, in other saints sufficient deepening or silencing of the surface mind and being is enough for higher spiritual experience to pour in. But in Buddha it is obvious that what happened was not mere silencing and deepening and detachment at the surface, but a complete cessation and annihilation of all that could give rise to the world of names and forms, a veritable "seedless" (*nirbīja*) *samādhi*. His dialogues (and also his statues and pictures) exude peace, self-recollectedness, detachment and yet compassion, all with a powerful transcendental impress.

Though rare, yet the experience is not an isolated phenomenon. We find this in Vedantic literature and in other developed spiritualities, though the terms and images of the form-creating power or principle need not be the same in all expereinces. Some have seen Godhead creating the worlds, oceans, stars, nights and days from his status of plenitude and self-sufficiency, by the creative power of his Word, or *chit-śakti*. We have Platonic and neo-Platonic images of the process of creation or manifestation. Others have seen God pouring Himself out in multitudinous forms and yet remaining essentially unaffected by His creation. In the Gita, we find Sri Krishna revealing his mighty Form to Arjuna: time and space, high gods and noble warriors, everything in the three worlds rising from and rushing headlong into his "gaping mouth; tremendous-toothed and terrible to see".

There are other experiences less theistic though not less transcendental. Some have seen the world of relative forms appearing and disappearing according to the laws of karma. Sāṁkhya provides another account. In it we see Prakriti, moved forward by its three *guṇas*, giving rise to the whole world of names and forms. At the time of dissolution the Prakriti in equilibrium withdraws unto itself all the forms and forces it created and goes out of manifestation. Buddha's experience is akin to the above in the sense that the process of creation or manifestation is not referred to a conscious principle, to a Purusha or the God, but to a Law as immanent and absolute as the former. In Buddha, the terms of the Law of Dependent Origination on which hangs all the world of names and forms, sound like ordinary facts of life, but the knowledge of their operation as revealed to him was transcendental.

Quite in keeping with the practical approach of Buddha, the terms of his Law are rather individualized: Karma, contact, consciousness, desire, etc. On the other hand, Sāṁkhya talks in the language of principles *tattvas*: *prakriti*, *mahat*, *ahaṁkāra*, *manas*, *tanmātras*, etc.

II

We have discussed the similarity and even the sameness of Buddhistic experience of Nirvāṇa with the Upanishadic experience of the Ultimate Reality. We must now also account for some of the differences, both primary as well as secondary. As one reads the literatures of Hinduism and Buddhism, one cannot help being impressed by the fact that the two create very different atmospheres or ethos. All transcendental experiences are incommunicable and inexpressible in the language of the mind, but the fact that one uses one particular language rather than another in reporting its mental impression of the transcendental experience is not accidental. It does convey, however imperfectly, something to the nature of that experience. The difference in language also conveys a difference in the nature of the spiritual experiences. But the differences do not invalidate the truth of One spiritual life, or One spiritual reality.

The Divine is capable of and permits multiple contacts which when expressed in human language may even seem, to an external view, to exclude each other, but which in reality indicate the fact that the Ultimate Reality which is One in essence is multiple in its expression and experience.

Dryness of Buddhism: its 'Abstract' Approach

As one studies the early Buddhist literature, one encounters a certain atmosphere of dryness, of narrow and laborious self-culture, of strenuousness. One misses the atmosphere of effortlessness, fullness, ease and self-abandonment, which one comes across, say, in reading Chaitanya, Mira, and Alvar saints etc. In Buddhism, though one comes into intimate contact with the transcendental realm, one is particularly struck by the omission of any reference to God or soul, those mighty facts of spiritual experience which, except for illusionist monism of Shankara, the philosopher (who is very different from Shankara, the *bhakta*), and scholastic renderings of Sāṁkhya, figure so much in the Upanishads, the Gita, the Mahabharata and in the religious consciousness of the country in general.

Regarding the nature of the Ultimate Reality, there are two traditions in India. One tradition images It impersonally as a featureless Brahma, as a formless, relationless Absolute. As one abstracted from the lesser and more mixed expressions and forms of the Ultimate Reality, one contacted Its highest attributes of *śānti*, *sat*, *chit*, and *ānanda*. The Supreme Reality could be experienced as peace or liberation, but It could also be experienced as Bliss and Consciousness. Further it was possible to abstract even from these attributes. Bliss, Peace, Liberation and Consciousness would recede and one would be left aware of One *Presence* alone, One *Isness*, Something ever-present without a "name and habitation". One could possibly abstract even from this Presence and might experience the Ultimate Reality as some Blank or *śūnya* or even a Nihil, *asat*.

Buddha, it would appear, was in line with this too abstractive approach to the Divine. A Buddhist Nirvāṇa, therefore, came to mean two things:

1. A rather too complete emptying out of the world and the

mind of all forms and relations and a complete dying out of all phenomenal consciousness; and

2. A rather too full abstraction from all the forms, attributes and planes of the Divine — even from the attributes of *sat chit*, and *ānanda*.

In the first sense, Nirvāṇa acquired several names all meaning more or less the same thing; emptying out the mind of all thought-forms and desire-complexes and even of all substantiality. It was called a letting go, a loosing hold, complete cessation, complete fading out, a relinquishment, the perishing of passion, the perishing of hatred, the perishing of infatuation etc. In this sense, Nirvāṇa was the beginning as well as the consummation of the Buddhist Way. It began with the practice of Buddhist *śīla* and ended in the dawn of Buddhist *prajñā*, the supernatural knowledge regarding the unsubstantiality and painfulness of earthly life and earthly goods and the way out of it.

The process of progressive abstraction is carried all along the line in order to eliminate all that is less than Nirvāṇa. The point is well brought out in the Buddhist accounts of a deepening trance. The first trance is characterized by *vitakka* and *vichāra* (reasoning and reflection), *pīti* (exaltation), *sukha* (joy). In the second trance, *vitakka* and *vichāra* cease. In the third trance, *pīti* also ceases and one acquires *upekkhā* (indifference). In the fourth trance, even *sukha* ceases and only *ekāggata* (one-pointedness) and supreme *upekkhā* remain. As the *samādhi* deepens, the process of negation and abstraction continues and one enters the region of the four kinds of the boundless and the vast. Of one who has entered the realm of the infinity of space, the perception of form has stopped; of one who has entered the realm of the infinity of consciousness the perception of the realm of the infinity of space has ceased; of one who has entered the realm of nothingness the perception of the realm of infinity of consciousness has ceased; of one who has entered the realm of neither perception nor yet non-perception, the perception of the realm of nothingness has ceased; of one who has entered the cessation of perception and sensation, perception and sensation have ceased. Beyond the four "infinities" lies the region of Nirvāṇa, the *asamprajñāna* of Pātañjala Yoga.

Saguṇa Brahma: *Bhakti*[6]

But this Ultimate Reality can be experienced not only as a featureless absolute, but also as the lord, a friend, a sustainer, a lover, a personal God to whom the secret aspirant in man gives his all, his mind, his soul, his strength, his heart. There is nothing petty or small or limited about this way of experiencing God. It is as vast, deep, sweet and total. It is the *purushottama* to the Gita Who can be experienced without any form or

[6][We have already reproduced Sri Rajagopalachari's comments on this essay. He was a sage and a great spokesman of Hinduism. His views command our greatest respect. But I beg to make one clarification. Sri Rajagopalacharya agrees that there was a great affinity between the Vedanta and the Buddhist philosophy, but according to him Hinduism saw in it a danger of being misunderstood and identified with a school which denied God and soul; and it met the danger by developing the school of *bhakti* and surrender. I believe Hinduism sensed no such danger and it did not panic into *bhakti* and surrender because of any such danger. The fact is Bhakti and surrender even as a "school" are older than Buddhism. They are great truths of the Spirit and, as is to be expected, they found their great expression in a comprehensive religion like Hinduism as did other great truths of the Spirit. At no stage, there was any intention of keeping Buddhism "out of the pale". Hindus regarded Buddha as a great teacher; many of them joined Buddhism, preached and propagated it; they built Buddhist monasteries, stupas and temples and fed Buddhist monks; they protected Buddhism and defended it when it was threatened; they gave refuge to Buddhists when they were persecuted in Persia, Khurasan, Iraq, Mosul by king Gushtasp and his descendents — in the same manner as they are doing it at present to Buddhist Chakmas fleeing from persecution in Bangladesh; they put Buddha in the pantheon of their avatāras. In this decade, in Kerala two idols of Buddha were found buried; they were recovered and consecrated. One was placed in the temple at Kamapuram and has found the highest place along with the main deities of the temple; the other was placed in the Sree Krishna Temple in Mavelikara town. Both are worshipped by hundreds of devotees daily.]

attribute, but Who also comes to His devotee in the Form in which he worships Him — and comes quite as fully and wholly. He is *param-ānanda, sanātana, pūrṇa*. He is not only transcendent, but immanent too. He is the sole Godhead Who also becomes the *jīvas* and the world. As Sri Chaitanya would say the Ultimate Reality is Sri Krishna, Who also becomes the Gopis, above all, Sri Radha, to taste and relish His own love-in-separation of Himself. Through Radha alone He knows how sweet, heart-ravishing and mind-and-soul-captivating He is.

Christianity and Islam charge that Hindus do not have a personal God. The charge is true in the sense that their God is not anthropomorphic and anthropopathic; nor is he a monolith, nor an aloof and incommunicable being who reveals himself only to a favoured individual called his Only Son or his Last Prophet. Hinduism conceives God differently, as an indwelling spirit seated in the heart of every seeker. Again, he is conceived not merely as a Judge or Father but also as a mother, a friend, a counsellor, a playmate, a consort, a lover and in hundred other ways. Sometimes some Christian saints and Muslim sufis too have done the same but their experiences went beyond the theological bounds of their own religions. The fact is that spiritual theism, like spiritual monism and spiritual polytheism — all have found their most profound expression in Hinduism. God is transcendent and Immanent; He is Impersonal and Personal; He is One and Many; He is Formless and yet He has his divine Form or Forms; He is Nameless, yet He has his Name or Names. In his personal manifestations, He indulges in His divine *līlās*, his divine Play and Pastimes; He has his divine Associates and divine Abodes (*dhāmas*). Vaikuṇṭha, Vrindāvana, Golok, Kailāśa are not mere images but transcendental realities of the highest order. Thus, the personalizing consciousness, like the impersonalizing one, has found its fullest play in Hinduism.

Anātta[7] (not-Self)

Another peculiarity of Buddhism is its denial of or rather silence regarding the individual human soul. Some hold that Buddha never denied the soul-principle; that what he denied was the ego, the human-personality or individual human mind which is generally mistaken for the human soul.[8] Plucking a

---

[7]There are definite statements by Buddha which clearly prove that he rejected theories which preached annihilation of Self altogether. Explaining why he refused to answer a certain monk in a simple yes or no, he said, "If I, Ananda, when the wandering monk Vacchagotta asked me 'Is there not the ego?' had answered: 'The ego is not,' then that, Ananda, would have confirmed the doctrine of the Samanas and the Brahmanas who believe in annihilation (*uchchheda-diṭṭhi*)."

On another occasion, complaining against those who called him "an unbeliever" preaching "the real entity's destruction, annihilation, dying away" he said, "what I am not, what is not my doctrine, that I am accused of."

8[Buddha's *anātma* is at heart Vedantic *neti, neti*. In dozens of places, Buddha repeatedly teaches that man's body or his mind, his psycho-physical being, is not his true self. In Chulla-sachchaka suttanta (Majjhima Nikāya), in Panchavaggīya sutta, in Sappaya (*sampreya*) sutta, Chakkhu-sutta, Rūpa-sutta, Na Tumhaka sutta (all of Saṁyutta Nikāya), he preaches that man's eye or his ear, and the material form they reveal (*rūpa*), and also his more subjective (*ajjhattā*) existence — *vedanā, saṁjñā, saṁskāra, vijñāna* — in short all, *dharmas* pertaining to him are *anātma*, are not his. They do not belong to him, nor does he belong to them; they are not *he* nor *his. They are all changeful* (anicca *or* anitya) *and sorrowful* (dukkha) *and it is better they are disowned. In* Sappaya sutta, *he asks whether it is proper to regard these things so transient and painful as, in anyway, yours or you or your ātman?*

[In the Upanishads, the *ātman* represents the principle of *consciousness* and *freedom*. But Buddha limited his discussion to man's "conditioned" life and release from it; therefore, there is no wonder that in him and the *anātma* principle has found prominence and the atmic principle remains in the background. In Andha-bhuta sutta, Buddha found that everything related to man's conditioned life is blind — his eye, his ear, the material forms they reveal, his feeling, his perception, his ego, etc., all are blind. Similarly in the Kukkul sutta and Upchala sutta, and again in the Aditta sutta, he saw all forms (*rūpa*), all the worlds (*lokas*), and everything in and about man on fire — his eye, his ear, his sensations, perceptions, his mind; they are all burning with desire, burning with hatred, burning with infatuation, burning with ego, etc. Buddha repeatedly warned his disciples not to confuse their "conditioned" self — their psycho-physical aggregate — with themselves, with their true, liberated status in *nirvāṇa*, with *ātman*, about which nothing can be said. But he knew that men are prone to this delusion and easily confuse the two; in Diṭṭhi saṁyutta, he tells us how men make this double mistake: how while they think of the *ātman* having material form, they regard their material form as their *ātman*.]

handful of leaves from the tree under which he was sitting, he told Ananda that as there were many more leaves on the tree than in his palm, similarly the truths which he had withheld were more numerous than those he had revealed (Siṁpsapa sutta, Saṁyutta Nikāya). "Soul" was one of these withheld truths. Revealing it would not have meant much. For, in the first instance, the truth of the soul cannot be described in human language. For another reason, because the affirmation of soul or any permanent self, either individual or cosmic, did not help the individual in arriving at those truths. That could only be done by a strenuous individual effort by negating all that was mutable, all that belonged to the phenomenal world. All thought-clusters, all sensation-groups, all form-constellations mistaken for permanent entities or abiding realities have to be negated.

On the other hand, affirmation of a permanent soul-principle (*sāssata-diṭṭhi*) would probably have been harmful. Aspirants tend to confuse or identify it with their body or mind; at least, almost invariably with the subtle and *sāttvika* modifications or states of their mind, when in fact even in its highest reaches, it is merely a *pudgala*, a *skandha*, a concatenation of various principles and therefore subject to change and destruction, and empty and *anātma*.[9]

Whatever be the truth, denial or silence, the lack of affirmation of the soul-principle in the Buddhist literature will have to be accounted for. For, the soul occupies a central

[9]That these *skandhas*, or sensation-complexes, or material-pyschic aggregates have no permanent reality or self is all the Emptiness Buddha avowed. This point is well brought out in a dialogue in the Saṁyutta Nikāya:

"To what extent is the world called 'empty', Lord?"

"Because it is empty of self or of what belongs to self, it is therefore said: 'The world is empty'. And what is empty of self and what belongs to self? The eye — all these are empty of self and of what belongs to self. So too are ear, nose, tongue, body and mind (and their appropriate sense-data, appropriate consciousness and the impression on them of their appropriate sense-data) they are all empty of self and of what belongs to self. Also that feeling which arises, conditioned by impression on the eye, ear, nose, tongue, body, mind, whether it be pleasant or painful or neither painful nor pleasant that too is empty of self and of what belongs to self. Wherefore is the world called empty because it is empty of self and of what belongs to self."

position in the religious thinking of all mankind in different ages. The "person of the measure of a thumb", the "dwarf seated in the middle", in the language of the Upanishads, is a recurring experience of those attracted by the Divine call and life.

At a first glance, the absence of the soul in Buddha seems to agree with at least one interpretation of the Vedānta which denies any permanent individual soul in man. But this view neither agrees with other views of the Vedānta nor with the general religious intuition of man.

Apart from practical reasons we have discussed above there could be two other reasons of a spiritual nature for the denial of or silence about the question of the soul. One is that in a deep trance, all sense of individuality — even of spiritual individuality — is lost and one is immersed in a Nameless, Cosmic or Transcendental, Incommunicable Consciousness, in a Limitless *śūnya* or in an Ocean of Self-Existence. Here the testimony of Sri Aurobindo would be very interesting. According to him it is not possible to situate Nirvāṇa as a world or plane for the Nirvāṇa push is to a withdrawal from the world and world values: it, therefore, is a state of consciousness and rather super-consciousness without habitation or level. It is an absolute silence of mind and cessation of activities, constructions, representations, which can be so complete that not only to the silent mind but also to the passive sense the whole world is emptied of its stability and reality and things appear as only unsubstantial forms without any real habitation or else floating in something that is a nameless infinite. This infinite or else something still beyond is That which alone is real; an absolute calm, peace, liberation is the resulting state. In his own experience of Nirvāṇa, Sri Aurobindo lost all sense of the individual soul, any trace of the Self, individual or cosmic. He says, "I myself had my experience of Nirvana and silence in the Brahman...; it came first simply by an absolute stillness and blotting out as it were of all mental, emotional and other inner activities... I did not become aware of any pure 'I' nor even of any self, impersonal or other — there was only an awareness of That as the sole Reality, all else being quite unsubstantial, void, non-real. As to what realized that reality, it was a nameless consciousness which was not other than that; one could perhaps say this, though hardly even so much as this, since there was no mental concept of it, but not more.... Consciousness (not this or that part of consciousness or an 'I' of any kind) suddenly emptied itself of all inner contents and remained aware only of unreal surroundings and of Something real but ineffable" (*Sri Aurobindo on Himself and on the Mother*, 1953, pp. 178-79).

So one need not discover one's soul or one's permanent individual principle, nor one need find the universal Self, the unchangeable principle behind the flux of things in order to make contact with the transcendental realm. One could begin by unloosening and dissolving that knot called the mind or the ego and directly seek and find release in some transcendence, in some nameless, formless, consciousness, which can neither be defined as Self, nor not-Self, which is aloof, incommunicable and without any *nāma* or *dhāma*. It could be the Nirvāṇa of Buddha, or the *śūnya* or Nihil of the later-day Buddhists, or the "supreme Eternal Brahma which can be called neither being nor non-being" of the Gita.

Transitoriness and Painfulness of Existence

Besides the above, there are other differences of nuances and emphases. These generally relate to the emphasis on the misery and transitoriness of this life. The Vedānta too has stressed the fleeting character of world's goods, but that is more than balanced by its emphasis on the bliss, peace, and freedom of the transcendental experience. That is why a reading of Hindu and Buddhist literatures leaves two distinctly different impressions on the mind.

The Vedānta has declared as much as Buddha did the impossibility of describing the transcendental experience in the language of the mind, but it did not shirk the responsibility of evoking it, conjuring it up, suggesting it by expressive images, symbols and parables. True, Buddha was a mastermind in the use of parables, but he used these to illustrate his discourses on morals and meditation, and on the "vanity" of all things, on the law of suffering and change which characterizes everythig. On the other hand, the Vedānta used these parables and suggestive terminology to suggest, however imperfectly, something of the beauty and joy and freedom of the transcendental experience. This explains why Buddhism leaves an impression of emptiness and transience, while the Vedānta leaves an impression of joy and freedom.

In Buddhism, the bifurcation or divorce between the phenomenal and the transcendental worlds is rather too complete, too trenchant. There is no point of contact or interchange between the two. The phenomenal world is all misery and flux while the world beyond the realm of birth and death is aloof and incommunicable. The two worlds completely exclude each other. There are no reflections, no echoes, no responses of the one in the other.

In the Vedānta it is different. Even in the interpretations most akin to Buddhism, the world and the *jīvas* derive their existence from the *māyāśakti* of the Divine. In the more affirmative interpretations, the world acquires a status of the fullest reality for the first time — a reality infinitely more full than the one given by materialists, if indeed their "reality" could be called by that name at all. True, the world is "nothing" without God, but there is no such world. Everything is derived from God, moves and has its being in God. God is behind, above, beneath and in the heart of everything. The human soul looks back to its Divine origin, and looks forward to its Divine destiny. It hungers for the Divine truth, its "pasturage" as Plato calls it, beholds it and in gazing upon it is "replenished and made glad", and fulfilled. In the language of the Gita and the *Kaṭha Upanishad*, the tree of life has its "*roots above*". The world and its existence is grounded in God: "On it all the worlds do rest." What could be a surer, more solid foundation for human life on earth? According to the Upanishads, *this* is full with the fullness of *That* and what is above is also below. The terrestrial reflects the celestial. This teaching finds its echo in the Egyptian-Greek Hermetic tradition too.

We have not only the phenomenon of the *jīvas* aspiring and ascending to Godhead, we find God coming down to the earth, putting on the limitations of our earthly life in order to save beings and help them in their spiritual evolution. So there is a loving interchange, and "open sesame" between Gods and men, between the Universal and the individual, between the Transcendental and the phenomenal. There is a relationship of antiphony between Bhagvān and His Bhakta. They live and move with their centres in each other. Each finds his perfect response, reflection, image and echo in the other. The Gita says that Gods and men are nourishers of each other.

Flowing from the above, there is another difference in the method of *sādhanā*. There being no loving God, in Buddhism one has to work out one's salvation alone and with diligence. In the Vedānta there is no lack of call on the personal effort of the aspirant, but this must very soon give place to a complete call on the Divine, complete surrender to the Divine will. "Abandoning all duties, all methods, all techniques of meditation, come unto Me alone for shelter. I will liberate thee from all sins," is the message of Sri Krishna in the Gita. The personal effort of the *sādhaka*, when it is sincere and persistent, evokes Divine help. The heavenly waters of Divine Grace fill him, inundate him, drown him. This difference in approach again makes Buddhism look dry, ascetic and arduous. While methods of *sādhanā* developed on the basis of the Upanishads are joyous and effortless.

But let us not stress the differences too far. As we have seen there is an important tradition of the Vedānta which is akin to the negating trends in Buddhism. Similarly, there are many schools of Buddhist philosophy and Buddhist methods of *sādhanā* which are akin to the more affirmative tradition of

Hinduism. In these schools, one does not pass into a void or *śūnya* effected through negation of all thought-forms or thought-complexes and through detachment from the world (the process called *ashtāṅgayoga* by the Hindus), but takes refuge in the "compassionate Buddha". Buddhism in these developments is no longer dry or flat, but rich and even luxuriant. But we have purposely refrained from a discussion of these powerful developments in Buddhism. For, we wanted to concentrate on those elements alone that are found in their earliest records and are agreed upon by all schools and determine where these elements stood in relation to Hinduism.

The nature of Buddhist *Nothingness* should not be misunderstood. In fact there is nothing peculiarly Buddhist about this *Nothingness*. It is the process of *self-noughting* enjoined by all religions and all mystic disciplines. For going into spiritual regions above it is necessary to pass through the doors of Nothingness. Therefore, an *arhat* has been defined as one in whom all *outflows*, all desires, sense-life have dried up.

Moreover *ceasing-to-be* is not a dry or life-denying process as many people outside the Mystic Way think. As useless sensations, mental constructions and idealizings, vital desires and sentimentalizings fall away from one's true being, one feels lighter, freer, happier. Life which was otherwise cluttered, dark, divided, painful, anxious and weary knows for the first time its true status of joy, freedom, light and power.

Nor the true nature of *dukkha* in Buddha which figures so much in his teachings and which prejudices people's thinking on Buddhism has been rightly understood. The status of *dukkha* is not psychological but metaphysical. At the level of duality and phenomenality, there can only be *dukkha* whether psychologically so manifested or not, or even when psychologically speaking, agreeable and pleasant sensations accompany the life at this plane. Indeed the basicality and universality of suffering is difficult to grasp and comprehend for a mind given to its usual life of sensations, pleasant or unpleasant. Buddha says, "It is difficult to shoot from a distance arrow after arrow through a narrow keyhole, and miss not once. It is more difficult to shoot and penetrate with the tip of a hair split a hundred times a piece of hair similarly split. It is still more difficult to penetrate to the fact that 'all this is suffering'."

The views of Hinduism and Buddhism on *dukkha* and *ānanda* are complementary, not contradictory. Looked at from below, from the viewpoint of duality and multiplicity, in divorce from the divine, the world is true to the Buddhist picture of suffering, misery, change and sorrow. But looked at from above, through the all-comprehensive view of the One or That, all is seeped in *ānanda*, everything is the ecstatic play of the Divine Mother, or the loving and rapturous *līlā* of Sri Krishna or Shiva — to use traditional Hindu images. As the *Taittirīya Upanishad* says: "Out of joy all this life came forth; by joy all this is sustained and into that joy all this will merge. *ānanda* is Brahma."

Where is the contradiction?

Concluding Remarks

In the above discussion we found that Buddha, his spiritual experiences and teachings formed part of a Hindu tradition. He belonged to the Upanishadic heritage. He cannot be understood in any other sense. The attempt to understand him in isolation divorced from that tradition which he confirmed, enriched and represented, has only led to misunderstanding and distortion of his teachings. He himself claimed no originality. He claimed to have "seen an ancient way," followed an "ancient road." Those who claim to love Buddha should also love and cherish that tradition, which was his cradle, foster-mother, guide and inner inspiration. A good Buddhist has perforce to be a good Hindu too. But some self-styled, latter-day admirers of Buddha go out of their way to denounce and malign that tradition. It only shows lack of understanding on their part.

Like Buddha and later on Ashoka, let an Indian lover of

Buddha learn to represent India again.[10] But let him also realize that India is the land not only of Buddha but also of Rama, Krishna, Yajnavalkya, and mighty Vyasa. Hinduism is not a one-book or one-prophet religion; it is the repository of man's nameless spiritual tradition and knowledge nourished by countless sages and seers. It does not give a neatly worked-out scheme of theological ideas; on the other hand, it tries to name the Nameless, express the Inexpressible, to give language to man's intuition of the Beyond with which he has tried to establish contact in many ways at different times, according to his capacity and preparation.

Hinduism is like a great reservoir of water from which many streams take their rise and to which they again repair after passing through many strange and fair lands. It is a great, creative matrix giving birth to many beautiful and living forms. Itself ahistorical, it has given birth to many sects and branches with interesting, chequered histories. Paying sole allegiance to the Guide within seated in the cave of the heart, it has put forward from time to time many teachers and sages of incomparable power and vision, incarnating the very Gods above and within.

Brahma-vāda, Advaita, Sāṁkhya, Buddhism, Jainism, Shkta-ism, Vaishnava-ism are noble children of the same mother. Each could be completely satisfying to its individual devotees so long as it does not forget its common heritage and common source. Accepted in a sectarian, exclusive sense, in forgetfulness of the whole, it becomes one-sided and even distorted. Hinduism is a lute yielding many sweet notes each deriving its meaning from its place in the total symphony. The

---

[10]Probably, in its world excursion, Buddhism followed the trail of Hinduism. It went where Hinduism was already known and honoured. There it made a permanent niche in the affections of the people and destroyed nothing. Nourished by their psyche, it acquired a new wealth and became thoroughly indigenous. It was not governed by a distant mother-church. On the other hand, it drew is sustenance from the soil of its adoption. This prevented it from becoming the handmaid of Imperialism exploiting from afar. Its centre and authority was always local. Therefore, it became the genuine voice of the people who lived by it.

Vedas say that there is one God but the wise call Him by different Names. Similarly, there is one Religion, one Perennial Philosophy, one Sanatana Dharma, the old name for Hinduism, which means the ever-living Law; but it is expressed in different ways. Different religions and sects that come and go in history are facets of the same Religion, different attempts to reach the Inaccessible. All are noble attempts and all bring their heart's offerings to the same altar.

Recapturing their lost consciousness of identity, regaining their sense of the divine and the transcendent, and uniting into a mighty force of living spirituality, let Hinduism and Buddhism, the two sister-religions, come forward and offer their healing message to a troubled world. In the absence of this message inferior religious and secular ideologies and life-philosophies are having a field day and are doing immense damage to humanity. Having conquered Europe, they have also made deep inroads into Asia. China is already under their cruel domain. But China's cultural and spiritual roots are deep and her people are patient and long-suffering; so she will undoubtedly survive the vandalism of her own rulers; and the gentler and nobler qualities of her people will again triumph after the current fever is over and the present iconoclastic wave has exhausted itself. In fact, the signs of self-revival are already there.

Indian people, too, are not above the attraction of these ideologies. New India looks upon her spiritual inheritance as a reactionary and undesirable burden. The class that now controls the political, cultural and intellectual life of the country proudly and openly proclaims atheistic beliefs and positivistic values. Today, India prides herself in being a "secular" State, a secularity which is more anti-spiritual than anti-communal in its temper. [In fact, anti-Hindu than anti-communal]. In order to qualify for Government grants, Shanti Niketan, the famous institution found by the great Rabindra Nath Tagore, the poet of the soul's Godward aspiration and a great representative of undying India, had to give up its Upanishadic motto: *satyam, śivam, sundaram.* These figures represent the deepest and loftiest that spirituality has conceived about man, his aspirations and destiny, his hopes and possibilities. But to the modern secular ears of the present-day rulers, these terms sound communal and antiquated.

These rulers have little understanding of, or sympathy or patience with Indias's age-old values. But there is no doubt that they would fail and India would again regain her *svadharma* in not too distant future.

Western imperialism has destroyed many parts of the globe not only economically but also culturally. The indigenous religions of the countries of the two Americas have been completely overwhelmed. In the African continent, the local religions are under a systematic attack from Islamic and Christian ideologies. Economic imperialism is withdrawing but religious and spiritual aggression continues to operate unchecked with unprecedented ferocity and zeal. This continuing onslaught is more destructive than the old-style imperialism.

The dominant ideologies of the day bear many names and appear in many forms. Some of them are secular; others don religious garbs. But they have certain common characteristics: they are dogmatic, narrow, self-regarding, pretentious and megalomaniac. They claim to know the truth and they presume to impose it on others too. They lack inwardness, deeper charity and larger humanism. They are all based on a partial definition of man or on a distorted vision of Godhead.

Not taking up the religious variety for the time being, let us consider, for the sake of illustrtion, two dominant secular forms: Communism and Liberal Democracy. Apparently, they are at loggerheads but in some ways they are also complementary forms and forces subserving the same psyche. For example, Soviet Communism is more aggressively atheistic but Liberal Democracy, as we find it in its manifestations in different countries, is more thoroughly hedonistic and individualistic. It increasingly understands and defines Truth and Ethics in pragmatic, positivistic and utilitarian terms. The sense of holiness, transcendence, and interconnectedness of things is fast going out of life. So the cults of emptiness and meaninglessness rule. Truth is merely that which is soft, odd and interesting. The sensation-seeking of this culture has already so weakened its people that this freer brand of materialism, so full of amusing dissipation, levity and casualness, may go down before Soviet Russia's more mechanistic and militant but also more austere and regimented variety.

On the other hand, while liberal democratic countries may lose politically, their current cultural values may win, particularly in the long run. Consumerism and hedonism are seductive and it is difficult to resist them. Their working is subtle and insidious. They seep, permeate, corrode like water. They undermine from within, with the willing co-operation of the victim. The frowning tyrant is no match for a smiling plutocrat. Where a stick fails, the carrot succeeds. The Brave New World scores over 1984.

This, of course, assumes that the present industrial culture will last indefinitely. But there are already signs of decay and exhaustion. The best minds of the day are prophesying doom. Psychologically, the system is already a failure. It no longer fulfills the deeper needs of man. The young men feel trapped and they are already in revolt. Knowing no better, it often takes them into undesirable directions.

In this confusion and crisis of values, in this general failure and forgetfulness, could some one re-awaken humanity, make it conscious of its spiritual heritage, conscious of its God-life and soul-journey? What part could India play in this re-awakening, re-affirmation — India that has been the priest of things belonging to the Spirit from very ancient times?

Chapter 4

Indo-European Encounter: An Indian Perspective

India and Europe[1] originally came out in German in 1981. The English translation which was originally published by the State University of New York in 1988 has now been brought out in an Indian edition and made available to readers in India. The English translation is a much enlarged version of the original German edition and the Indian edition carries a special Preface by the author. The book contains 604 pages divided into three sections sub-divided into twenty-four chapters. The first section divided into ten chapters deals with "India in the History of European Self-Understanding". It is probably the best portion of the book and very useful to an Indian reader. It presents valuable historical material well digested and analysed. It deals with important sub-topics like India as seen by the Greeks of the Classical period, India as approached by the missionaries as Europe entered its modern period, India as seen by the Europe of Deism and the Enlightenment, and shows how its own internal controversies were given an edge or even shaped by Indian presence. It gives us the history of Indology, it tells us what some of the greatest European thinkers like Voltaire, Herder, Hegel, Schelling and Schopenhauer thought of India. In this sense, the book is also Europe's own self-portraiture.

The second section, again divided into ten chapters, deals

---

[1]Wilhelm Halbfass, *India and Europe: An Essay in Philosophical Understanding*, Motilal Banarasidass Publishers Pvt. Limited, Delhi, 1990.

with "The Indian Tradition and the Presence of Europe". It discusses mainly Neo-Hinduism, or Hinduism as modified by the influence of European concepts and categories, a Hinduism unable to speak for itself but which used European categories of thought for its self-presentation and self-assertion. This section maintains the erudition of the first but lacks its sweep.

The third section called "Appendices" contains additional material added to the English edition. This section deals with certain key concepts such as "Experience" and "Tolerance". If one was inclined to regard them as Indian contributions to the East-West Dialogue, one must be ready for disappointment for the author finds the two concepts "ambiguous" and questionable. Following the inclination of the book, the author at the end (Chapter 24) adds an important discussion on the "Europeanization of the Earth", a subject on which the author also spoke on January 4, 1989 at the India International Centre, New Delhi.

After this brief summary, let me deal with some important points of discussion more fully. I keep close to the language of the author even in places where I do not directly quote him. I take full advantage of his erudition and freely draw from his researched material but I offer my own conclusions and a different schema.

II

India and Europe opens with the "Philosophical View of India in Classical Antiquity", or India in the old Greek tradition. It assumes that Classical Greece provides Europe's antiquity and that the two are related in some special way. It is a debatable point but it has been assumed here as axiomatic. The fact is that at the time when Greece represented a living culture, it did not know Europe, nor Europe of that time knew Greece.

The Greeks knew themselves as Hellenists, not Europeans. And whenever they sought the origins of, or influences upon, their own philosophy and religion, they thought of Egypt, Chaldea and India, not of Europe. They received little from Europe and they bequeathed not much to it, at least at the time when they represented a living culture. In fact, Christian Europe as it was taking shape first grew in opposition to and later in forgetfulness of Greek culture. Christian Europe in its early period used Greek language and Greek philosophy to establish itself; then it attacked ferociously Greek culture. Christian Europe in its early period used Greek language and Greek philosophy to establish itself; then it attacked ferociously Greek religion and culture; it destroyed Greek literature, its schools and libraries.[2] The work of destruction was so

---

[2]Even before it was adopted as an official religion, Christianity indulged in destroying the shrines of the Pagans. Christian mobs under the leadership of their bishops and saints went about seizing and destroying the temples of their neighbours. Two Hindu temples too became the object of their iconoclastic furies. The temples were built by an Indian colony settled in the Canton of Jaron on the upper Euphrates The Indians had built two temples with the images of deities 18 and 22 feet high. St. Gregory the Illuminator (240-332 AD) destroyed them in 304 AD, according to the Syrian writer, Zenob.

When Christianity became the state religion of the Roman Empire, destroying Pagan temples became a state policy. Theodosius, the fanatic Christian Emperor ordered that the Pagan temples be destroyed and he appointed officers of high rank who were directed to shut Pagan temples and confiscate their property for the benefit of the Church.

The pehenomenon enveloped the whole Empire. There was a respite during the time of Julian, but the Christians were already powerful. The altar of Cybele at Pessinus was overturned almost in the presence of the Pagan Emperor. Similarly, in the city of Caesarea in Cappadocia, the Pagan temple, the only one that had survived, was destroyed by Christians during the reign of this Pagan Emperor. The attacks were organized by the most pious Christians, monks and bishops. Gibbon tells us that the "holy Martin, bishop of Tours, marched at the head of his faithful monks, to destroy the idols, the temples, and the consecrated trees of his extensive diocese". In Syria, "the divine and excellent Marcellus", as he is described by Christian chroniclers, a bishop, destroyed many stately temples within the diocese of Apamea. He was accompanied by numerous troops of soldiers and gladiators, and "he successfully attacked the villages and country temples." He was slain by furious villagers.

In Alexandria, the great temple of Serapeum, with its stately halls and exquisite statues, "displaying the triumph of the arts", as Gibbon describes, it was destroyed under the leadership of Theophilus, a *saint*, and friend of St. Jerome. The Serapeum...

complete that even the memory of Plato and Socrates was obliterated and for a thousand years Christian Europe grew in complete ignorance of what it calls its classical antiquity.

...also preserved treasures of ancient learning and housed the famous Alexandrian library. All were reduced to ashes. A church was built in honour of Christian martyrs on the site of the ruined temple.

Libanius, a contemporary writer, rails at these "black-garbed" monks "who ate more than elephants". Poor elephants! they are temperate animals."

Many temples were appropriated by the Christians. The temple of Venus at Carthage, whose sacred precincts formed a circumference of two miles was converted into a Christian church. The same thing happened to the majestic Pantheon at Rome. Built by Marcus Vipsanius Agrippa (63-12 BC) and reconstructed in the 2nd century AD by Hadrian, it became a Christian church in the 7th century.

St. Sophia, the church at Constantinople, was built by Constantine in 325. Enlarged, rebuilt, destroyed at various epoch, the present structure is virtually that erected by Justinian. Over 10,000 workers were employed for seven years, and the rich materials used were taken from nearly every celebrated Pagan temple in all parts of the Empire. Its altar was made of molten gold weighing 320,000 lbs. In 1453, Turks conquered Constantinople, and the church was converted into a mosque.

Ancient rites suppressed

The ancient rites were abolished. These including luminaries, garlands, frankincense, and libation of wine were especially enumerated and condemned. The offender was subjected to the forfeiter of the house or estate where those ceremonies were performed. And as Gibbon says even "the harmless claims of the domestic genius, of the household gods, are included in this proscription." The ruse of these "profane and illegal ceremonies" subjected the offender to the forfeiture of the house or estate where they have been performed.

We are told by Gibbon how "The monks (a race of filthy animals, to whom Eunapius is tempted to refuse the name of men) are the authors of the new worship, how in these shrines, and instead of the Gods conceived in beautiful images, were worshipped the salted and pickled heads of the so-called martyrs, those infamous malefactors".

There were laws against Judaizing Christians, against Paganism, against folk practices. Lex Visigothorum, XII, 2, 16, (642-52) deplores "pretended belief in Christ" and prescribes penalty for those who "have renounced a good religion for a bad one." It says that a "cruel and astounding act of presumption should be extirpated by a still more cruel punishment". The Edict declares that whenever it is proved that a Christian born of Christian parents has practised circumcision or any other Jewish rite, "he shall be put to an ignominious death by the zeal and cooperation of Catholics, under the most ingenious and excruciating torture that can be inflicted"...

When Greek learning revived again, it was too late for it to exert a living influence on anyone. It had died as a living tradition and it was now a thing belonging to museums and libraries and was a topic only for learned dissertations. But even in this form, it began to invite fierce opposition. The Reformation was a revolt against the classical Renaissance, a "reaction of backward minds", or a "protest of antiquated spirits", as Nietzsche saw it. The call to go back to the Bible and to Jehovah was in a very deep sense a repudiation of the Greek tradition, whether spiritual or intellectual. Today what Europe calls the Greek learning is not the learning as it was seen by the Greeks, but as it is understood by the Europeans through their own categories of thought. To the Greeks, Homer and its Gods were great realities, part and parcel of their lives; to Europeans of the Renaissance period, they were legends and interesting tales.

Even earlier, during the first centuries of Christianity, it was clear that the Greek and Christian approaches to the life of the

---

...The precept of King Childebert I of France (c. 533-58) threatens such of his people "which does not keep the precepts of bishops." It declares: "We order that any men who, once admonished, shall not at once cast out images and idols, dedicated to the devil, made by men, from their fields, or shall prevent Bishops from destroying them, shall not be free..."

Again, Lex Visigothorum VI, 2, 4, (642-52) declares punishments for "magicians and invokers of tempests". "Such persons" shall be publicly scourged with two hundred lashes; shall be scalped; and shall be dragged by force through ten villages of the neighbourhood, as a warning to others.

In other places, this infringement was put to a profitable use. Lombard Italy: Liutprant 84.I (727) says that anybody going to a soothsayer "shall pay half his price in the Sacred Palace, according as he is valued.. and he shall also do penance according to the Church canons. In the same way he who worships at a tree which the rustic call holy and at springs, or performs sacrifice or incantation, shall similarly pay half the price." Any one who does not denounce them or conceals them suffers the same penalty.

Pope Gregory the Great writes to Mellitus, Abbot of France on his way to England to tell Bishop Augustine "that the temples of idols in that nation should not be destroyed, but that the idols themselves that are in them should be...since, if these same temples are well built, it is needful that they should be transferred from the worship of idols to the service of true God."

spirit were incompatible and Christianity waged a relentless war against the Greco-Roman approach; and when the Greek learning revived again, the old incompatibility was still there undiminished. But if the Greek learning still found a certain receptivity the reason was that by this time, it was totally misunderstood and misconceived. For any truly classical revival, Christian soil was very inhospitable indeed.

This however does not mean that modern Europe had no link with old Greece. An unknown link connected the two intimately and the link was established when Sanskrit was discovered. When this discovery was made, it became obvious that India, Greece, Rome and Europe had great linguistic, spiritual and ethnic affinity and even a common ancestry derived probably from India and Sanskrit. But this suggestion was soon resisted by rising European colonialism. To counter such a suggestion, it postulated on the other hand a third, conjectural source still more remote in time and also far removed from India. But according to all the testimony available at present, the old affinity between these regions and peoples, particularly in its spiritual dimension, is still best represented by India. The Christian interlude in Europe and the Muslim interlude in Iran are merely distorters or aberrations of this old affinity.

But while one need not subscribe to Professor Halbfass's unproved assumption that old Greece represents modern Christian Europe's classical antiquity, there should be no difficulty in readily agreeing that the author's treatment of the subject of "India in Greek Tradition" is able and competent. It brings together many traditions on the subject within the confine of one chapter and it is useful for interested readers. One could of course still point out some obvious omissions. For example, Apollonius of Tyna, the great sage of the Greek world who is reputed to have come to India to meet its sages, is mentioned just to be told that his biography by Philostratus is "legendry". There is nothing improbable in a saint of the Greek world visiting India, but even if the biography is legendry, it is known to have been written by 220 AD, and even as a legend it is a good witness and tells us where India stood in the estimation of Greek sages and philosophers of an early date. It tells us that the Pythagoreans of Greece and the Naked Philosophers of Egypt had derived their doctrines from the "Wise men of India".

Professor Halbfass follows a scholar's methodology in determining the extent of Indo-Greek contact. He is determined to find a document, some written mention, some journey relating to this contact before he would admit it, but by their very nature such evidences can only be very rare considering the time that has lapsed and the changes that have been wrought. But if Professor Halbfass had followed a more inward method or criterion of looking at Greek literature, he would have easily found plentiful evidence of a living Indo-Greek contact, particularly at the deeper level of the spirit. Both shared a common spiritual approach; both intuited man and his world in the same way; both expressed their spiritual intuition in the language of *Gods*; both taught *ātma-vāda*, and the theory of Two Selves and Two Ways; both taught the theory of *karma*, rebirth and *moksha*. In fact, the Greece of Pythagoras, Plato and Plotinus has more in common with Hindu India than with Christian Europe.

III

Then a long period of more than a thousand years intervened — a period of triumph and consolidation of Christianity in Europe. Already Christianity had successfully fought Greek as well as several Eastern spiritual influences in the shape of Mithraism, Gnosticism, etc. An ideological iron-curtain fell on Europe and its spirit underwent a process of systematic Semiticization. Thanks to this sustained conditioning, the European spirit became incapable of appreciating and understanding Indian spirituality. This spiritual impediment was reinforced by a physical one when Islam triumphed in the

Middle East and swayed over the sea and land routes connecting the Mediterranean with India.

During these long years of lost contact, India became a legend. But contact was resumed when a new route to India was discovered and Vasco da Gama landed in 1498 at Calicut with soldiers, missionaries and traders. Thus the first modern contact was military-cum-missionary-cum-commercial, and any subsequent academic intellectual interest grew out of this and it contained the qualities of the first encounter.

India and Europe includes a very interesting chapter on the "Missionary Approach to Indian Thought". Most missionaries had a very dim view of Hinduism which they regarded as unmitigated evil. St. Xavier thought that Brahmins, a highly revered class, stood between Christianity and the heathens and that this class should be destroyed. He requested the king of Portugal to use the secular arm for the conversion of the Hindus.

But there were certain missionaries who had a livelier idea of the difficulties and their situation. They proposed the strategy of using Hinduism against Hinduism, a strategy which has its Biblical precedent in the practice of St. Paul. Robert Di Nobili, representing this school, made a distinction between the social customs of the heathens and their religious ceremonies. He preached that while the former could be accepted, only the latter should be opposed. He also pointed out that the Brahmins were mainly teachers and priests and their function was social and educational and not religious; and therefore they need not be opposed but only neutralized and, in fact, the respect accorded to them could be used to promote Christianity. He himself pretended that he was a Romanic Brahmin and the teacher or Guru of a lost Veda, *Jesurvedam*, which he offered to teach to his fellow-Brahmins in India.

While most missionaries saw Hinduism as a handiwork of the devil, some also saw in it the remnants of an old monotheism, probably borrowed from Christian and Judaic sources, but now distorted and defaced beyond recognition. B. Ziegenbalg (1682-1719), a Lutheran missionary, wrote back to his patrons in Europe about this original monotheism which had been subsequently lost because Hindus "allowed themselves to be seduced by the devil and their ancient poets into believing in a multitude of gods".

IV

These reports reaching Europe had an unintended effect; they were used to support a very different line of reasoning — a line of reasoning which was even anti-Christian. In order to understand this, we shall have to understand the Europe of those days.

After the Crusades came to nothing, Europe was in an intellectual ferment and was learning to question some of its cherished ideas and dogmas. A pamphlet "On the Three Impostors" (Moses, Jesus and Muhammad) came out in 1598 and had a wide clandesting circulation When the Greek learning was revived, stoicism, the old Greek religion, was also rediscovered. Many advanced thinkers saw that it was deeply religious and highly ethical, and yet it had no revelation and no mediator; it also spoke in the language of reason and conscience and it had a universality of approach quite unknown to Christianity.

Under these new influences, a school grew in Europe which spoke of a "natural religion" and "natural theology". It said that man's "reason" and "conscience" were enough to account for God and morality and they needed no revelation and no mediators. Thomas More (1478-1535), an English statesman and author, expressed this idea of a "rational religion" and "natural theology" in his famous *Utopia*.

This view also agreed with man's enlightened commonsense. Therefore, when reports reached Europe from the Far East of a religion — Confucianism — which had no heaven-mongering and yet was highly ethical and humane, it had a warm reception in certain highly intellectual circles. Leibnitz (1646-1716), the German philosopher and mathematician, thought that Chinese missionaries should visit Europe in order to instruct the Westerners about the questions of “natural theology” and commonsense.

It was at this time and in this climate that India entered Europe. India was already known for its natural theology. Quite early even Shahrastani (1086-1153) in his *Kitb al-Milal wa'n-nihal* had noticed that prophets were unknown to the Brahmins and that they tended towards a kind of rationalism which does not depend on revelation.

India not only taught high morals like the Chinese, but unlike them it also did not neglect the metaphysical dimension. Some, like Schopenhauer, were in search of a “philosophy which should be at once ethics and metaphysics”. India did not disappoint them. Schopenhauer (1788-1860) found it in the Upanishadic *tat tvam asi*, “that thou art”. Earlier J.G. Herder (1744-1803) had found that Indians' morals were “pure and noble”, and their concept of God “great and beautiful”. Indian thought satisfied those who sought spiritual transcendence without an anthropomorphic God who is always thundering, threatening, and promising and also an ethics embodying man's innate moral nature and not arbitrary commandments from an external agency. This thought, in one of its lower expressions and movements known as Deism, made a wide appeal in Europe. It even affected many European administrators and residents abroad. William Carey, a Baptist missionary, complained that “India swarms with Deists”.

V
Original Home of All Religions

It did not take long for the question to acquire another dimension, the dimension of time. India gave a religion which was not only *rational* but was also *prior* to all other religions. In 1760, Voltaire acquired a copy of *Ezourvedam*, a forgery of the Jesuits (most probably of Di Nobili). But even this served an unintended purpose. Voltaire with his acumen saw even in this document the voice of an ancient religion. While he praised Brahmins for having “established religion on the basis of universal religion” of religion in its oldest and purest form. He described India as a country "on which all other countries had to rely, but which did not rely on anyone else". He also believed that Christianity derived from Hinduism. He wrote to and assured Frederick the Great of Prussia that "our holy Christian religion is solely based upon the ancient religion of Brahma".

This view was held by many European thinkers and writers. F. Majer (1771-1818) said: "It will no longer remain to be doubted that the priests of Egypt and the sages of Greece have drawn directly from the original well of India." And again: "Towards the Orient, to the banks of the Ganges and the Indus, it is there that our hearts feel drawn by some hidden urge — it is there that all the dark presentiments point which lie in the depths of our hearts... In the Orient, the heavens poured forth into the earth."

J.G. Herder also saw in India the "lost paradise of all religions and philosophies", the "cradle of humanity", the "eternal home", the "eternal Orient...waiting to be rediscovered within ourselves". This is high praise, indeed, but it does not mean that he ever thought that India supplanted the West. Any such thought was far from his mind. What he meant was that India represented humanity's childhood, its innocence, as Hellenism represented its "adolescence" and Rome its "adulthood". Similarly, while Indians were "the gentlest branch of humanity", Christianity was the religion of "purest humanity".

The thesis of Indian origins of Christianity found a warm reception in many quarters and it continued to be propagated by Rosicrucians, Theosophists and individual scholars and philosophers like Schopenhauer, L. Jacolliot, A. Lillie and F. Nork.

But the traditional Christianity did not yield easily and it argued furiously for the primacy of the Mosaic-Christian Revelation. A. Dacier, J. Bouchet and Th. La Grue argued for the priority of Biblical Chronology. Even Newton was involved in the controversy and argued for the primacy of the Biblical Chronology. But the growing knowledge of history and older civilizations was against them.

Orthodox Christians took recourse to another line of argument. While yielding a certain chronological priority to India they upheld Christianity's moral and spiritual primacy. They said that even if India had known some kind of religion at an early date, its essential truths were badly corrupted and it needed the living waters of Christianity to revive them. To them, India offered a classic example of a tradition that had been unable to safeguard its original purity against its pagan superstition and priestly fraud, and disgusting barbarism — a warning and reminder to others. An article on "Brahmins" in *Encyclopaedia* says that a Christian could not fail to see the "effect of divine wrath" in such decay and deprivation. Professor Halbfass informs us that India's example was often cited to illustrate the theme of the eclipse and suppression of "natural light" through superstition and ritualism, and that this theme enjoyed a great popularity among thinkers of the Enlightenment.

VI
A New Phase

Soon the Indo-European encounter entered a new phase. Indian texts began to be translated into European languages. Works of Roger, Dow, Holwell, Wilkin's translations of the *Bhagavad Gita* and the *Hitopdesha* and W. Jones' *Shakuntala* created a taste for Indian thought. Western scholars read in translations such things as: "Vishnu is in you, in me, in all beings"; or "See all men in your own soul"; or "Banish the delusion of being different". Though later on, the missionary writers tried to dismiss such teachings under the label of "pantheism", many Western thinkers heard such sublime thoughts and ethics for the first time and were deeply stirred. The stir was Europewide, but it was most conspicuous in Germany. F. Schlegel, one of the pioneers of the Oriental Renaissance, wrote about India: "Here is the actual source of all languages, all the thoughts and poems of the human spirit; everything, everything without exception comes from India." Later on, of course, he changed his views when he became a

Roman Catholic and not to India but to Biblical Mesopotamia gave the palm of being the "cradle of mankind", but his contribution to the Oriental Renaissance remained outstanding.

Another great name belonging to this movement was that of Schopenhauer. His interest in Indian religion was first aroused by reading Anquetil Dupperon's Latin translation of *Oupnekhat* (1801-1802), itself a translation from a Persian version. He was deeply moved and he found its reading "the most rewarding and edifying", and its philosophy "the solace of my life and will be the solace of my death". After this he continued to take a deep interest in India. In Indians, he found the "most noble and ancient people", and their wisdom was the "original wisdom of the human race". He spoke of India as the "fatherland of mankind", which gave the "original religion of our race" and "oldest of all world view". He thought of the Upanishads as the "fruit of the most sublime human knowledge and wisdom", documents of "almost superhuman conception" whose authors could "hardly be thought of as mere mortals". He expressed the hope that European peoples "*who stemmed from Asia...would also re-attain the holy religions of their home*" (Italics added).

Sanskrit

Europe's discovery of Sanskrit also worked in the same direction. F. Sassetti had observed as early as the second half of the sixteenth century that Sanskrit and Europe's classical languages were related in some way. Jones also saw the basic similarities between these languages and soon some basic concepts of linguistics and history were revolutionised. The discovery of Sanskrit proved a great event in Europe's intellectual history. It upset Europe's self-image; it showed that its Semitic association and identification were brief and accidental and that its linguistic and, therefore, its philosophic, religious and cultural roots lay elsewhere. Europe's close affinity with India could no longer be a matter of speculation; it was written all over in the languages of Europe, classical or modern. J.G. Herder asked himself: "All the peoples of Europe, where are they from?" And he answered: "From Asia."

Sanskrit was found to be the oldest of all Aryan languages and therefore also their ancestor. Hegel, no admirer of India, admitted: "It is a great discovery in history — as of a new world — which has been made within rather more than the last twenty years, respecting the Sanskrit and the connection of the European languages with it. In particular, the connection of the German and Indian peoples has been demonstrated." German Oriental Renaissance was erected on Bopp's linguistic foundation.

The enthusiasm for Indian culture was widespread. Amaury de Riencourt in his *The Soul of India* tells us that philosophers like Schelling, Fichte, Hegel, Schopenhauer and Schleiermacher, poets such as Goethe, Schillar, Novalis, Tieck and Brentano, historians like Herder and Schlegel, all acclaimed the discovery of Indian culture with cries of ecstasy: "India, the home of universal religion, the cradle of the noblest human race, of all literature, of all philosophies and metaphysics." And he adds that "this enthusiasm was not confined to Germany. The entire Romantic movement in the West put Indian culture on a lofty pedestal which the preceding Classical Movement had reserved for Greece and Rome."

Tolstoy, a late-comer, was also deeply influenced by Indian religious thought. Like Wagner, his introduction to it was through Burnouf and Schopenhauer. Beginning with his *Confessions*, there is no work of his "which is not inspired, in part by Hindu thought", to put it in the words of Markovitch quoted by Raymond Schwab in *The Oriental Renaissance*. He further adds that Tolstoy also "remains the most striking example, among a great many, of those who sought a cure for the western spirit in India".

Thus we see that India's influence was widespread throughout Europe, but it was the greatest in Germany. In fact, Germany was called "the India of the Occident". Hugo said that "Germany is to the West what India is to the East, a sort of great forbear. Let us venerate her". These words (September 1870) might have been said though in order to flatter Germany in the hope that she would spare Paris which her armies had besieged.

Importance of Indian Influence

While the Oriental Movement expanded the West's intellectual horizon and influenced it at a deeper level, it was also used in the current controversies and polemics of the day. Some used it in support of the forces of Enlightenment and rationalism to give themselves an example of high-minded religion and ethics which did not depend on revelation and dogmas; others used it against the naive rationalism of the eighteenth century.

Some found that the Bible's Hebraic tradition with its narrow-mindedness, intolerant monotheism, its coarse materialism and lack of mysticism had a corrupting influence on European culture and they found their answer in Indian religious culture which was both rational and mystical.

Oriental Renaissance was also used against classical Renaissance, particularly in Germany. For long, Germans had been accused, particularly by Latin people, of being Teutonic barbarians who destroyed the great Mediterranean culture. In return, the Germans by identifying themselves with the more ancient Indian culture rejected the cultural superiority of the Latin races and especially of French Classicism. Thus by identifying themselves with ancient India and by claiming a new lineage, the Germans restored their self-respect and equality with their accusers.

VII
Opposition

Thus the Oriental Renaissance came to tread over too many toes and its results were disturbing even to many Orientalists who had intended their labour to yield a different kind of harvest. For example, H.H. Wilson, a celebrated Indologist,

Boden Professor, translator of the *Ṛg Veda* and the *Viṣṇu Purāṇa*, speaking at the University of Oxford in 1840, said that the objects of Indian studies were "to contribute to the religious enlightenment of a benighted, but intelligent and interesting and amiable people"; another object was "to confute the falsities of Hinduism". Earlier William Carey had said that the purpose of translating Sanskrit texts was to show they were "filled with nothing but pebbles and trash". But the results were just the opposite. Many of the best minds of Europe thought that these texts were sublime, and the possessors of those texts could not be benighted and needed no foreign aid in religious enlightenment. Some also used these texts to show the inadequacy of Christianity.

Oriental Renaissance began to invite opposition. Missionaries were one obvious source of it. Another source was Imperialism. European powers were becoming self-conscious imperialists and they could not rule with a clean conscience over peoples who were proud possessors of great cultures. Therefore they opposed views which exalted the ideological status of their colonies. Another source, a natural result of Imperialism, was growing Eurocentricity. Europe became less and less inclined to believe that anything worthwhile could be found anywhere outside of Europe. Therefore, the Oriental Movement began to be downgraded. It was called "romantic", and even "fanatic"; its fascination for India was a form of "Indo-mania". Others dealt with it in a more intellectual, but equally hostile way. They admitted a certain antiquity and even priority for Indian people and their culture, facts which could no longer be denied, but they saw in it no reason for departing from their low estimate of India. Hegel, for example, admitted that India "was the centre of emigration for all the western world", but he said that it was merely a "physical diffusion". "The people of India have achieved no foreign conquests, but have been on every occasion vanquished them-selves."

Similarly, though he admitted the fact of India's cultural spread arguing that Sanskrit lies at the foundation of all those further developments which form the languages of Europe — Greek, Latin, German — but he also found in this cultural diffusion only "a dumb, deedless expansion", which "presented no political action". No wars, no forcible conversions, no cultural impositions; therefore, worth nothing much, nothing creditable!

Others dealt with the problem in other ways. They retained old facts but gave them a new rendering; or they retained some facts and changed others and offered a new combination. For example, Indians were allowed to possess the Vedas, the oldest literature of the Aryans, but the Aryans themselves were made to migrate, this time from Europe to India as conquerors. Thus the tables were turned. Migration remained but its direction changed. India which was hitherto regarded as the home of European languages and people now became the happy hunting ground of the same people who came and conquered and imposed their will and culture on India. The theory of Aryan invasion was born. History was written in support of the new hegemony and power relations.

Other scholars made other kinds of attempts. Considering that Europe's religious and philosophical tradition was a late comer, some European thinkers had derived it from India, a common enough practice in the academic field in such matters. But William Jones now offered the hypothesis of a *third unknown source*. He said that India was not the original home of the religious and philosophic tradition of the West, but itself represented an old offshoot of an original source common to both East and West. "Pythagoras and Plato derive their sublime theories from the same fountain with the sages of India", he said. As the attitude in Europe changed, the *hypothesis* was lapped up and it was accepted as *fact*.

The hypothesis of a third lost source began to be applied to many fields but more particularly to linguistics. Some scholars even began to reconstruct this common source and invented "Indo-European roots". These roots were a logical construct and the already existing Sanskrit roots could have done as well, but possibly a psychological motive was at work. Though Sanskrit had the oldest literature, the idea that it could have some sort of a primacy in the Aryan family of languages was not acceptable. Therefore they accepted the next best hypothesis that both Sanskrit and European languages had a common source still more ancient but now lost. To own a filial relationship with India was no matter of pride for Europe; so the next best thing under the circumstances was to make this relationship collateral and push it as far back in the past as possible. Things may change and India's social status may improve after its political and economic status improves.

Hegel

Europe, at the head of a far-flung empire, had to assert its superiority at all levels: military, commercial, religious and philosophical. It could not countenance a view which exalted the peoples of the Orient in any way Missionaries were always on the war-path but on the level of philosophy, Hegel led the attack and his attack was as unsparing and ungenerous as that of the former. But while the missionaries used the language of theology, Hegel used the high-winded language of intellectuality, or just sheer "confused, empty verbiage", according to Schopenhauer.

Herder had thought that India represented man's living past, his *innocence*, but Hegel believed that the World-Spirit (*Weltgeist*) moved from East to West, and in the Oriental tradition, Europe faces, in a sense, its own petrified past. He believed that the Occident had already superseded the Orient and the Orient has to be "excluded from the history of philosophy". In fact, Hegel himself gave us a "philosophy of history", a scheme which brought non-European cultures and thought in historical subordination to Europe. After Hegel, many European scholars have engaged in this labour and in Marx it touched new heights and achieved much concrete, political results.

According to Professor Halbfass, Hegel and others "reflected

Europe's historical position at the beginning of the 19th century. It claims intellectual, moral and religious superiority over the rest of the world." The author tells us that Hegel "even tries to justify the historical necessity of Europe's colonial activities". In his *The Philosophy of History*, Hegel praises the British for undertaking "the weighty responsibility of being the missionaries of civilization to the world".

Following Hegel's lead, though the lead was hardly necessary, Indian philosophy began to be berated. Professor Halbfass writes a whole chapter entitled "On the Exclusion of India from the History of Philosophy". But there is nothing surprising about it. In the same spirit and with the same level of understanding, Indian religion, art, sciences and technology, social and political thought were also either omitted or berated. But what is really incomprehensible is that India's own elites under the spell of Europe have shown no appreciation and commitment to their country's intellectual and creative contribution.

In a sense, this omission is no deprivation but in fact a blessing. Exclusion does no harm and inclusion brings no honour. In fact, inclusion is far worse than exclusion. The fact is that Europe is not spiritually prepared to take Indian higher thought into its purview and, therefore, it is better that it is left out altogether. But on occasions when Europe does speak about it, it speaks vaguely about something it does not comprehend. For example, take Hegel himself. Speaking about Yoga, he says that the "ascent to Brahman is brought about by utter stupefaction and insensibility". The comment is simply laughable. Similarly, he often speaks, probably more than any other European philosopher, of *consciousness*; but he does not seem to be aware, even conceptually, of a state of consciousness which is liberated from its own images, thoughts, stored impressions, its opacity, duality and ego, a state of consciousness about which Indian Yogas speak. In this state, the consciousness is joyful (*viśoka*), and luminous (*jyotishmatī*), truth-bearing or truth-filled (*ritam-bharā*), and those who attain it live on truth (*rita-bhuj*), and dwell in truth (*rita-sad*).

VIII

India entered Europe as a widening and deepening force and it was looked upon with respect and admiration by some of its greatest thinkers like Voltaire, Schelling and Schopenhouer, But the vested interests and forces of narrowness and obscurantism were powerful and they banded together and made a determined stand. Eventually the Euro-Colonial-Missionary forces triumphed, represented by soldier-scholars like J.S. Mill, Hegel, Macaulay, Marx and many others. They were thoroughly Eurocentric and they looked at India and other countries of the East with contempt and condescension. But they became popular not only in the West but in India and Asia as well. They taught several generations of Indians how and what to think of themselves and of Europe. The Indian elites began to look at their country and people through European eyes and European categories. They even borrowed the West's contempt for their own people. Traditional India, during its recovery and reaffirmation, finds itself most fiercely opposed by these elitist forces at home. These forces have intimate intellectual, organizational and financial links with the West.

Neo-Hinduism

This *anti-Hinduism* of the Hindus, their Missionary-Macaulayite-Marxist view of themselves, their own culture, religion and history, is the most powerful legacy the European contact has left behind. But Professor Halbfass does not discuss this at all. On the other hand, he discusses, in the second section of his book, what he calls Neo-Hinduism, a Hinduism shaped by and during the presence of Europe but which is not anti-Hindu and which, in fact, defends Hinduism though not in its native idiom but in the borrowed idiom of Europe. According to Professor Halbfass, Neo-Hinduism took shape "in a historical setting created by Europe", and it "has difficulties speaking for itself"; it "speaks to a large extent in a European medium".

To some extent, this is true; but the limitation is not all on the side of Neo-Hinduism. If it is to engage in a dialogue with the West, it must speak in the idiom best understood by the listener. Though the West is an acute linguist and it has mastered many languages but it is not so nimblewitted in understanding the peoples who spoke them.

Moreover, Neo-Hinduism does more than justify Hinduism; it also justifies Christianity, Islam and many other non-Indian cults. As it uses Western categories to defend Hinduism, in the same spirit it uses traditional Indian categories to promote Semitic religions. In its insatiable desire for "synthesis" and similarities, it seeks and finds Vedānta in the Bible and the Quran and in Das Kapital too; it says that Jesus and Muhammad and Marx all are incarnations and Rishis, and that they all say the same thing. The net result is that Semitic prophets are as popular among the Hindus as their own. Western Rationalism had rejected Christianity not only for its miracles but even more so for its exclusive claims which offend rationality, but it is now coming back under Hindu auspices and promotion.

IX
Hindu Passivity

At more than one place, Professor Halbfass gives us what he regards as a basic characteristic of the Indo-European dialogue or encounter. In this encounter, he tells us that while Europe's role was active, that of India was passive; that while she never went out to study or preach or proselytize, the West has been, on the other hand, in search of India in a variety of ways. It has looked there for analogies and origins; it has even used India for its own self-definition; it has tried to define its identity "by demarcating it against, and reflecting it in, the otherness of India". India, on the other hand, has never tried to find Europe, but discovered it when she was herself discovered, and "started responding to it while being discovered, subdued and objectified by it".[3]

What Professor Halbfass has said so graciously has been said less civilly by many others. H.U. Weithrecht, for example, makes no such intellectual ado and states quite brutally that India's contact with the outer world "has been mainly through immigration of foreign invaders".

We thank Professor Halbfass for his civility and we also think that there should be no difficulty in agreeing with his observation in a broad way. But what he says has many unstated implications and it also raises some deeper questions which should not go unmentioned.

The author presents the East-West encounter as an intellectual enterprise in which the West played, on the whole, the part of a disinterested pursuer of knowledge and truth. It wanted to know others and it went out in search of this knowledge. Perhaps, sometimes it was too eager and, therefore, indiscreet and even aggressive, but all this was in the pursuit of knowledge. History however does not support this rosy view and reveals a different story. It tells us that the East-West encounter was a very cruel affair and the intellectual component was the least important part of it. Its main expressions were piracy, gunboat diplomacy, political domination, religious arrogance, economic enslavement and cultural genocide. These things have not even been mentioned by the author.

And looking at "knowledge" the encounter generated, we find that though its quantum is impressive its moral worth is very little. It abounds in censuses, surveys, reports, maps, charts, atlases, tables, chronicles, archives, transactions and

---

[3]Is it really true? Has Europe, particularly Christian Europe, been really so alert and curious as Professor Halbfass claims? According to E.R. Bevan, far into the medieval ages Christian Europe drew its conception of India mainly from books written before the middle of the third century BC and the additions of this period "never equalled in substance or interest the older books" (*The Cambridge History of India*, p.383).

other such data useful for ruling over a country; it contains laborious studies of castes and creeds and other social divisions so that these could be used for "divide and rule", and even studies of history and religions so that these could be used for subversion. All this is "knowledge" of a sort but it is worthy of administrators and generals and, not of scholars and philosophers of cultures and civilizations. Data-collection is not knowledge and knowledge is not wisdom.

But even those works pretending to study other peoples' cultures are most of the time worthless. Take, for example, the *Encyclopaedia of Religion and Ethics*, in twelve volumes; it is written by more than 450 scholars, Europe's best minds, great linguists and top-notch theologians. The volumes study world cultures, past and present. But with all their scholarship, they constitute a hate-book, a declaration of war against all non-Christian cultures and peoples. They prove that European intellect is profoundly inadequate for dealing with other peoples' cultures. It has neither the necessary sympathy nor the insight for this kind of task.

While on the subject, we may also make a comment or two on the intellect of the West. In contrast to its eastern counterpart, it is supposed to be objective but facts show that it can be quite credulous and careless about facts. For example, we know how for centuries, it believed in a legendary Prester John, the ruler of "the three Indies", the "illustrious and magnificent king...and a beloved son of Christ", the centre of many legends whose support the Christian world hoped to gain against Islam. Similarly, we now know the story of Barlaam and Josaphat, two fictional characters in a story of Siddhartha Buddha taken over and after suitable adaptations converted into two real saints of Christendom whose feast day falls on 27th November. We also know how strong is its belief in Apostle Thomas visiting India which though found to be a myth continues to be promoted for extraneous reasons. All these facts do not speak for an alert, objective and disinterested European intellect.

Now let us also give some thought to the author's perspicacious observation that India's role in the intellectual encounter has been passive. This is true, at least apparently. India's behaviour conforms to its basic attitude in the matter. India believes that there is such a thing as higher learning; and in this kind of learning, one learns best about others by learning about one-self. This kind of learning about others does not analyse, compare and judge all the time, but it *accepts* them as they are. This method gives a benign, a compassionate knowledge of others. In fact, in this kind of knowledge, there are no others. India has known mankind in this benign sense from the beginning. In this sense, India can also have no true xenology of European fancy though the author discusses it at length in a whole chapter, Traditional Indian Xenology (Chapter II), where one can also see Indology at work in all its intellectual irresponsibility.[4] Hindus have their own pride but they have no

[4]Here the author follows the lead of Indology quite uncritically. The discussion is set in the framework of the theory of Aryan invasion as already a proven fact. We are told of the Aryans as "a closely knit group of conquerors and immigrants who gradually took possession of the Indian sub-continent", and of aboriginals who were "vanquished and subdued by Agni", an Aryan God. We are told that the conquerors had already "a clearly recognizable, though somewhat mythical awareness of the surrounding world of foreign or hostile powers or groups or people". How this awareness was both clear and mythical at the same time is not explained but treating it so makes it easier to regard myths and parables as history. We are also told that according to the testimony of the Vedas themselves, the subdued people were "excluded from the Aryan community and its ritual performances" (and blamably not "compelled to come in"), and were described as *dasyu* or *dāsa*, and as *aśraddha*, *ayajña*, *avrata*, *anyavrata* and *akarman*.

In this scheme, the pre-Vedic conquest proves the Vedic epithets which in turn prove a pre-Vedic conquest. But, really, have the epithets to be applied to a conquered people? They could as well be applied by moralists to the members of their own society who in their eyes were not worshipful and observant enough. Manu does it often and advises that even kings and Brahmins who do not perform sacrifices (*ayajña*) are not to be honoured (3.120). But in all probability and in most cases they were applied by Rishis to all mankind, to man at large, to his inner life, his seeking and struggle, to his soul which seeks kinship with Gods but which is also subject to the opposite pull of impiety, lack of faith, worship and spiritual effort.

Taking a leaf from the Orientalists' book, could we argue that the words like gentiles, heathens, infidels, pagans, servants, slaves and serfs which abound in...

concept of an *ummah*, and a divinely ordained mission, and therefore no true xenology though they could have words indicating praise and censure and even hostility. In point of

---

...European religious and social literature assume a conquered people? Could we also hold that the Biblical words like *sklero-trachelos* and *qesheh oreph* (stiff-necked) are physical descriptions of those people as "noseless" (*anāsa*) *dasyu* of Orientalists? Could we further say that the Bible's words like ignorant (*agnoeo*), unbelieving (*apeitheo*), heedless (*aphron*), unrighteous (*adikos*), lawless (*anomia*) and accursed (*anathema*) are not moral judgements but epithets applied to conquered peoples of various grades?

But even if we take the Vedas to be history, we must apply a chosen criterion consistently and not pick and choose according to our convenience. In a *Ṛg* verse (7.6.3) which speaks of the foolish, the faithless, the rudely-speaking, the niggardly, of men without belief, sacrifice and worship (*nyakritu*, *grathina*, *mṛdhra-vāc*, *paṇi*, *aśraddha*, *avriddha*, *ayajña*), we are also told that "Far, far away has Agni chased those dasyus, and, in the east, has turned the godless westward", a direction which is just the opposite of what the Orientalists have been telling us — not eastward and southward but westward. Why neglect this testimony?

Let me take another example of this intellectual irresponsibility. Beginning from the beginning and tracing the tradition of Indian Xenology, Professor Halbfass quotes P. Thieme to show that "while in Greece the word for foreigner (*xenos*) becomes the words for 'guest' or 'host' the corresponding word in India [*ari*] becomes a term for the enemy" (p. 175). Well, we do not know whether the word *ari* in the Vedic lore ever meant a stranger which in time began to mean an enemy, but such things are possible and words do change their meanings in response to many factors (for fuller discussion, see our *The Word As Revelation: Names of Gods*, Voice of India, New Delhi). A word of a living language responds, among other things, to the collective experience of its speakers. A stranger is not always a friend and sometimes he comes as a guest but stays back as the master as the experience of native American-Indians proves and the word has to incorporate and convey such new meanings too.

But turning away from these larger speculations, let us turn to the concrete case in hand. We are not sure whether such a change of meanings as suggested by Thieme took place in India but it did take place in Europe. If Professor Halbfass had carried his etymological investigation a little further, he would have found that the Greek word *xenos*, a stranger, is akin to Latin *hostis*, a stranger, a guest, an enemy, acquiring in Medieval Latin the sense of 'army' (from the plural *hostes*, enemies) giving us the word 'hostile' in English; it is also the parent of the word 'hostage', a person kept in pledge. Akin to this was also the Latin *hostia*, an expiatory victim offered to a deity, a sacrifice. The sense is still actively retained in the Church's most important rite, the *eucharist*, in which they eat (*substantially*, Christian theologians insist) the flesh of the sacrificed victim, Jesus Christ, the Son of God. Perhaps the...

fact, Hinduism has concerned itself with humanity, with man, nay with all beings, animate and inanimate, past and present and future, on all planes, visible and invisible.[5] "The European Tradition and Presence of India", which could discuss Neo-Christianity and Neo-Europe, modifying their idiom under the influence of Indian thought. There is no dearth of data, but there is a reluctance to acknowledge that kind of data under the inertia of an old habit of thinking. For this reason, even Gandhi appears most briefly and perfunctorily in the book though he earned a wide audience in Europe and America, and not as an Indian political leader but as a Hindu thinker and saint; he is also treated as a representative of Neo-Hinduism, and not one who contributed to the shaping of a Neo-Christianity.

The fact is that India has been exerting a great influence though it often remains unacknowledged and unnamed. For example, India's *Pañchatantra* began to be translated from an early date and it saw more than fifty translations and its stories are found in two hundred adaptations though without any knowledge of their Indian origin. The Indian influence has been silent but sure. For example at present, the Hare Krishna movement and the Saiva Siddhanta are visible but partial forms of a great invisible but abiding influence. Under this influence, many are taking to vegetarianism, hundreds of thousands of Western brothers believe in the Law of Karma, and in rebirth, and millions have participated in some kind

...word retains the memory of the days when they sacrificed their first-born to their God, perhaps later replaced by a stranger, then by a living animal and then by a consecrated bread or wafer, the host. The word reveals the steps in European Xenology and its etymology helps in constructing European history. Or, this would if India has its Occidentalists and they were as bright as Europe's Orientalists.

[5]But increasingly faced with a world of strong nation-states and religious ecclesias organised on *ummah* principles, Hindus like other Pagan peoples found themselves at a great disadvantage (for example, while not successful in converting the Muslims, St. Xavier said: Give me out and out pagans). Therefore they tried to develop a measure of political nationalism and religious solidarity (*saṅgaṭhana*) of their own under the leadership of people like Swami Dayananda, Swami Vivekananda, Lokamanya Tilak, Sri Aurobindo and Mahatama Gandhi, but these sentiments still retain the full imprint of universality.

of meditation sessions. Traditional Christianity has hitherto spoken the language of dogma, authority and superiority, but under this new influence, even it is forced to speak the language of "experience" and reluctant "plurality". The Bible does not even know the word "consciousness", but under the influence of Indian thought, even the televangelists are embracing the word though without realizing that the word properly belongs to a different spiritual ethos and has little meaning in the Christian tradition.

X
Experience

Such overwhelming evidence of the influence of Indian spirituality has made it difficult to avoid its discussion altogether. So the author turns to it at the end of his book and in two separate chapters discusses two key concepts, Experience and Tolerance, concepts quite new to Christian-Western vocabulary. Dean W.R. Inge says that the "centre of gravity in religion has shifted from authority to experience". Professor Halbfass also finds the word "most significant" and "most conspicuous in works on Indian religion and philosophy, and in the so-called dialogue between India and the West". But apparently he does not think much of it. He quotes H. Cox who speaks slightingly of a "gluttony of experience". He also regards the term "most ambiguous and evasive" and seems to agree with H.G. Gadamer who says that the word is the "most obscure of all philosophical concepts" and also "among the least clarified concepts".

For that matter what concept is not ambiguous in philosophy? Is "experience" more ambiguous that the concepts of "East and West", or "encounter", "tradition", "Europe" and "understanding", concepts which are so much used by the author and some of which even decorate the title of his book? Most scholars do not seem to share this view and they have found the word good enough and clear enough for ordinary use. William James, the celebrated American philosopher and psychologist, wrote his famous *The Varieties of Religious Experience* (1902). Similarly, only recently, about a decade ago, Sir Alister Hardy, a zoologist, established a Religious Experience Research Unit (RERU) at the University of Oxford, England.

Tolerance

Professor Halbfass's discussion on "tolerance" is also out of focus. He uses his erudition to confuse the straight meaning of the word. In this discussion, he introduces one Paul Hacker (1913-1979) and gives him a place quite disproportionate to the importance of his ideas. Paul Hacker says that "Hinduism has inclusivism instead of tolerance", and that "what seems to be tolerance to the Europeans, is almost always inclusivism". According to him the terms "tolerance" and "intolerance" are "inappropriate for the description of Hinduism". H. Von Glasenapp, who missed tolerance in Hinduism paraphrased Hacker's "inclusivism" as "non-violent fanaticism".

Professor Halbfass discusses "tolerance as a modern European idea", and finds it inapplicable to traditional Hinduism because it "does not recognize the idea of man, and of human freedom and equality, which constitute the background of the modern concept of tolerance". Here, it is obvious that he neglects to take advantage of a larger perspective that is needed in discussing such inter-civilizational issues. Particularly, a deep culture like Hinduism based on a profounder definition of man and a wiser under-standing of what makes for true human freedom and equality needs more than this kind of cavalier judgement.

The author discusses the modern context of Europe's idea of tolerance without mentioning a word about its practice of intolerance in dealing with Asian and African countries. Tolerance, as a "modern European idea and ideology", acquired "special significance in connection with the tensions between different Christian denominations since the period of Reformation", he says. Thus the question is treated as an intra-Christian question, a question of relationship between different denominations of Christianity. The larger question of how Christianity views other religions is simply glossed over. There is not a word about the vast missionary apparatus, a living monument of intolerance, doctrinal and practical. Perhaps, this apparatus and its work are included in the modern "European idea of tolerance". It seems that Professor Halbfass's view, in this matter again, has failed to rise above the Western-Christian horizon.

The argument that treats tolerance as a "modern European idea or ideology" is of one piece with the arguments of missionaries. For example, Searle Bate in his *Religious Liberty: An Inquiry*, a missionary-sponsored work, argues that since Hindus did not practise persecution, they did not know tolerance! For the very lack of persecution itself "did not raise clear issues of compulsion or liberty". And he further adds that "it is only in the political development of recent years [that is when the British were leaving], in the missionary introduction of fresh Christian undertakings, that the issue of religious liberty had become apparent". According to this view, if Hindu India questions some of these "Christian undertakings", it will prove that it lacks and denies religious liberty. But when India was under the British and no such questions were raised, that was true religious liberty of "modern European idea or ideology".

XI
Europeanization of the Earth

In the last chapter, Professor Halbfass discusses the concept of the "Europeanization of the Earth", a conviction and predilection which philosophical Europe too has shared with religious and political Europe. Christian Europe has always believed that it has the divinely ordained mission of bringing all heathendom under the domain of the Church; similarly at the dawn of modern period, Imperial Europe felt heavily the "white man's burden of civilizing the world"; philosophical Europe too felt that it had an equally "onerous task of understanding others" under its "idea of truth which requires and authorizes it to understand other cultures", to put it in the language of M. Merleau-Ponty.

The thought found its first most powerful expression in Hegel and lately in E. Husserl. Professor Halbfass tells us that Hegel believed that the European horizon transcends the Asian horizon, that Asian thought is comprehensible and interpretable within European thought but not vice versa, and that European thought has to provide the context and categories for the exploration of all traditions of thought. Europe has an "innate entelechy" which urges it on towards an "absolute idea", a universality beyond the reach of other cultures.

Husserl believes that Europe has acquired the spirit of "true philosophy" and "pure science", "autonomous thinking" and an "attitude of pure theory" and "freedom from prejudice"; and, therefore, is especially equiped to understand other cultures while other cultures lacking in these qualities cannot understand Europe. "European mankind" has a "universal human mission". Its culture "comprehends and cancels other cultures".

Not that other cultures lack reason altogether, but it is of a merely human, pre-philosophical kind. "As animal reason is to human reason, pre-philosophical reason is to philosophical reason." This philosophical reason provides to the West a kind of "self-trasnparent omniscience". This gives the West a great advantage over others. Others will have to Europeanize themselves, "whereas we, if we understand ourselves properly, will never, for example, Indianize ourselves", Husserl says. Naturally, the "Europeanization of all foreign parts of the world" is the destiny of the earth. God made Europe in His own image, and now the rest of mankind will be made in the image of Europe. M. Heidegger also refers to the "complete Europeanization of the earth and of mankind", but he is less proud about it. Recently, Dr. Francis Fukuyama, a scholar and official of the United States, wrote an essay, *The End of History*, which was widely discussed. It celebrated the "triumph of the West, the Western idea".

But what does "Europeanization of mankind" exactly mean? Does it mean that European rationalism will triumph over Asian intuition? And European sciences, forms of knowledge and technology and even social and economic forms replace sciences, forms of knowledge, technology and social and economic forms developed elsewhere? Let us remember that developed cultures like India, China and Egypt were masters of many sciences.

A measure of Europeanization in the sense of some dominant European influences is quite on the cards. The last several centuries belonged to Europe and the rest of mankind was on the retreat. In these days, economic and political colonialism went hand in hand with intellectual colonialism. Many Western ideas and ideals were successfully planted. Even highly developed cultures like those of India and China were under a tremendous psychological pressure to accept the world-view, the value-system, intellectual fashions and preferences and political and social forms of the West. Many Afro-Asian countries tried to go western in the hope of acquiring the West's power or even approval, but without success. They were de-indigenized without being Europeanized. Some of these countries like Brazil and Mexico failed even in the more external forms. They tried to adopt Western patterns of industrialization but their harvest has been colossal debts, inflation, economic bankruptcy and great social upheaval. It is clear that whatever the adjustments it is necessary for the non-European countries to make, the path of imitation is hardly the path of their salvation.

Then there is also the question of desirability. Thanks to the West's glamour and its technological achievements in many fields, it is not widely and fully realized that Europeanization has also meant the externalization of the Spirit and its impoverishment. The Europeanization of the earth started long ago. It started with the Europeanization of Europe itself; let us remember that there was a time when Europe was not Europeanized in the modern sense; its Europeanization started with the Semiticization of its religious feeling and thinking, and then invaded other departments and expresssions of its life; Europe began to lose its roots; and while it underwent inner contraction, it started on the path of outer expansion, recognizing on the way no one else but itself. It began to seek Europeanization of the earth.

But will it do any good to anybody? What will happen if the Afro-Asian countries also became consumers and polluters on the Europeans scale? What the earth, including Europe, needs is not Europeanization, but a new philosophy, a new life-style which is in harmony with man's spiritual nature and ecological system.

Europeanization of the earth may satisfy the West's ego, but the satisfaction will be short-lived. The West does not realize how deep is man's, including its own, present spiritual crisis. In the depth of this crisis, it is not above learning from developed Hindu-Buddhist culture of Asia. This culture could teach us innerness, respect for plurality, ways of frugal, harmonious and compassionate living.

Chapter 5

Development in Huxley's Thought: Hindu-Buddhist Influences

Hinduism-Buddhism has been making a great impact on the West's religious thinking. C.E.M. Joad even called it a "counter-attack from the East". This is a kind of impact however which cannot be measured in terms of "converts". The influence remains even unacknowledged. But it works nonetheless unconsciously and at a deeper level. "Karma", "Yoga", "Experience", "Consciousness", "Meditation" and other such intimately Indian concepts are very much current. Fully 23% American young adults believe in Reincarnation. Under this influence, there is less belief in dogmas and official Saviours, but there is more emphasis on an experimental approach, on personal experience and on finding for oneself. The Church is no longer regarded as the sole vehicle of grace except in die-hard circles; on the other hand, there is a new awareness of the spiritual wealth of non-European and non-Christian nations and cultures, a thought quite new to the West's traditional religion. This new universality and wider appreciation are the best gifts of Hinduism-Buddhism to the West since it discovered the East.

This broadening did not take place in a day. It took more than two hundred years and it began in developments whose results were unforeseen at that time. The initial contact of India with the West was not happy. The Europeans were not curious visitors. They came as conquerors; and soon they developed a contempt proper to their status for the culture and religion of the conquered people. It worked further to the disadvantage of

Hinduism when they adopted the views of the preceding Muslim invaders regarding it. Hinduism was idolatrous, polytheist and out of grace with God.

In this mood, the new rulers began to translate Indian religious, philosophical and legal texts. The initial motive was political and administrative, though some scholars did come to their task with genuine curiosity and open-mindedness. The Missionaries had their own approach which is illustrated by William Carey who wanted these translations so that they could show that the Hindu Sanskrit texts are "in reality filled with nothing but pebbles and trash".

But once these translations were available, they went beyond intended results. They won admirers amongst some of the best minds of Europe. In some cases, they even turned the Christian apple-cart. After reading them, Schopenhauer found them the "solace" of his life and death, and also found his mind "washed clean of an early engrafted Jewish superstitions". Kant found that the Hindus were "gentle", that "all nations are tolerated amongst them". This fact also explained to him why they were "subdued by the Tartars". These texts in translations won the admiration of Emerson, Thoreau, Walt Whitman, Tolstoy, Victor Hugo, Romain Rolland, Hermann Hesse, Henrich Zimmer, Sir Edwin Arnold, Yeats, Jung, Toynbee and many others.

The Indian influence was not restricted to some outstanding individuals alone; through Theosophy, it become a popular movement. Theosophy spoke of "ancient wisdom" by which it meant mainly the wisdom of ancient India.

In post-World War II Europe and America, Transcendental Meditation (TM) of Mahesh Yogi has attracted wide attention, and literally hundreds of thousands have attended some kinds of meditation-camps. The two other more important movements are the Krishna Consciousness and the Saiva Siddhanta Church. They offer more than some selected or edited ideas of Hinduism; they represent its mainstream sects in their flesh and blood, in their full-fledged philosophy, symbolism, modes of worship *sādhanā* and even their rituals. The Saiva Siddhanta Church even brings out a monthly journal, *Hinduism Today* (Hawaii), the first of its kind, which is doing an important work in consolidating international Hinduism.

Aldous Huxley

Aldous Huxley is one of those who enriched the West greatly with the wisdom of the East. Though he came late on the scene, his influence was nonetheless real and deep. Himself a great intellectual, he spoke to the intellect of the West — its most effective medium of communication.

Huxley's initial reaction to India was far from being warm. In fact, he started by rejecting its spirituality altogether and finding it no good to anyone and even to itself. During 1925-26, he visited India but left it quite dissatisfied. He landed at Bombay "hot, muggy and expensive" on 2nd October and left India in early February the following year, "rather glad to escape". In *Jesting Pilate*, his travelogue, he says that "one is all for religion until one visits a really religious country". But he does admit that there are some admirers of Indian 'spirituality', whose "admiration actually survives a visit to India". Elaborating on the theme, he further says: "Admirers of India are unanimous in praising Hindu 'spirituality'. I cannot agree with them. To my mind 'spirituality' is the primal curse of India and the cause of all her misfortune." He felt that religion is a "luxury", which India, at least, in its present condition, "cannot possibly afford". He added that if he were an Indian millionaire, he would leave all his money for an "endowment of an Atheist Mission". Perhaps discouraged by India's material problems, he says that "Ford seems a greater man than Buddha".

Three years later, he repeats his rejection of Indian spirituality through a character in his novel *Point Counter Point*. "What a comfort it will be to be back in Europe again! And to think there was a time when I read books about Yoga and did breathing exercises and tried to persuade myself that I didn't really exist! What a fool."

In due course, Huxley was more than reconciled to India's spirituality, but physical or geographic India still disappointed him. He visited it briefly in 1961 at the invitation of the Tagore Centenary Celebration, and he found it "almost infinitely depressing". During mid-twenties, Huxley put the word Indian "spirituality" under quotes to indicate that it was suspect in his eyes and that it needed being warned against. A decade had to pass before he adopted it himself and became its warm admirer and able exponent. The new influence radically changed his views on metaphysics and morality, on life and death, on man and his universe and his norms of conduct and excellence.

Rational World

What accounts for this transformation? It has to do with Huxley's own deeper seeking. From his early youth he was a collector of "psychological varieties" ("the only things I have ever thought it worth while to collect", he says in one of his essays in his *Music At Night*), world-views and life-views; he was also a critical analyzer and earnest explorer and seeker. He sought to find man's place, purpose and significance in the universe. In this search, he passed through many terrains and reviewed many philosophies, paths and creeds.

In this search, the first guidance came from the intellectual world in which he lived. This world subscribed to materialism in philosophy; it was positivist in outlook and relativist in morals. It was shaped by Rationalism of the 17th and 18th centuries as reinforced by evolutionary and historical theories of the late 19th century. Freud and Pavlov made important contributions. The net result was that the age denied God; it denied the "other world"; it denied any higher purpose and destiny for man. Not excellence or self-exceeding but Benthamite happiness was the Highest Good; not the heightening of the Consciousness to contact a higher order of reality but an adjustment with the sense-world was the admired, scientifically approved and sanctified goal or ideal.

These movements provided powerful influences and they find eloquent formulation in Huxley's writings of the early period. Their impact was reinforced by his own precocity and the stimulation he received from his immediate intellectual quarters. As a young man, he had occasions to spend considerable time at Garsington, six miles from Oxford, at the Elizabethan manor, maintained by Lady Ottoline, wife of Philip Morrell, a liberal M.P. The place provided retreat and hospitality to many intellectuals and *avant-gardists* in moral fashions. It was here that Huxley first met Bertrand Russell, John Maynard Keynes, Lytton Strachey, D.H. Lawrence, T.S. Eliot and many others. It was here that Russell had his well-known affairs with Lady Ottoline. Sybille Bedford, Huxley's biographer, tells us that the atmosphere of the place was permissive and "constancy and the loyalties of the heart were looked upon as philistine and a bit ridiculous".

Indian Influence

Huxley's earlier writings are powerfully coloured by the prevailing intellectual atmosphere. But increasingly he began to find them unsatisfying. The materialist philosophy denied the spiritual dimension; his growing mind refused to take it as the final explanation. He began to reject Freudianism and Behaviourism which made man's mind a prisoner of its own lower powers. He felt that vague intimations of "another world" could not all be illusory. It was at this stage of his intellectual questioning and seeking that Indian philosophy and religion came to him. In a vague way, they were known to him already, but at this stage they came with a new impact. They opened up new vistas; in them he found answers to his intellectual and spiritual seeking. They provided not only answers but also a *method*, a *praxis*. They became interwoven with and part and parcel of his spiritual quest.

Can one trace their course satisfactorily in his life? At what stage did he change from a rational truth-seeker to a seeker of the mystic truth and at what stage did this seeking take on a decidedly Indian turn? In short, when did he become a mystic, become an *advaitin*? Was the change accompanied by inner conflicts?

Huxley provides no direct answer. He wrote no autobiography. He was reticent and he hated to speak about himself. Even his biography written by Sybille Bedford does not throw much light on this subject in this form. The biographer does give events in Huxley's life in their chronological sequence, but she undertakes no specific study of Hindu-Buddhist influences as such on Huxley.

However, this omission proves no great handicap. Huxley's best life consisted in his thoughts and they are lucidly expressed in his novels, essays and letters. If we study them, we find in them an "increasing purpose", a trend progressively expressing Hindu-Buddhist influences.

Under these influences Huxley's views on man's most intimate concerns changed fundamentally. He began to look at the world through different eyes. His ideas on man, morals, life and death were transformed. The subject is large, but we shall take up some illustrations to make the point clear.

Love-making

Following the new usage of his time, Huxley's early novels abound in philandering and love-making. He explores, mainly intellectually, sexuality in its various facets: committed and open-ended, dogmatic and experimental, prosaic and romantic, illicit and open, guilty and remorseless, critical and passionate. One does not know where his own sympathy lay for while describing the one he also knew the other. In one of his essays of the period, "Fashions in Love", he brings out the relativity of love and says that love has its styles, schools and influences. But his aesthetic restraint makes him describe only a few of these fashions in his novels. Each school is an idea on legs; each offers its intellectual justification, the permissive often making a better case for itself.

In his *Those Barren Leaves*, published in 1925, Huxley depicts the "love of the parallels"; different pairs make love on different terraces of a large villa, each in its own style, the more philosophical types using their philosophies, as birds use their plumage, to attract their mates. A moralist does not like the permissive atmosphere, but Mr. Cardan, a philosopher, counters that "everyone has his own favourite vice". Another regards love-making as "the best indoor game".

His *Brave New World*, published in 1932, leans on Freudian wisdom and makes love-making free, plentiful and compulsory for its citizens in order to create a people who have no knots, no complexes, no emotional and spiritual conflicts, and, therefore, are happy and sociable, and docile and easily governed.

In another novel, *Point Counter Point*, belonging to the same period, sexual exploration continues. But in his writings of the War and post-War period when he had come under the influence of Hindu-Buddhist tradition where *brahmacharya* (abstinence) holds a high position, there is less interest in the subject and it takes a different direction. Sexual encounters are retained but they belong to the mundane world, *saṁsāra* as it were, and are depicted on the outer walls of the shrine and are kept out of the inner sanctum. In his *Ends and Means*, he came to regard chastity as a "necessary pre-condition to any kind of moral life superior to that of the animal"; he began to think of it as "one of the major virtues" for without it, "societies lack energy and individuals are condemned to perpetual unawareness, attachment and animality". But he also distrusted it if it did not serve the major virtues of charity and intelligence. Associated with and in the service of a lower spiritual ideology, it became merely puritanism which was historically associated with "militarism and capitalism, with war and persecution and economic exploitation".

In Island,[1] Huxley's last novel published in 1962, we find that love-making does not cease but it is done under and as a spiritual discipline. It is done with *awareness*, and "awareness transfigures it, turns love-making into the Yoga of love-making."

Meaninglessness

There was a phase when Huxley believed like so many other thinkers and philosophers of the day that the world was purely physical and had no spiritual dimension. He had no use for "airy assertions" about God and such like things. "God, we psychologists know, is a sensation in the pit of the stomach, hypostasised," he said. Similarly, he held, in the same vein, that the "Other World" was merely an "invention of the human fancy". It took him much time, influences of a very differnet kind and much self-reflection before he changed his views and concluded that the Other World was neither a human invention, nor *other* or *alien* but was one's true home and shelter, but that these truths have to be discovered by each person for himself.

This purely physical and chemical view of the world also gave birth to its own kind of sociology and ethics; it gave us a world which had no meaning, no significance, no morality, no value.[2] "It is obvious, there are no moral laws; there are only

[1]It is Huxley's Utopia situated in an island in South-East Asia and called Pala by him. It had the luck of never having been a colony. It had no harbour, and therefore it escaped "an Arab invasion in the Middle Ages", and its people could stay "Buddhists or Shivaites". Later on, it escaped the "infestations" of the Portuguese, the Dutch, the English. "No Dutch, no English, and therefore no planters, no coolie labour, no cash crops, no systematic exhaustion of our soil. Also no whisky, no Calvinism, no syphillis, no foreign administrators. We were left to go our own way and take responsibility for our own affairs," explains one inhabitant of the island.

[2]The philosophy of meaninglessness did not embody one single idea; it was made up of many ideas all psychologically interlinked. Generally those ideas went together but each idea had also its special appeal and one could choose and reject according to one's temperament. Huxley roughly summarizes them in the following language: that life is without significance, that values are illusory and ideals merely the inventions of cunning priests and kings, that sensations and animal pleasures...

social customs," says one of Huxley's characters. But his ideas changed radically when he embraced Upanishadic thought. In this new phase he asked the question again whether the world as a whole possesses the value and meaning we often attribute to certain parts of it (such as human beings and their works). And his answer is very different. He says that this is a "question which, a few years ago, I should not even have posed. For, like so many of my contemporaries, I took it for granted that there was no meaning." He gives two reasons for holding this view. One was because he shared the common belief that the scientific picture of an abstraction from reality was a true picture of reality as a whole. But he also confesses to some "non-intellectual reasons". He says he had "motives for not wanting the world to have a meaning". Explaining these motives and these non-intellectual reasons a few pages away, he says that for himself, as no doubt, for most of his contemporaries, "the philosophy of meaninglessness was essentially an instrument of liberation". They objected to morality because it "interfered with our sexual freedom", he explains. He expounds that similar tactics were adopted during the eighteenth century and for the same reason when many thinkers went 'philosophical'. They preached that people should be "free from prejudices — above all, prejudices of a sexual nature".[3]

... alone possessed reality and were alone worth living, that there was no reason why anyone should have the slightest consideration for anyone else, that those who find rape and murder amusing, rape and murder are legitimate activities for them.

[3]He also explains that in some ways the philosophy of meaningless was a reaction to Christian ethics which found meaning in most abominable things they did. "Christian philosophers have found no difficulty in justifying imperialism, war, the capitalist system, the use of torture, the censorship of the press and ecclesiastical tyrannies of every sort, from the tyranny of Rome to the tyrannies of Geneva and New England. In all these cases they have shown that the meaning of the world was such as to be compatible with, or actually most completely expressed by, the iniquities I have mentioned above. . . In due course there arose philosophers who denied not only the right of these Christian special pleaders to justify iniquity by an appeal to the meaning of the world, but even their right of find any such meaning whatsoever. . . One unscrupulous distortion of the truth tends to beget other and opposite distortions."

Now in the new phase, he came to regard the world as supremely good and meaningful and in the process of realizing it he became a regular mystic philosopher. The ultimate reality is "the peace of God which passeth all understanding", he said and "goodness is the way by which it can be approached". To realize that the world is good one had himself to be good. "Virtue (Buddhist *śīla* or *yama* and *niyama* of the Pātañjala Yoga) is the essential preliminary to the mystical experience," he said.

Bridge-Building

But to arrive at this conclusion, Huxley had to traverse a long road. First he had to overcome, in his own, thinking the powerful bias of the age: world's essential materiality and meaninglessness. He took the first step by recognizing a plurality of dimensions; he thought that the world exists on many planes and in many modes, each on its own, and the problems was to bring these different planes in some sort of unity or at least relationship. In *Those Barren Leaves*, Calamy, a philosophical character, reflects on his own hands, of course while in bed with Miss Thriplow — perhaps a novelist's device to make philosophy living and even loving; he speculates that his hand exists in many modes: electromagnetically as a structure of molecules; biologically as part of a larger living organism; amorously as at that moment with power to excite and exhilarate; ethically when it does good and executes evil. "Universe on top of universe, layer after layer, distinct and separate." In these early novels, Huxley, through his characters, is very much occupied with "bridge-building", in synthesizing these multifarious universes in one grand philosophy.

After he came under the Indian influence, he saw his universes and his task differently. He saw two orders, *saṁsāra* and *nirvāṇa*, as being different and yet the same. There is a Godhead, Brahman, Clear Light of the Void which is the Unmanifest principle of all manifestations, which is at once transcendent and immanent. Both are held together in a mystic vision, in the unity of consciousness, in an act of unitive knowledge. Both are at heart the same. *This* is also *That*. The soul is akin to God and it can grow into his likeness.

Passionate Life

In his early writings, Huxley had no use for thinkers and moralists who talked of "true" selves and 'true' Gods, who preached that men should shape their lives in their image. He opposed the "stoic's brutal sacrifice of the physical, instinctive and passionate life" and "the ascetic's self-castration". He said that aspiration for a "consistent perfection" was "aspiring towards annihilation". And then praising the Hindus where the praise was not due, he said that they "had the wit to see and the courage to proclaim the fact" that "Nirvana, the goal of their striving is nothingness". Later on, he had a different view of Nirvāṇa.

At this time, he held the current scientific view that man was no more than a physical-biological being and the spiritual dimension tended to be neglected or it was equated with the intellectual and artistic faculty. Therefore he came to the eminently reasonable view that a man should be what he really is and should not try to be different. If man was a worm in reality, he should not try to be a butterfly. "Fate has decreed that we shall be worms; so let us resign ourselves to being worms; nay... let us be worms with gusto, strenuously; let us make up our minds to be the best of all possible worms. For, after all, a good worm is better than that nondescript creature we become when we try to live above our station, in the world of wings. No amount of trying can convert a worm into even the worst of butterflies."

Partly at least, this view was a revolt against so many theologians, moralists and utopians who were around and, who in the name of a "consistent perfection" and an "ideal" society and an "ideal" man, exercised great tyranny. The theologians taught that there was no good in man and yet he should do good[4] and then dictated what that good was. Huxley's ideas on human goodness, aspiration and perfection changed when his view of man changed, when he realized that man is secretly good and divine.

Multiple Selves

In his earlier novels, Huxley teaches the gospel of "noble savagery"; he wants man to be a "life-worshipper". Man should learn to live not only mentally but also "viscerally"; he should admit not only the claims of his heart and mind but also claims of "the bowels, the loins, the bones and skins and muscles".

Huxley's own constitution was highly intellectual and ascetic. In his essay Squeak and Gibber (*Music at Night*), he says that he finds the life of pleasure boring and painful, that it has do with his temperament, not any ethical theory. Probably pretty girls attracted him, but he found them boring — nothing wrong morally but spiritually raw, bothersome and uninteresting.[5]

---

[4]There are other variations on this theme. For example, Albert Schweitzer holds that though from the view-point of scientific thought, there is no good in the universe yet man should do good by an act of self-will. In his *My Life and Thought* he says: "My knowledge is pessimistic, but my willing and hoping are optimistic." He was lucky. Not many can live with their mind and heart so irreconciled and be good on their own without invoking some principle of godliness and goodness in man and the world.

[5]Some yogic practices prescribe that to keep a woman at bay one should meditate on her body (and also on one's own) as heap of bones, as a bag of impurities. Perhaps, Huxley had already practised some of these meditations in his previous life. Even before he turned to Indian Yoga, he thought of women under some other general ideas though not of the same old type but some modern and sociological ones which were equally effective and kept him away from them. For example, in the twenties, after a bout of illness, he visited a sea-side resort in the Mediterranean and went into a hotel to stop there "for weeks, if necessary". In the evening, at dinner, he found at the table perhaps forty guests — all English, and all except himself and an English clergyman, women. He saw spinsters and widows, widows with daughters who had been once pretty but were now fading into a definite unmarriageableness, widows with daughters who had never been pretty at any time Huxley contemplated the scene and found the spectacle of so much age and virtue ...

Therefore, many of his characters even while in the midst of a passionate love-affair find it a "dreary and fatiguing routine". They remain also aware of another dimension, the dimension of the spirit which they would like to plumb if they were free from their present obsession. However the spirit is willing, the flesh is weak. Weak in pain but still weaker in pleasure, they reflect.

Therefore, he developed an ethical theory which had room both for instincts as well as the intellect. He said that man is not *one* but *multiple*; He is not one self, but a colony of selves. He must live all his selves and all his parts, and live them not moderately but fully. In his essays on *Pascal* and *Spinoza's Worm* both included in his anthology, *Do What You Will*, published in 1929, he developed the theory of "balanced excess". He preached that the life-worshipper of his conception would be "at times a positivist and at times a mystic; derisively sceptical and full of faith"; he will be "by turns excessively passionate and excessively chaste"; he held that "all the manifestations of life are godlike, and every element of human nature has a right — a divine right, even — to exist and find ex-

...and ugliness, so much frustration and refinement, so much middle-class pride on such small fixed incomes, so much ennui and self-sacrifice. . .painfully distressing and grotesque. And then suddenly it occurred to him that the whole Riviera, from Marseilles to Spezia, was teeming with such women. "In a single appalling intuition I realized all their existences. At that very moment, I reflected, in all the cheap hotels and pensions of the Mediterranean littoral, thousands upon thousands of them were eating their fish with that excessive middle-class refinement which makes one long, in the Maison Lyons, for the loud bad manners of provincial France or Belgium. Thousands upon thousands of them trying to keep warm, trying to keep well through the winter, trying to find in foreign parts distraction and novelty and cheapness... The only distraction is the chat of other women of their kind. The only novelties are the latest things in semi-evening dresses and semi-precious beads... Income remains irrevocably fixed — and so do morals and intellectual interests, so do prejudice, manners, and habits." In the midst of this contemplation, the Anglican chaplain, the only other man around, tried to get into conversation with him. "Beautiful evening," he said to him. "Beautiful," Huxley agreed. "Staying long?" he asked. "To-morrow. Have to make a very early start," Huxley said.

pression." He said, quoting Pausanias in the *Symposium* of Plato, that "all the Gods ought to have praise given to them."

Plato had also described such a man who was sensualist and ascetic alternately, who fasted one day and gormandized the other. But according to him, this life was chaotic and it belonged to one who had no metaphysical and moral standards left, and whose soul was heading for a tyrannical life.

Under the influence of Indian religion and philosophy, Huxley also radically changed his view-point. He gave up the doctrine of the "multiple man" and embraced the one of the "higher man". Probably he still remained a "life-worshipper", but under a very different definition. Life now meant life of the soul, higher life, immortal life. He came to believe that "enlightenment is the supreme end of man", the highest *purushārtha* of Hindu thought. In *Ends and Means*, an early work written under Hindu-Buddhist influence, he said that "the ideal man is the *non-attached* man. Non-attached to his bodily sensations and lusts. Non-attached to his craving for power and possession. Non-attached to the objects of these various desires. Non-attached to his anger and hatred; non-attached to his exclusive loves. Non-attached to wealth, fame, social position..."

Spirit and Body

On purely materialist principles, a life even when lived "fully" — as the word is understood — has little meaning. Its best accomplishments are a mere vanity and vexation of the spirit. There is even less to justify the lives of the poor. Huxley once shared these views. Like the rest of his intellectual community, he believed in one life. No after-life, no rebirth, no resurrection. While in India in the mid-twenties, he asked himself the question — to what end millions upon millions of people are born and painfully live? He was honest enough to admit that it is hard enough to find a reason anywhere, West or East. But in India, he thought, there was no conceivable answer to the question, at any rate in terms of the present existence. And therefore, he added, "Metempsychosis had to be invented, and the doctrine of *karma* elaborated with a frightful logic, before the serried, innumerable miseries of India could be satisfactorily accounted for." The explanation was in the spirit of sciences of the day.[6]

Huxley was never a thorough denier. He recognized the Spirit and its life, but he identified it with Intellect, or with aesthetic or with art. It was also thought to be at the mercy of the body. "Sooner or later every soul is stifled by the sick body; sooner or later there are no thoughts, but only pain and vomiting and stupor.. The Spirit has no significance; there is only the body," says a philosophical character in *Those Barren Leaves*.

Here again, Huxley follows the lead of Western Science. In it, the fact of pain and death is used to deny immortality, the body is used to deny the soul; but in India, the facts of human sickness, old age and death led its sages to seek a status of the soul where "there is no old age, no death, no sorrow" (*vijro vimrityurviśoko*), to put it in the language of the Upanishads.

Dying

In Western thought, the body holds the soul; in Indian thought, the soul holds the body. After Huxley adopted the

---

[6]He was not so indifferent to the question of life after death as it would appear here. He took interest in the findings of Psychical researches like C.E. Broad and M. Rene Sudre who believed in the survival of a "psychic factor". In one of his essays, Sqeak and Gibber, published in 1931, he says that probably the dead survive "but only fragmentarily, feebly, as mere wisps of floating memories." In *Time Must Have A Stop*, published in 1944, he describes the "after-death experiences" of Eustace Barnack in terms of these floating memories. His drama *The World of Light* published in 1931 deals with the same subject though in a somewhat different way.

But his interest in "survival" or even of repeated incarnations ceased when his spiritual interest deepened. He was now interested in liberation, in immortality, in "participation in the eternal now, not persistence in one of the forms of time." In his *The Perennial Philosophy*, he quotes *Yoga Vāśishṭha* which says: "Troubled or still, water is still water. What difference can an embodiment or disembodiment make to the liberated? Whether clam or in tempest, the sameness of the ocean suffers no change".

Indian view, the body and its death lost their primacy. They were seen as *accidents* in the larger life of the soul. In 1955 when Maria, his wife and companion of thirty-five years, was dying, he was guiding her on her next journey according to the teachings of *Bardo Thodol, The Tibetan Book of the Dead.* He continued whispering into her ears that her essence was love and light, that she should now forget her body and the time in which that body had lived, that she should leave her old memories behind, that regrets, remorses, apprehensions — all these were barriers between her and the Light. "Peace, Joy, Love", he kept on whispering into her ears. In 1963, when Huxley was himself dying, Laura, his second wife, provided him similar guidance.

In Hinduism, dying is an art. In the higher reaches of Yoga, one can choose at will when to quit and where to go. Under certain circumstances, voluntary death — *prāyopaveṣaṇa*, *sallekhana* or *santhārā* — is admitted. The art of dying however is the same as the art of living. Noble life and noble death go together. In the *Mahābhārata*, Arishtanemī, a *tapasvin*, sings; "Death holds no sway over us, for we have lived a noble life."

One conquers death by ceasing to cling to life. In *Island*, the inhabitants, who are "Buddhists or Shivaites" when they are not "Tantrik agnostics", are taught, among many other sciences, the science of thanatology, "the ultimate science"; it consists in dying in *awareness*. It is different from the ordinary, modern-day dying which is described by Huxley in his *Time Must Have A Stop*: "Ignore death up to the last moment; then, when it can't be ignored any longer, have yourself squirted full of morphia and shuffle off in a coma. Thoroughly sensible, humane and scientific, eh?" It is this kind of dying, in its still more scientifically organized form, that takes place at the "Park Lane Hospital for the Dying", described in the 14th chapter of the *Brave New World*, the scientific utopia.

The premise of the new mode of dying — dying in awareness is different. It is based on the vision of an "immortal" life. In Hinduism, Immortality has its own connotations; here it does not mean prolongation of an unregenerate life in time but rather a life lived in *Gods* and in *eternity*. Huxley adopted this view and presented it ably in his *After Many A Summer*, published in 1939. In another still later novel, he says that man's problem is not Black Death but the Grey Life — a life without aspiration and experience of divine life.[7]

Monotheism

Huxley always distrusted monotheism from the earliest days of his intellectual life. And even when his views changed radically, monotheism was no beneficiary of this changed outlook. In an article 'One And Many' written in an early phase he says that "monotheism, as we know it in the West, was invented by the Jews". Living in a desert, they found nothing in the surrounding bareness to make them suppose that the world was richly diverse. And their belief in monotheism "prevented them from having any art, any philosophy, any political life", and that "except for a little literature, the Jews and Arabs produced nothing valuable until they left their deserts, and came into contact with the polytheistic races and absorbed their culture". He said that Christian God was a "magnified and somewhat flattering portrait of Tiberius and Caligula".

When Huxley accepted the spiritual view of life, his opposition to monotheism remained and in fact deepened. He could not be reconciled with the Christian God, the Father — and a habitual whipping father too — the wholly other. He sees sadism in this God. In *Island*, a very late work, one of his

---

[7]Here one may also mention Huxley's idea of modern medicine. He says that it has marvellous antibiotics but absolutely no method for increasing resistance. Similarly, fantastic operations but nothing in the way of teaching people the way of going through life without having to be chopped up. Good for patching up when one is falling apart, but bad for keeping him healthy. And of course it knows nothing of integrated treatment as it knows nothing of integrated life. It knows nothing of the higher and positive consciousness and therefore there is no attempt to help a man to "open himself up to the life force or the Buddha nature".

character says: "Somebody ought to make a historical study of the relations between theology and corporal punishment in childhood. I have a theory that, wherever little boys and girls are systematically flagellated, the victims grow up to think of God as — 'Wholly Other'... A people's theology reflects the state of its children's bottoms. Look at the Hebrews — enthusiastic child-beaters. And so were all good Christians in the Age of Faith.[8] Hence Jehovah, hence Original Sin and the infinitely offended Father of Roman and Protestant orthodoxy. Whereas among Buddhists and Hindus education has always been non-violent. No laceration of little buttocks — therefore *Tat tvam asi*, thou art That, mind from Mind is not divided." Continuing he mentions Augustine and Martin Luther, as the "two most relentlessly flagellated bottoms in the whole history of Christian thought"; and how their flagellation-theology is carried to its logical conclusion by Calvin and others. "Major premise: God is Wholly Other. Minor premise: man is totally depraved. Conclusion: Do to your children's bottoms what was done to yours, what your Heavenly Father has been doing to the collective bottom of humanity ever since the Fall: whip, whip, whip!"

No Sudden Conversion

All these changes took a period of gestation to mature. Even at an early stage, Huxley had read Jakob Boehme and William Blake (who had read Charles Wilkin's translation of the *Bhagvadgītā*) with "fascinated interest", though also with a

[8]When Europeans reached the American continent, the Red Indians were astonished to find that white people whipped their little children. They thought it cruel. Not long ago, London had shops where parents who could not themselves whip their children could go and hire professionals to do it for them. Guprun Dimmbla Hangantysdottir, sagely author of *Odsmal*, tells us that after Iceland was taken over by Christianity, kids began to be regularly whipped on Good Fridays, that they were so terrified by this threat that "some went off and hid, only to be found dead later on".

"good deal of scepticism".[9] He was also aware in a broad way that to receive intimations from the higher world, one must have the mind wide and open. He knew that our sublime thoughts are "gracious visitants", but our intellect uses its "rattling" and "noisy cleverness" to scare away these "wide-winged birds from settling in the mind".

But at this stage all this was tentative and experimental. The spiritual view was one of many views, and unlikely to be a true one in the scientific sense. At best, he was neutral between these many views and entertained them all as philosophical and literary occasions demanded. But when the Hindu-Buddhist influence matured, the spiritual view became the foremost and he became its ardent champion. The change came without any dramatic conversion, accompanied by no apocalyptical vision. The new influence worked silently, benignly, by suggestions and hints as it were. At no stage was there a sudden, offensive and unwanted intrusion, no taking of heaven by force.

One notices a definitive turn in *Eyeless In Gaza*, published in 1936, the change becoming irrevocable in *After Many A Summer*, published three years later. Here Huxley begins to

---

[9]Of these sentiment, "fascinated interest" was the more important and seminal; scepticism, and even suspicion, were expected at this stage as something had yet to open up in Huxley before the Gita became a great scripture for him. The two negative attitudes were pretty visible when during his tour of India he visited the Ghats of the Ganges at Benares. There he also saw, among many other things, men in meditation, men sitting cross-legged with closed eyes, with their hands dropped limply and palm upwards communing with their deity. There was nothing unusual in the sight or the posture; it is a traditional and quite common way of worship practised in private as well as in public by many in India as a daily routine. But to Huxley at this stage the sight was incomprehensible and he saw in those worshippers merely "nose-gazers", contemplating "the brown and sweating tips of their noses". However, as he had read his Gita with care, he easily recalled that this "mystic squint" is prescribed by it (5.27 and 8.10); and his reaction not unexpectedly was characteristic of the stage of his spiritual development at that time. He said that "Lord Krishna. . . knew all that there is to be known about the art of self-hypnotism". It was only later on when he had reflected more deeply and developed a new insight that he began to look at these things in a new light.

speak of the need to get beyond personality, "beyond this piddling twopenny-halfpenny personality, with its wretched little virtues and vices, all its silly cravings and silly pretensions"; he begins to see "I am not my body, I am not my sensations, I am not even my mind"; his God also "is not absent from anything, and yet is separated from all things".

In these works, he also quotes Buddha's repeated instructions on Mindfulness for an aspirant for higher life: "Constantly retain alertness of consciousness in walking, in sitting, in eating, in sleeping". It is a variant of the Gita's instruction on the same subject: "Seeing, hearing, touching, smelling, moving, sleeping, breathing, one should remember that I am not the doer." In *Grey Eminence*, a work of great erudition, published in 1941, when Huxley's spiritual thoughts had greatly deepened, he tells us that a "totally unmystical world would be a world totally blind and insane".

Self-Understanding

Huxley wrote all his future works under this new influence, which gave him a new orientation, a new power and purpose. *Time Must Have A Stop*, which belongs to this period, is probably his best novel and certainly the one which, as he himself says, he "most enjoyed doing". Here he depicts a character, Bruno, who is the most moving and transforming. He is compassionate and understanding and speaks of the "unutterable weariness, the silly and degraded horror, of being merely yourself, of being only human". He teaches impersonality and believes that man is more than human.

He also teaches self-understanding. The lower life too has its unity. According to the Pātañjala Yoga, attachment, anger, craving, Ego and Nescience go together and support each other. Following this teaching, Bruno says that the "shortest distance between two cravings is violence", that the "square on lust is equal, so to speak, to the sum of the squares on vanity and idleness".

Therefore when someone commits an offence, it is useful to

draw up not so much its balance-sheet of merits and demerits, but its "genealogy", its family tree. One should trace its ancestors, its collaterals and its descendants, its antecedents and its necessary consequences. An eminently Yogic way of dealing with moral problems.

In this novel, Huxley reestablishes God and says that Humanism is not enough. "To the surprise of Humanists," he says, "the abolition of God left a perceptible void. But Nature abhors vacuums. Nation, Class and Party, Culture and Art have rushed in to fill the empty niche." He had already learnt to see that "painting, music, literature, thought — they're not enough". They may take you for a time to the "other world" as he says in *Eyeless in Gaza*, but it "isn't other enough"; he now wants something still "heavenlier, something less human".

The Perennial Philosophy

During the same period, came *The Perennial Philosophy*, the Sanatana Dharma of the Hindus. It is an important book on an important subject with an important message and, therefore, needs a special mention. In this book, Huxley discusses the "minimum working hypothesis" of a truly spiritual and tolerant philosophy and its various supporting ideas. The very first chapter is on the Upanishadic message: That Thou Art; other chapters discuss Immortality and Survival, Non-attachment (*anāsakti*), Self-Knowledge (*ātma-jñāna*), Religion and Temperament (*svadharma*), all peculiarly Hindu concepts.

It is a fashion to think that the Perennial Philosophy has no form and face (*svarūpa*) of it own, that it is compatible with all kinds of dogmas, belief-systems and practices, that it rejects nothing and makes no spiritual demands and calls for no change in belief or orientation and nobody need to give up anything in order to follow the tenets of Perennial Philosophy. But Huxley does not seem to agree; he thinks that the Perennial Philosophy has quite a face of its own and it makes great demands and is incompatible with many belief-systems.

Discussing the problem concretely, he finds that both in its spirit and deeper conceptualization, the Perennial Philosophy is opposed to and is also opposed by the so-called "revealed religions" which make salvation and God's truth dependent on a unique and single revelation in history, dependent on an authorized mediator, and makes it a privilege of a particular church or *ummah*. Perennial Philosophy recognizes no such historical fatality, no priviledged intermediaries, no surrogates, no authorized proxies. Spiritual life is a lawful process, not a lucky accident or piece of history, a happenstance. Salvation is man's assusured possession, not a chance windfall. God is not a pie in the sky who appeared from nowhere at a particular time and became operative in human affairs; he has been active from the beginning. The great spiritual life resides in the heart and its truths are open to all sincere seekers. Man has known, possessed and lived those truths long before "revealed religions" were heard of.

Mysticism

However, Huxley tries his best and closely looks at Christianity and Islam for elements of Perennial Philosophy. In the process, he discovers that it is difficult to reconcile them with any developed form of mysticism. According to him, the difficulty arises, taking Christianity as an example, "because so much Roman and Protestant thinking was done by those very lawyers whom Christ regarded as being peculiarly incapable of understanding the True Nature of Things". So under the cicumstances, what does Huxley do? He meets the situation partly by leaving out these lawyers altogether; which has meant leaving out almost all the Popes, the Church Fathers, the Church Councils and most Church theologians. He has also to leave out all the Church dogmas: Sin, the historical Jesus, the Vicarious Atonement, the Missionary Vocation of the Church, and many such things. He quotes Paul but to prove the 'not-1' of Jesus, that is, for opposing the claims of a historical Jesus, which is unpardonable heresy according to all branches of mainstream Christianity.

The other expedient Huxley adopts is that he quotes from unrepresentative mystics like Eckhart or he quote the unrepresentative statements of orthodox mystics like St. John of the Cross.[10] Eckhart, for example, is the most quoted Christian mystic (32 times). But it is well known that his death saved him from the clutches of the Inquisition and that Pope John XXII had condemned him after his death for many of his sermons which contained "error or the blot of heresy". We are assured by A. Pouplain, a Catholic theologian and author of *The Graces of Interior Prayer*, that the Church never reckoned Eckhart "amongst her mystics, or even amongst the mystics".

Huxley realizes his difficulty. He knows that mysticism is not native to Christianity and has been an uneasy implant from outside. In his *Grey Eminence*, he shows how through "neoplatonism and along with it, at several removes, the most valuable elements of Hindu religion,[11] entered Christianity and became incorporated, as one of a number of oddly heterogeneous elements, into its scheme of thought and devotion". In a lecture, *Man and Religion*, delivered in 1959 at the University of California at Santa Barbara, he goes over the subject again and shows the incompatbility of Christianity with mysticism. He says that religion as a system of beliefs is a profoundly different kind of religion, and it is the one which has

---

[10]Huxley often quotes St. John of the Cross (19 times) whom he regards as the last great representative of the Dionysian tradition of mysticism and who is also orthodox. But about him Abbot John Chapman, a Benedictine monk and a spiritual director of the early part of this century, says that he "is like a sponge full of Christianity: you can squeeze it all out and the full mystical theory remains. Consequently, for fifteen years or so I hated St. John of the Cross and called him a Buddhist. I loved St. Theresa and read her again and again. She is first a Christian, only secondarily a mystic. Then I found that I had wasted fifteen years so far as prayer was concerned."

[11]E. Hermann says that the Neo-Platonic doctrine of *via negativa* "from Dionysius onwards took an Asiatic rather than a Greek from". She does not explain what its Greek form was and how it differed from its "Asiatic" (Indian) form.

been the most important in the West. He adds that the two types of religion — the religion of direct acquaintance with the divine and the religion of a system of beliefs — have co-existed in the West, but mystics have always formed a mino-rity in the midest of the official symbol-manipulating religions, and the relationship has been a rather uneasy symbiosis. The members of the official religion have tended to look upon the mystics as difficult, trouble-making people. They have made even puns about the name, calling mysticism 'mystischism' — a foggy, antinomian doctrine, which doesn't conform easily to authority. He also quotes from a letter of Abbot John Chapman, a well-known Benedictine monk, in which he speaks on the "great difficulty of reconciling — not merely uniting — mysticism with Christianity".

In this lecture, Huxley also relates how mysticism acquired a "tolerated position" in Western Christianity by an early "pious fraud". About the sixth century, a Neoplatonic writer, a convert to Christianity, wrote a book on Mystical Theology under the name of Dionysius the Areopagite, who was mistaken for one Dionysius who was the first disciple of St. Paul in Athens. Under this mistaken identity, the book was well received. In the ninth century, it was translated by John Scotus Erigena[12] and thereafter it entered into the tradition of the Western Church. It was not until recent times that the fraud was recognized for what it was, but by then it was too late.

[12]He was born between 810-815. He is reputed to have travelled to Greece, Asia and Egypt. When he becomes first known, he was at the court of king Charles the Bald. He translated *On the Heavely Hierarchy* and other works of pseudo-Dionysius the Areopagite. They were Neo-Platonist in approach and considered bad influences. He wrote a book on *Eucharist* in which he denied the real presence of Jesus Christ. Another work of his, *Divisions of Nature*, earned for him the accusation of pantheism. Pope Nicholas I complained to the king in 867 and Erigena had to leave his court. He retired to a monastery in England where, it is said, he was "pieced with the iron-pens of the boys" and died. Though he died in disgrace, he left behind important influences which lasted for many centuries. Four hundred years later, during the Albigensian crusades, Pope Honorius III condemned his works and ordered them to be burned publicly (1255).

Huxley says that "in one of the odd, ironical quirks of history, this curious bit of forgery played a very important and very beneficent part in the Western Christian tradition".

According to Huxley, St. John of the Cross was the last great representative of the Dionysian tradition of mysticism who was also orthodox.

Huxley faces the same difficulty with Islam. It is strange that in a book containing hundreds of quotations ("about 40% is not written by me," says Huxley about this book), there is not a single quotation from the Quran in support of the Perennial Philosophy. He only quotes from Rabia, Bayazid, Abu Sa'id and Rumi who do not propely represent even the *sufi silsilas*, the mainstream Islamic Sufism.

Are All Religions the Same?

Huxley was looking for elements of Perennial Philosophy and he acknowledged them wherever he found them. But in all his wide-faring and conscientious research, he found nothing to lead him to conclude that all religions are expressions of a Perennial Philosophy and therefore they are basically one.[13]

[13]"Unity of all religions" has been a special infirmity of the Hindu mind. It has its doctrinal and historical reasons. Brought up in his own religious tradition, a Hindu could not even conceive that a religion could teach persecution. And though its continuing victim for a thousand years, he thought there was a mistake somewhere and its perpetrators had not understood their own religions. In this state of mind, he began to paint for himself and for those who would take him seriously a picture of these religions quite different from the one which their own followers knew and practised. It was a self-deceiving picture but it satisfied him and he wanted to go no further into the matter.

There is also a historical reason. Christianity and Islam have been great and systematic attackers and persecutors of various cultures and religions in various parts of world. In Greece, in Rome, in Egypt, in Europe, in Syria, in Persia, in Central Asia, old cultures and religions were almost completely wiped out. The Hindu culture too has been under a similar attack but it withstood it. However, though it survived, its body and psyche were badly damaged. It survived by lying low, by submission, by deference, even by self-denial and self-repudiation, by having no word to say about itself, by making no claims for itself — in fact it...

On the other hand while discussing Christianity and Islam, he found in them a great deal which was opposed to Perennial Philosophy, and he said so in so many words on many occasions.[14]

He finds these religions exclusive and dogmatic; he finds their cosmology and theology unsatisfactory and God-eclipsing. He finds that they are obsessed with time and events and values of the time and there is very little of the eternity-principle in them. This makes them intolerant and violent and Huxley is forced to refer on many occasions to the spirit of persecution that characterizes them. He observes that while historical religions have been violent, eternity-philosophies like "Hinduism and Buddhism have never been persecuting faiths, have preached almost no holy wars and have refrained from that proselytizing religious imperialism, which has gone hand in hand with the political and economic oppression of the coloured peoples."

Huxley tells us how the time-worshipping Catholicism institutes Inquisition and how it "burns and tortures in order to perpetuate a creed, a ritual and an ecclesiastico-politico-

---

...made all the claims for its persecutors and their religious ideologies. The old habit continues and has become a part of the Hindu psyche.

[14]Huxley rejected some of the most cherished dogmas and fondest rites of Christianity. He rejected the Biblical God and the Biblical Saviour; he rejected as violent and even "obscene" the Christian doctrine of man's redemption by the death and blood of Jesus. He notices that there is no blood in Buddhism. Gautama lived till eighty and died from being too courteous to refuse bad food. Violent death always seems to call for more violent death. "If you won't believe that you're redeemed by my redeemer's blood, I'll drown you in your own."

Similarly, he had already rejected the Catholic Eucharist even during his rational days. He had written how the "Holy Ghost comes sliding down", and how "His hosts infect Him as they rot; the victims taking their just revenge". When he accepted a spiritual view of life, he felt no need to revise his older view and rehabilitate the Eucharist.

In the same way, he also rejected the Protestant doctrines of the man's total depravity, predestination and salvation by faith and grace alone. He has a lot to say about Luther and Calvin in his novels and essays.

financial organization regarded as necessary to men's eternal salvation"; he tells us how "Bible-worshipping Protestants fight long and savage wars, in order to make the world safe for what they fondly imagine to be the genuinely antique Christianity of apostolic times".

In his *Grey Eminence*, Huxley wishes that Catholicism knew Buddhism properly for in its teachings it "would have found the most salutary correctives for its strangely arbitrary theology, for its strain of primitive savagery inherited from the less desirable parts of Old Testament, for its incessant and dangerous preoccupations with torture and death, for its elaborately justified beliefs in the magic efficay of rites and sacraments. But, alas, so far as the West was concerned, the Enlightened One was destined, until very recent times, to remain no more than the hero of an edifying fairy tale" — the reference is to the story of *Barlaam and Josaphat*, a garbled version of the life of Buddha in the person of a legendary Barlaam who becomes a Christian saint.

Huxley also notices "Islam's black record of holy wars and persecution — a record comparable to that of later Christianity".[15]

Personal God

Huxley continues to speculate on reasons that made Christianity and Islam violent and persecutory. One reason of course is because they are time-philosophies; another reason often mentioned by him is their belief in a personal God who is considered as "the Lord of hosts", or a "commander-in-chief".

---

[15]At one place in his *Ends and Means*, Huxley says: "It is an extremely significant fact that, before the coming of the Mohammedans, there was virtually no persecution in India. The Chinese pilgrim Hiuen Tsang, who visited India in the first half of the seventh century and has left a circumstantial account of his fourteen-years stay in the country, makes it clear that Hindus and Buddhists lived side by side without any show of violence. Each party attempted the conversion of the other; but the methods used were those of persuasion and argument, not those of force. Neither Hinduism nor Buddhism is disgraced by anything corresponding to the Inquisition; neither was ever guilty of such iniquities as the Albigensian crusade or such criminal lunacies as the religious wars of the sixteenth and seventeenth centuries."

Illustrating the point he says: "The Moslems who invaded India brought with them the idea of a God who was not the order of the army of being, but its general. *Bhakti* towards this despotic person was associated with wholesale slaughter of Buddhists and Hindus. Similarly *bhakti* towards the personal God of Christianity has been associated, throughout the history of that religion, with the wholesale slaughter of pagans and the retail torture and murder of heretics." Huxley adds "that it is the business of the rational idealist to harp continually upon this all-important fact", so that "the evil tendencies which history shows to be inherent" in "belief in a personal deity" could be mitigated.

Huxley repeats this idea often enough in his writings. At one place he says that much of the "folly and wickedness" of those who follow the Bible can be traced back to its "mistaken view of the world". He says that "The Hebrews of the Bronze Age thought that the integrating principle of the universe was a kind of magnified human person, with all the feelings and passions of a human person. He was wrathful, for example, he was jealous, he was vindictive. This being so, there was no reason why his devotees should not be wrathful, jealous and vindictive. Among the Christians this primitive cosmology led to the burning of heretics and witches, the wholesale massacre of Albigensians, Catharists, Protestants, Catholics and a hundred other sects."[16]

[16]Huxley is unnecessarily harsh on a "Personal God". There is nothing wrong with this concept as such but it becomes mischievous like any other concept when it represents an inadequate spirituality, when the Personal God is non-yogic and is projected by an impure psyche, when he forms part of a fanatic theology, or is himself a fanatic idea rather than a spiritual being. According to the Upanishads, self-purity is the first requirement. A God who does not represent the purity of the Self becomes a Moloch and his worshippers become his sacrificial and draught animals. Huxley is aware of this and, at one place quoting William Law, he speaks of the mischief of those who turn to God without turning away from themselves. Such people, he says, perpetrate abominations "which nature, left to itself, would be ashamed to own". Huxley sees the continuity between these religious crusaders and the modern secular ones. In the past, they committed their wickedness in the name of their 'God' or 'the Church', or 'the True Faith'; today they kill and torture and exploit in the name of 'the Revolution', or simply 'the Future'.

The Book

Huxley finds that it is no good to anybody to have Religions of the Book. Writing to his brother, Julian Huxley he says: "One sees the immense good fortune of Buddhists in not being cursed with a sacred book or an impossible dogma".

A sole sacred book is undesirable for two reasons. First it sets up an external authority when the real authority is man's reason and his own deeper spiritual intuition. Secondly these so-called holy books contain much that is undesirable. Huxley says that the early Christians made the enormous mistake of burdening themselves with the Old Testament, which contains, along with much fine poetry and sound morality, the history of the cruelties and treacheries of a Bronze-Age people, fighting for a place in the sun under the protection of its anthropomorphic tribal deity. . . Ancient ignorance had been sanctified as a revelation. . . Those whom it suited to be ignorant. . .could find in this treasure house of barbarous stupidity justifications for every crime and folly. Texts to justify such abominations as religious wars, the persecution of heretics, breaking of faith with unbelievers, could be found in the sacred books and were in fact used again and again throughout the whole history of the Christian Church. . ."

Pluralist View

Another reason advanced is that they lack a pluralist view of God, man and his nature or what the Hindus call the "doctrine of vocation". This makes all the difference. According to this doctrine, "the Indians admit the right of individuals with different *dharmas* to worship different aspects or conceptions of the divine. Hence the almost total absence, among Hindus and Buddhists, of bloody persecutions, religious wars and proselytizing imperialism."

Animal World

Huxley notices the same difference in the treatment of the animal kingdom by the two philsophies. He says that while great eternity-philosophies like Hinduism and Buddhism have taught a morality inculcating kindness to animals, time-philosophies like "Judaism and orthodox Christianity taught that animals might be used as things, for the realization of man's temporal ends. Even St. Francis' attitude towards the brute creation was not entirely unequivocal. True, he converted a wolf and preached sermons to birds; but when brother Juniper, a beloved disciple of his, hacked the feet off a living pig in order to satisfy a man's craving for fried trotters, the saint merely blamed his disciple's intemperate zeal in damaging a valuable property.[17] It was not until the nineteenth century, when orthodox Christianity had lost much of its power over European minds, that the idea that it might be a good thing to behave humanely towards animals began to make headway.[18] This new morality was correlated with the new interest in nature which had been stimulated by the romantic poets and the men of science. Because it was not founded upon an eternity-philosophy, a doctrine of divinity dwelling in all living creatures, the modern movement in favour of kindness to animals was and is perfectly compatible with intolerance, persecution and systematic cruelty towards human being.

[17]In his essay 'Francis and Grigory', Huxley gives a fuller version quoted from Francis' biographies. On the request of a sick Brother who wanted a pig's trotter to eat, one Brother Juniper, highly thought of by Francis, went out, took a knife, fell upon a feeding pig, cut off its foot leaving it maimed, cooked it and gave it to the sick man who ate it greedily. When the owner of the pig protested, Juniper did not understand "why should he be so disquieted, seeing that this pig, whose foot I cut off, is rather God's than his". St. Francis' objection was why Brother Juniper should have given "so great a scandal". Huxley adds that the "fact that Francis called donkeys his brothers and bull-finches his sisters is not enough in itself to prove that he lived in any kind of fraternal communion with his adopted family".

[18]W.E.H. Lecky reaches the same conclusion. Discussing the problem in his *History of European Morals*, he finds that while the ancient Greek and even the classical and late Roman world had great teachers life Pythagoras, Empedocles, Xenocrates, Apollonius of Tyna, Virgil, Ovid, Lucretius, Juvenal, Epictetus, Porphyry, Plutarch and many others who practised and taught kindness to animals, there is "no adequate parallel...in the Christian writings for at least seventeen hundred years". Man was too special to his creator and any notion of duty to animals was "dismissed somewhat contemptuously, as an idle sentimentalism".

Young Nazis are taught to be gentle with dogs and cats, ruthless with Jews. That is because Nazism is a typical time-philosophy, which regards the ultimate good as existing, not in eternity, but in the future. Jews are, *ex hypothesi*, obstacles in the way of the realization of the supreme good; dogs and cats are not."

Vegetarian Diet

Some may regard the dietic question too lowly and think that it should not rub shoulders with such sublime concepts as *brahman*, *śūnya*, God and Soul. But in Indian spirituality, it holds a high place. Dietary is more than gastronomy; it involves fundamental attitudes and views. Vegetarianism also represents a great cultural and religious value of India and it has found emphasis wherever Indian religious influence has gone. "Vegetarianism is one of the priceless gifts of Hinduism," as Mahatma Gandhi says. Today under this influence, it is already making an appeal in the West on more than health grounds. It stands high in the spiritual discipline of all those movements which follow Indian inspiration.

Following the Indian lead, Huxley finds a "correlation between religion and diet". He even sees a close link between the Semitic "personal God" and what His followers eat. In his *Eyeless In Gaza*, Huxley says: "Christians eat meat, drink alcohol, smoke tobacco; and Christianity exalts personality... teaches that God feels anger and approves the persecution of heretics. It's the same with Jews and the Moslems. Kosher and an indignant Jehovah. Mutton and beef and personal survival among the houris, avenging Allah and holy wars. Now look at the Buddhists. Vegetables and water... They don't exalt personality; they try to transcend it... What worlds away from Jehovah...! The fact is, of course, that we think as we eat."

Huxley says through the mouth of a doctor of Buddhist persuasion that frozen meat, by being widely available, has become the "greatest enemy of Christianity". It has filled the Christians with "scepticism and despair", so that only "the most violent stimuli will rouse them to purposive activity, and what's worse, the only activity they undertake is diabolic". The doctor tells Anthony Beavis, his meat-eating patient, that the latter's "intestines are ripe for fascism".

Art

Hindu art has been incomprehensible to most Western critics, particularly of the colonial era and they often used harsh epithets like 'barbarous', 'ugly', etc., to describe it. But it was not so with Huxley. He found much in Indian art to appreciate even while he used Western standards of judgement. He could also see though obscurely that Indian art was in some radical way different and it was trying to express another feeling, another dimension. But at this stage, he had no proper comprehension of this dimension and also no intellectual sympathy with it. Therefore, after going about in India, it confirmed him even further in his European standards. He tells us with great self-satisfaction that a visit to India "makes one realize how fortunate, so far at any rate as the arts are concerned, our Europe has been in its religions". He said that while in its Pagan traditions, the Olympian deities were men made gods, in its Christian tradition, the Saviour was God made man. But in neither the artist was asked to go beyond the boundaries of real and actual human life. However, it was different in Hinduism, which though it permitted the representation of the human, thought that "the human is not enough". Hinduism, he said tried to represent the superhuman and the metaphysical and, as a result, "Hindus have evolved a system of art full of metaphysical monsters and grotesques". Carrying on the discussion, he concluded that the "Hindus are too much interested in metaphysics and ultimate reality to make good artists. Art is not the discovery of Reality — whatever reality may be... It is the organization of chaotic appearance into an orderly and human universe".

But all this was changed when he accepted the spiritual dimension. His definition of "Reality" changed; his understanding of what is "human" changed. He developed different standards and different criterions of judgement. He developed a new eye for Hindu-Buddhist art. He also began to look at European art, music, and literature from a new angle; for example, now he began to notice the absence of a "detached character" in Shakespeare. Similarly, he began to see that the higher transcendental dimension which he had now begun so much to value was either missing or was at least very inadequately expressed in European art tradition. This point becomes clear when we read, for example, his essays on 'Variations on a Baroque Tomb', or 'Variations on El Greco' contained in his *Themes And Variations* published in 1950. Discussing baroque art of the seventeenth century, he speaks of its failure to find an adequate artistic expression for the mystical experience, even when its artists were rendering saints in ecstasy who were often shown gesticulating and swooning under an epileptic fit; they were often represented not with God, but with their physiology in a state hardly distinguishable from that of sexual enjoyment. He points to Berini's statues of Blessed Ludovica Albertoni and the more celebrated St. Teresa in ecstasy and his failure to deal with the subject.[19] At the end, he concludes that "no fully adequate rendering of the contemplative life was ever achieved in the plastic arts of Christendom".

According to Huxley one great symbol through which, in the past, the spiritual life has been most clearly and powerfully expressed is landscape painting. He observes that from time immemorial deity has been associated with the boundlessness of earth and sky, with the longevity of trees, rivers and mountains, and space and time on the cosmic scale have been

---

[19]He repeats this idea on several occasions in his writings. For example, in his *Ends and Means*, he says that in rendering the ecstasies of the saints "baroque art is hysterical, almost epileptic in the violence if its emotionality", that these ecstasies "are represented...as being frankly sexual", and that from "this orgy of emotionalism and sensationalism Catholic Christianity seems never completely to have recovered".

symbols of the infinity and eternity of Spirit. He points out that the first artists to concern themselves with the spiritual significance of Nature were the Taoist landscape painters of China, and that when long after landscape painting was discovered in Europe, the artists had no philosophy to explain and justify what they were doing — that work was left to poets like Wordsworth, Shelley and Whitman. To show the contrast between the the Western and the Far Eastern approach to nature, he quotes from the handbook on painting by Cennino Cennini whose recipe for mountains is: take some large jagged stones, arrange them on a table, draw them and, lo and behold, you will have a range of Alps or Apennines good enough for all the practical purposes of art. Huxley observes that in China and Japan mountains were taken more seriously. The aspiring artist was advised to go and live among them, to make himself alertly passive in their presence, to contemplate them lovingly until he could understand the mode of their being and feel within them the workings of the immanent and transcendent Tao.

Huxley also says that another form in which man has expressed his deep spiritual vision is a human figure. In fact, a human figure in response is the best symbol of life in God or even of God himself. But this presupposes a very different understanding of man and divinity than the one found in Semitic religions. In this approach man in his innermost being is divine (not sinful as in Christianity), and Indian art has tried to express this being, this inner divinity as best as it could. This however presupposes a great science of contemplation and a developed art of inner exploration. In Indian art-tradition, when Gods are rendered into visual art-forms, they must first be contacted on subtle planes through meditation. The sculptor undergoes a strict regimen of fasting and meditation until he is ready to "receive" their transcendental-form or forms; the forms thus revealed in meditation (*dhyāna-rūpāṇi*) are then translated into visible forms (*vyakta-rūpāṇi*). Christianity has no idea of an inner-man, or of man's inner depths; and therefore there is nothing to search or find there. As a result, in the Western art-tradition, the problem has been very much simpler and it hardly caused any complication. According to John P. Lundy, author of *Mounumental Christianity*, God the Creator is often represented by Jesus; in Venetian Mosaics, a young and beardless young man is breathing into man the breath of life, or handing to Adam a little spirit with butterfly wings; in illumined Bibles of the fifteenth century, he is shown with cruciform nimbus creating the world. In these representations he is often shows with a beard and about thirty years old. In the sixteenth century, he is often replaced by the figure of Pope. The Pope is shown in full canonicals creating Eve or appearing to Job seated in clouds and holding the globe in his hands and also embodying the Trinity. W.E.H. Lecky tells us that in Christian art, when the Father began to be painted, in "Italy, Spain, and the ultramontane monasteries of France, He was usually represented as a Pope; in Germany, as an Emperor; in England, and, for the most part, in France, as a King".

Christianity treated its other 'pious' subjects with no greater vision. The depiction of Jesus passed through many artistic styles and followed many fashions into which we need not to go here, but a few salient facts may be mentioned. In early representations, Jesus was sometimes rendered as a chubby and sunny youth in imitation of Greek Gods who had beautiful forms. But precisely for that very reason in order to oppose and spite them, Jesus was also painted ugly and deformed. Many important Christian theologians taught that Jesus was "the ugliest of the sons of men"; others taught that Jesus was a "man of sorrow", a man who never laughed. Even so, however, inadequate in conception, some of these early depictions were devout and succeeded in expressing piety and solemnity of a sort. But, eventually, Christian art settled for expressing suffering, cruelty, horror and loathsomeness. It specialized in portraying the legends of martyrs, the agonies of the lost, the hot fires in which the heretics burned. Jesus himself was often shown as a tortured figure hanging on a cross with a crown of thorns pressing on his brow and the wounds on his side dripping blood. All this had little spirituality in it but it appealed to a perverse imagination and a morbid mind.[20]

According to Huxley, though peace that passes all understanding was often sung and spoken in the writings of such mystics as Eckhart, Tauler and Ruysbroeck, but it failed to find expression in Christian art. He notices that nowhere there are "equivalents of those Far Eastern Buddhas and Bodhisattvas who incarnate, in stone and print, the experience of ultimate reality".

Is this omission accidental or has it deeper causes? Huxley does not discuss this question directly, but, I think, his answer is clear. In one sense and on its own plane, Christian artistic performance was not unimpressive. Christian artists were talented and innovative; they performed all the tasks set for them by their religion and fulfilled all its needs for what they were worth. They portrayed a sky-god, thrones, clouds and winged angles; and with equal profusion they portrayed devils who had their own iconography; they portrayed the Virgin and the Apostles; they portrayed the Day of Judgement and the resurrection of the martyrs clamouring for revenge; they painted hell-fire with great conviction and fervour; they por-

---

[20]Similarly, Mary's portrayal too passed through many phases and expressed various theological ideas. From quite early days of its power, Christianity gave her an assured official status as a *Virgin* as the *Mother of God* — though quite significantly never as *God the Mother*. Therefore, during many, many centuries of Christian art, Mary was often portrayed as madonna with a child, or as a sorrowing mother — her statues and images are often shedding tears. The portrayal was often sentimental, but it did not offend good taste and revealed a religious feeling at work. But in later times, Virgin was completely secularized and she frankly became a voluptuous figure, the artist not unoften painting his mistress as Madonna. Lippi (1406-1469), famous painter and Chaplain to the nuns of Santa Margherita at Prato, used Lucrezia Buti, a nun and his mistress as his model for Madonna and later on simply abducted her from the nunnery. Savonarola thundered week after week against artists who "painted prostitutes in the character of the Virgin". It is said that his invectives gave bad conscience to many artists. Botticelli gave up his pencil altogether; Fra Bartolomeo retired into a monastry; the poems of Michelangelo reveal that he was troubled by doubts if his art had been sinful.

trayed the blessed and the damned and the joys of the former at the sight of the agonies of the latter. That there is little spirituality in all this is another matter. Similarly, they discovered important techniques like perspective and foreshortening by which they could portray the third dimension, and render horizons and depths in space. But this did not help them to render the spiritual dimension, the spiritual horizons and depths of man's being. That required a different kind of preparation and Christianity gave them no guidance in that direction.

The fact is that Christian art failed at a deeper level. It failed not in execution but in conception and vision, and this failure was at bottom failure of Christian theology in which mysticism is rudimentary and peripheral. Christian theology has no concept of transcendence, non-attachment, recollectedness, equality (*samatā*), liberation (*moksha*), the vast (*bhūmā*) and the infinite (*ananta*), compassion (*kuruṇā*), of cosmic action emanating from restfulness at the centre; therefore, it felt no call to try to convey them in its art-forms. A deeper iconography needed the support of a deeper theology and vision.

This explains why Christian art has no equivalents of Far Eastern Buddhas and Bodhisattvas as Huxley notices. The Eastern tradition was shaped by Hindu religious thinking and sensibility. Hindu art tried to portray the inner man: the Man behind the man, the Eye behind the eye, the Seeing behind the seeing, man's inner *prāṇika* or life-currents, the nodal points in his subtle body where the individual meets the cosmic. It portrayed man's inner physiognomy. Christian theology knew nothing of this inner physiognomy, and it remained unportryed in its art. Christian artists were often great anatomists and they painted attractive figures of lovely curves with draperies tastefully arranged; they studied and understood the structure of human body and rendered it in various postures and motions with their muscles and sinews. But they portrayed the external man; there was no portrayal of the inner man, the luminous man, the transcendental man.

The idea behind Hindu-Buddhist art was to convey inner

realities through figures and symbols. The underlying idea of Christian art was to narrate Biblical stories or to propagate a creed or dogma through picture-forms. In this task, it succeeded very well.

Very little can be said about Muslim art, at least in the sense in which we understand the word. Much of it is funerary art. In India, Huxley saw many specimens of Muslim architecture and he thought that as a whole "Mohammedan art tends...to be dry, empty, barren, and monotonous". Huxley also visited the Taj at Agra and he was much disappointed. He found the building expensive and picturesque but architecturally uninteresting. He thought that it was elegant but its elegance was of a "very dry and negative kind", and its classicism came not from an "intellectual restraint imposed on an exuberant fancy", but from "an actual deficiency of fancy, a poverty of imagination". He compared it with contemporary European buildings in the neo-classical style of the High Renaissance, and he found it inferior in comparison. Comparing it with Hindu architecture, he said: "The Hindu architects produced buildings incomparably more rich and interesting as works of art. I have not visited Southern India, where, it is said, the finest specimen of Hindu architecture are to be found. But I have seen enough of the art in Rajputana to convince me of its enormous superiority to any work of the Mohammedans. The temples at Chitor, for example, are specimens of true classicism". According to him, its fabulous "costliness is what most people seem to like about the Taj", and that because it is made of marble. But "marble", he say, "covers a multitude of sins".[21] Its costliness makes up for its lack of architectural merit.

It could be said that art is not Islam's forte as it repudiates it

[21]It seems that these remarks on Taj wounded the *national* sentiment of some Indians — that is the only kind of national sentiment many have; and when he briefly came to India again after thirty-five years in 1961, he was made to visit the Taj again in the hope he might revise his old opinion. But he saw no reason for doing it.

and, therefore, it has not developed it. But there is a another and even more important side of the question. The fact is that Islam also did not need much in the way of art. It had little to convey or communicate in the way of deeper spiritual truths. Its God was best satisfied with demolition of the shrines of "other Gods", and it was in that direction that Islam found its best self-expression, both religious and artistic. In this, it was not alone. It shared this passion of demolition with other iconoclastic religions including Christianity — we forget what it did in its heyday. But the facts cannot be kept under the carpet for all time. The question is opening up again and the iconoclastic ideologies are under interrogation.

Chemical Doors

For more than a decade, Huxley had been preaching a mystical view, the presence of another world beyond the veil of the mind. But his empirical mind still sought verification of the world of which his deeper intellect was already assured. This came in 1953 when he took mescalin. It brought to him some wonderful visionary experiences.[22] Later, he experimented with LSD and Marijuana (about ten times in all). In the experiences induced by them, a deeper dimension was added. He saw the "togetherness" of all things and their essential "alrightness". He described his visionary experiences in his *The Doors of Perception*, and discussed the problem of visions in a larger theoretical framework in his *Heaven And Hell*. Unfortunately, these books provided intellectual support to the psychedelic drug movement that enveloped America and Europe in

---

[22]It seems that Huxley was not altogether unaware of these visions. In *Eyeless in Gaza*, he describes one such vision of one of his characters which is likely his own. It says: "That last glass of champagne had made him the inhabitant of a new world, extraordinarily beautiful and precious and significant. The apples and oranges in the silver bowl were like enormous gems. Each glass, under the candles, contained, not wine, but a great yellow beryl, solid and translucent...Even sound was frozen and crystalline."

the sixties. Drugs could not have done much harm to Huxley, for he was already internally prepared; but the story was different with thousands of young men who came under the sway of the drug movement.

Huxley had always some use for drugs in influencing the mind. In his *Brave New World*, citizens use Soma to suppress any suggestions of a higher reality and ideal; in his *Island*, Moksha-medicine is used to provide occasional glimpses into higher reality, "an hour or two, every now and then, of enlightening and liberating grace". The rest depends on you whether you choose to "cooperate with the grace", or continue to behave like "silly delinquents". Habitual meditation is one of the ways in which one cooperates with those gratuitous graces. It helps in cultivating a state of mind where dazzling ecstatic insights become a permanent and assured possession. It helps man to know himself to the point that one is not "compelled by one's unconscious to do all the ugly, absurd, self-stultifying things that one so often finds oneself doing".[23]

That Huxley held to this view till the end becomes obvious from his posthumous work, *Moksha*, edited by M. Horowitz and C. Palmer, where the story is told through his letters, extracts from his previous works, his addresses to learned societies, and his articles in journals,both scientific and popular.

In many cultures, some people do resort to drugs for heightened and out-of-the-way experiences, but higher Indian spirituality disfavours it. It prescribes only the method of *yama, niyama, śīla, tapas, samādhi and prajñā for higher*

---

[23]Meditation for Huxley did not have this kind of significance before. It acquired this significance when a shift came in his fundamental viewpoint. Earlier meditation for him was no more than navel or nose-gazing as we have already seen; or even a form of dozing, "the doze's first cousin", as he described it. He said that people who are "insufficiently nourished" or are "reduced to an Indian diet" meditate willy-nilly. But when he embraced the spiritual view of life, meditation for him became the food of the soul, the method of self-discovery and of contacting higher reality.

aims of liberation. Godly life is holy ground; there should be no gate-crashing here, no short-circuiting. The path has it own lessons and beauties and the destination itself is in the path.

East and West

European soldiers, traders, missionaries — later on ably assisted by its colonial ideologies and scholars — opened up the East to the influences of the West. But Huxley belonged to that small group of European thinkers and seekers who opened up the West to the influence of the East — a more arduous task and in the long run perhaps more important too. He did not seek this role, it was merely a bye-product of his search for truth.

Huxley was one of the finest products of Europe — of a new Europe seeking its old roots, of a Europe no longer satisfied with mere technology and science and rationality but seeking a new dimension of the spirit, a Europe self-critical and in search. He was also a profound student of Europe's various traditions, religious, literary and artistic, and he discusses them with great knowledge, insights, authority and intimacy. In his hands, cultural Europe becomes alive. A critical discussion of Europe by such a sympathetic insider is meant to help, to fecundate; it can do no harm but will only help Europe in its spiritual rediscovery. In opening up to India and China, it would merely be opening up to an ancient tradition which was lost by her but preserved and developed in India and China.

Mahabharata and Ramayana

Though Huxley came late but his name stands high on the list of those who have opened up the West to the philosophies of the East. He however spoke to a highly intellectualized audience. Perhaps it was necessary at that stage; Europe had to be approached through its intellect. But now a different channel of communication is needed. The message too has to have a more vital clothing.

I believe that the Ramayana and the Mahabharata fill the bill. They represent embodied spirituality and reveal the higher dimension when it becomes dynamic in life; they give us "life-creations" of the Vedānta philosophy on which Huxley wrote so much (sixteen articles for *Vedanta for the Western World* and ten for *Vedanta for Modern Man*).

We all, whether in the East or the West, need their message. Not only do they offer the highest yogas, and the highest spiritual wisdom, they also offer the great social ideals, which we need badly today. At present, our social relations — filial, parental, fraternal, conjugal, civic — are tending to become empty. They revolve round a mere utilitarian nexus and have lost the higher dimension and therefore, they bring no fulfilment. The Ramayana and the Mahabharata can help in restoring this lost dimension.

Chapter 6

The Hindu View of Education

A nation's theories about education depend upon its theories about man. Its definition and understanding of education depend upon its definition and understanding of man.

If we regard man as a physical entity, our approach to education would be of one kind; if we regard man as a mental being, our approach would be of a different kind. But if we regard man as a spiritual being, our educational formulations are bound to be different.

Only for the sake of clarity and analysis, we have set these definitions apart. In actual fact, they cannot be kept apart. For man is one and he is an amalgam of all the three elements. Therefore, no nation can build exclusively on one definition or even two. No one of these definitions could be neglected completely. But it is a question of emphasis and that emphasis lends its particular colour and turn to the whole educative effort.

In India, from time immemorial, Hindus have regarded man predominantly as a Spirit. I say predominantly, for man's physical and intellectual natures were not denied. Rather they were regarded from the vantage-point of the Spirit; they were moulded in the life of the Spirit; and they subserved the life of the Spirit. This emphasis on Spirit as the true shaping reality of man gave Indian education and culture a peculiar colour and individuality.

But what does it mean, this definition of man as a Spirit? Let us raise this question and find out if this is more than a slogan, more than a pleasant-sounding phrase.

According to the ancient Indian seers, there is a greater Life beyond and behind this apparent life; there is a larger World enveloping this apparent world. They saw that the life of the senses and the mind is only a segment of a greater life of the Spirit. They also saw that this larger life of the Spirit is also man's true life, his true home — anywhere else he feels a stranger. So these seers taught that man should live in the spirit of this eternal and infinite life and claim his citizenship of this larger Kingdom of Heaven. According to these seers, the purpose of education is to make man aware of this larger life and to teach him how to reach it.

They taught: Give up egoistic life; give up narrow considerations and petty thoughts; give up hankering and desiring; develop fellow-feelings; enlarge your sympathies; widen your horizon. In short, shed your narrow "I". That will open the gates of a deeper "I" where all powers and blessings and fulfilment reside.

These seers were not content in merely formulating a philosophy of education; they developed an appropriate practical discipline to achieve it. They developed what is generally denoted by the word "yoga". Yoga teaches a practical method of going within and even looking out and of exploring new and larger life and worlds.

They found that this more intense and deeper inner life was not a substitute for the ordinary work-a-day life. On the other hand, it provided a vantage-point from which to live the latter life more fully. The Spirit enriched the life of the mind and the body, gave it meaning, comprehension and vista. Without the inner life, the outer life is blind, feeble, empty and self-estranged. Therefore, an education which only deals with man's secular concerns is self-defeating. That explains much of the emptiness and revolt of the modern youth in Western schools and colleges.

True, a time came in Indian spirituality when Yoga was used for suppressing the life of the mind and the body. But that was not its true and original aim. Self-absorption, though it has its attractions, was a secondary aim, a means to an end, not the end itself. A truer aim was self-unfoldment and self-expression, the expression of our higher Self.

This aim is formulated with utmost brevity in the famous *Gāyatrī Mantra* which is daily recited by hundreds of thousands of people all over India. The Mantra prays for arousing, activating, animating and manifesting our mind and understanding. Several Upanishads begin with this prayer: "Make strong my limbs, my speech, my vitals, my eyes, my ears and other senses".

India's education had two aims, both organically linked. One was to strengthen our body and mind, our nerves and vitality. If the Indian teaching on this subject is followed faithfully, it ensures full, vigorous, healthy and long life. Similarly, it ensures health and unimpaired senses and a mind with undiminished powers. According to the Hindu Psychology, a man's mind and senses are powers of the soul. Therefore, they should be strengthened, widened, deepened, purified. "May I see and hear clearly and abundantly", is the repeated prayer in the several Upanishads. Another variant of this prayer is: "May our eyes see the good, our ears hear the good." To see and hear and desire better, purer, finer and deeper is the first aim of Indian education. This means strengthening character, controlling desires and impulses, increasing powers of concentration and will. Not only this opens up our hidden powers, but this is even the basis of any fruitful life at all. If our senses and mind run their unbridled course, uninformed by any higher light, they will lead to self-destruction. But purified in the light of the soul, they become a blessing. This is also the teaching of the Greeks. According to Plato, there is a higher soul and a lower soul. The process of education consists in bringing the lower mind increasingly under the control of the higher.

There was yet another aim of Hindu learning to which we would make a barest reference here. The ancient seers would like to go to the principles of a thing, its source and foundation. They would not be satisfied with half-way houses. For example, in their system of education, their aim was not to seek or provide bits of information on random subjects, but to form and mould the mind itself which receives, processes and analyses all information. Similarly, in their search for knowledge, their aim was not just external half-knowledge about a stray subject. On the other hand, they sought knowledge of a deeper kind, and they sought that source-knowledge which is the fountain-head of all knowledge and all sciences. They thought and meditated and found that "mind is the uniting-point of all intentions"; and similarly, they found that the "heart is the uniting-point of all sciences and knowledge". So if mind is the source of all intentions and resolutions, then we could conquer the latter by conquering the former. Similarly, if heart is the source of all sciences and knowledge, we could master all sciences by entering into the heart. Many of the sciences came to India through this process, through this churning of the heart-ocean.

The Hindu system of education had its higher aims, but it also included that aim which the modern education would like to achieve but which eludes it, namely, a restful mind. The ancient Indian education helped to conquer what are called the *vikshepas* of the mind, like inattention, distraction, confusion, perplexity, lassitude, restlessness. To-day even the brightest minds suffer from these infirmities. A man may be very bright and intelligent in certain ways; he may be capable of certain high achievements in certain directions; he may be a good engineer, a good chemist; but his mind remains diffused and scattered, distraught and crazed. The modern mind is restless, distracted, ill-at-ease, in conflict with itself. The whole modern culture tends to be sick at heart and sick in mind. In America, the psychiatrist is doing a roaring business.

But modern education offers no cure for this sickness.

The ancient educators had prescribed *japa* and meditation for overcoming this sickness of the soul and these infirmities of the mind. There can be no healthy mind without these two aids. This is simply impossible. Any system of education which wants to plan for happiness and mental health must adopt these two aids.

The Hindu seers also believed that fellow-men are brothers, that the world and nature around are friendly. Therefore, they also founded their education on this vision. They taught for happiness, for integrity, for service. They taught harmony with oneself, harmony with our neighbours, and fellow-men, harmony with our environment. Modern education is based on another vision, the vision of man in conflict with himself, with his fellow-men, with his environment. Therefore, modern schools educate young men for competition and conflict. This is inevitable in a society which is based on the creed of maximum personal consumption, and maximum exploitation of our fellow-men, exploitation of the animal world, exploitation of our mother-earth, and exploitation of the elements of Nature. It is a world in which no one has rights except man. No wonder when we sow such ample seeds of conflict and exploitation, we reap a rich harvest of pollution, of neurosis, of crime, of drugs and of insanity.

The ancient educational thinking also emphasized the importance of a certain atmosphere in which alone any worthwhile education is possible. First, there must be a complete rapport between the teacher and the taught. "May we study together. May God protect us both. May we never spite each other", that is the prayer of the teacher and the pupil with which several Upanishads open. There must be an atmosphere of serious inquiry, of hankering for truth for its own sake, of affection, deference, service and respect. Hindus believed that without this environment, no higher education is possible.

Hindus also believed that a serious student should observe simplicity, austerity, chastity and faith. Without these attributes, higher learning could not be imparted. Not that the teacher was withholding anything, but the capacity of the student seeking pleasure was badly impaired for receiving higher truth. In the

Praśnopnishad, the sage-teacher tells the pupils who approach him for instruction in *brahmavidyā* thus: "Dwell with me a year, with austerity, chastity and faith; then ask what question you will."

The spirit of inquiry and the feeling of reverence tend to disappear from modern centres of learning. No doubt, a certain percentage of bright students still manage to do well in their learning, but their attainments remain only intellectual. Their deeper minds remain unprepared.

In the West, rightly famed for its scientific achievements, the atmosphere of learning is suffering a decline. In America, machines are replacing minds, computers are replacing teachers. The best minds go not to teaching but to research supported by big Corporations and the biggest Corporation of all, the Government. In all this there is a certain utility and pragmatism, but no deeper qualities of the mind come into the fore. The students imbibe a certain measure of scientific knowledge and technical competence but lack a broad humane culture. They remain uneducated in the right sense of the term.

The lack of the spirit of reverence has played havoc with the West's educational institutions. To call these institutions centres of learning would be to stretch the meaning of the word. They are degenerating into sanctuaries of all kinds of excesses, drinking, drugs, promiscuity, riots. In New York, we are told, teachers teach under the protection of the police. Glass-panes, windows, light-equipments are broken which cost the State millions of dollars every year. Now, we are told, the schools are built inside a blind, solid wall. In the higher centres of learning, in what are called Multiversities, things are no better. Corruption prevails amongst the professors and deans. The students are not for higher standards of learning, but for the right of free sex and free obscene speech. I do not want to emphasize these negative features, but we must become aware of what we want to import if our means permitted. We must develop our own system of education which is in harmony with our best thoughts.

There were also certain other characteristic features in the old Indian system of education of which we would like to make a passing reference. Those features are worthy of imitation by us even now. The old educational system was economical and democratic. It was open to all irrespective of caste, creed or sex. Pupils belonging to widely different conditions shared a common life under a common teacher. Princes rubbed shoulders with plebeians. We all know the stories of Krishna and Sudama, and Drupad and Dronacharya of ancient times. But the same is true of times less distant past. Prof. Radhakumud Mukherjee in his *Ancient Indian Education*, quotes from the Jataka stories and other literary sources to bring out this point. He shows how the teachers at Taxila drew students from all over India. These students belonged to different conditions of life. Princes, nobles, merchants, tailors, all studied together. Education was open to all except perhaps to Chaṇḍalas. There is a story in the Jataka according to which a prince of Benares leaves for Taxila with a "pair of one-soled sandals, a sunshade of leaves, and a thousand pieces of money as his teacher's fees, of which not a single piece he could retain for his private use". There is another story of a prince who took away some sweets from a vendor's basket without paying for them. The matter was reported to the teacher. The teacher caused two lads to take the young fellow by the two hands and smote him thrice upon the back with a bamboo stick, bidding him take care not to do it again. The democratic spirit in education continued to prevail till recently. I have seen an old account of a school of the last century in a village of Tamil Nadu by an official of the East India Company. It said that while the teacher was a Brahmin, the scholars belonged to all castes. But now a new stratification is coming, the one based on money. From the kind of school a boy attends, one could guess his father's income. This is bound to happen in a country where education is becoming increasingly costly. Costs may not improve the quality of education, but they do keep the populace out and give education a class-character.

II

We have been discussing the principles of old Hindu education as it existed in olden days and the vision that supported those principles. I have no doubt that they throw a flood of light on the problems of education of today. I believe that if we kept those principles in mind while planning our education, we shall have a standard to follow, however we may deviate from it in practice. I believe that even if a little of these principles are put in practice, that would raise our educational standards and improve the quality of our lives. Above all we should give up the barren path of imitation. We should develop our education according to our own historical development, experience and needs.

One can see the Indian tradition still in action in all neighbouring countries wherever Indian influence went. Indian monks carried this tradition of scholarship and education whereever they went. B.H. Chamberlain, in his *Things Japanese* (London, 1898), says: "All education was for centuries in Buddhist hands; Buddhism introduced art, introduced medicine, moulded the folklore of the country, created its dramatic poetry, deeply influenced politics and every sphere of social and intellectual activity. In a word, Buddhism was the teacher under whose instruction the nation grew up." A.S. Geden, while quoting the above passage, further adds that "In a larger sense of these terms, Japan owes more educationally to Buddhist influence and instruction than perhaps any other nation, with the possible exception of the Burmese". When Europe forced its way into Japan, it found that most Japanese, men as well as women, could read and write. They were educated by Buddhist monks in their "temple-huts", known as *tera-koya*. Attendence at these schools was entirely voluntry. "There were also schools open for girls, which were, it may be assumed, always under the direction of the nuns" (*Encyclopaedia of Religion and Ethics*, Volume 5, pp. 181-2).

It is the same story in other parts of Asia like Thailand. The

Encyclopaedia Americana (1952) says: "Traditionally, Siamese boys have been educated in Buddhist monastries, and more than 77 per cent of the local public schools, and 23 per cent of the government schools, are located in monastries." In Thailand, literacy was pretty high compared to other countries in Asia.

III

Today, youth movements and student movements all the world over tend to stand for dissipation and distraction. They are governed by tendencies and impulses which are not always for the good. They are permanently in revolt and most of the time they are talking of their rights. The campuses are becoming places of turbulence, unrest and agitation.

We know what kind of influences are running riot in our country. Our youths are increasingly being seduced by alien ideologies, by ideologies of materialism, hedonism, nihilism, communism, disunity and division. Under their influence, many unsuspecting and idealist young men become strangers to their own good. They become agents and allies of people who have their eyes on our country, who want to enslave us. In the past, these forces combined to divide our country. They are combining again and are set on an open war-path in a bid to annex what remains of a once united India.

A much talked subject these days is: "Educational Planning in a Developing Country". I do not believe that the subject is happily worded. "Developing country" is a euphemism for a backward or "under-developed" country. In fact, till recently, countries of the East were called by this unadorned name. But now we are supposed to have arrived at a "take-off" stage and consequently we have been promoted from an under-developed country into a developing country. After this "break-through", our cultural and educational leap is assured; henceforth, we shall leap with geometric progression till we land God knows where. Or, perhaps, this promotion is a concession to our sensitivity. We may be backward but we are also human. We could afford being flattered a little.

Nor does Planning always solve problems. On the other hand, many times it deepens them, particularly those connected with the deeper cultural life of the country. For the Planning Commission is West-oriented. It must be having on its staff and as its advisors hundreds of men fresh from the Harvard University. Our ruling elite sees in India nothing but backwardness and wants to solve all problems by wholesale import and imitation.

Today, India may be backward in certain material performances but it was never backward in philosophies, theories and speculation that concern the deeper aspects of man, his happiness, his self-discovery, his education. India's literacy-ratio may be low today, but its education is still one of the highest. As Gandhiji pointed out, in a country where the Ramayana is recited by the low-lowliest, in the remotest corners, the incidence and the quality of its education must be very high indeed.

Planning India's education is a vast and difficult subject. It is difficult even to describe where to begin. It could be regarded under various divisions and aspects — all legitimate aspects. All these divisions and sub-divisions have their specific problems and requirements and all perform specific needs. The vocational or technical education is important in a society where old skills are dying out and new ones have yet to be acquired. Child Education is in itself a vast subject. Then there is the question of the education of the more gifted students in the more abstract and advanced learning and more sophisticated technologies. A nation's very life depends on the mastery of these new masters. A nation must also attend to the demands of a more liberal and humanistic education which more truly moulds a nation in the long run. Education must also strengthen national consciousness and unity and prepare men for the rights and duties of citizenship. Then there is the economic side of education, like the question of allocation of funds to education as a whole and to its various departments. Then there is the question of a *lingua franca*, the question of a medium of instruction, the question of appropriate text-books. All these are important questions and a nation is called upon to tackle them.

My subject in this essay is: The Hindu View of Education. What has India thought about education? Is there a definition of education or are there certain principles of education which could be called Indian or which expressed the soul of India faithfully?

I believe that the question is not without a bearing on the current controversies and problems of education. If we want to be the architect of our true future, we must understand our past. It may be that while exploring the past, we may come by some seed-ideas which are true for all times. If that happens, those ideas may give us some direction and guidance in our current educational planning.

Chapter 7

Educational System During Pre-British Days

Ancient India was celebrated for its learning all over civilized Asia and Europe. Megasthenese (ca. 302 BC) was struck by the depth of this learning during his mission to the court of Chandragupta. Fa-hien, the famous Chinese traveller (399-413 AD) spent some years at the Pataliputra and Tamralipti monasteries. He also spent two years in Ceylon which too had its monasteries after the India fashion. These monasteries were a big affair, housing and teaching several hundred monks each. Two centuries after came Hiuen Tsang undertaking a hazardous journey across Central Asia and northern parts of India. During the seventeen years he spent in India (629-645 AD) he visited many monasteries belonging to the Mahayana and the Hinayana schools. He visited Hiranyaparvata, the Golden Hill (Munghir), a city on the bank of the Ganges, which had 10 Sangharamas with 4,000 priests, and 12 Deva temples. At Tamralipti (at the mouth of Hoogly), there were 10 monasteries with a thousand monks. The same story is told of many other towns he visited.

I-tsing (671-695 AD) came to India by sea-route. He spent ten years studying at the Nalanda University, the most dominant at his time. It was supported by a revenue of 200 villages and housed more than 3,000 monks. The building contained eight halls and three hundred apartments. On the way back, he spent seven years in Sribhoja (Sumatra), which was a cultural extension of India.

In the face of continued Muslim onslaught from across the

north-west frontier, Hindu Buddhist sciences began to retire into the ineterior. Alberuni tells us how "Mahmud ruined the prosperity of the country (India)", how they (Hindus) were turned into "atoms of dust scattered in all directions", how "this is the reason, too, why Hindu sciences have retired far away from those parts of the country conquered by us, and have fled to places which our hand cannot yet reach, to Kahmir, Benares, and other places." As time passed and the Muslim inroads became deeper, Hindu centres of learning were destroyed in the interior too. Eventually, from there they reitred into neighbouring countries like Tibet.

Tibet preserved as best as it could, what India was no longer in a position to do. For example, 4000 books belonging to the Sanskrit, Pali and Prakrit literature were translated into Tibetan language. Today, about 3800 of them are no longer even known in India. They were so completely destroyed. The work of destuction was so complete. Today much of old India is found in neighbouring countries like Tibet and Siam and Cambodia; and India's old past history cannot be reconstructed except with their aid.

The Nalanda University continued its glorious existence for a thousand years till it was destroyed by the Muslims. Bakhtiyar Khilji invaded Bihar in 1197 AD and found that at Odantapuri (present-day Bihar-Sharif in Patna District) "most of inhabitants were Brahmins with shaven heads. They were put to death. Large number of books were found there, and, when the Muhammadans saw them, they called for some persons to explain their contents, but all the men had been killed. It was discovered that the whole fort and city was a place of study. In the Hindi language the word Behar (*vihār*) means a college" (Elliot and Dowson, *The History of India*, Vol.II, p.306).

After this, India entered an era lasting over several centuries which may be called its dark period. Hindus came under the repeated attacks of the Muslims who destroyed their places of worship and learning. But their hands could not reach everywhere; and even in places where they were more securely established, their rule did not remain undisputed for long. As a result, Hindu India and its institutions, though badly mauled, still survived.

European Era

As we enter the period of European conquest, we find that the European travellers and administrators bear testimony to the great veneration in which the Hindus hold learning and instruction. One of the earliest observations made on the subject of indigenous education was by Fra Paolino Da Bartolomeo. Born in Austria, he spent fourteen years in India (1776-1789). Recalling what Megasthenese wrote, he says that the method of teaching and writing was introduced into India two hundred years before Christ, and that he still found it in practice. "No people, perhaps, on earth have adhered as much to their ancient usage and customs as the Indians," he says. He tells us that the Greek historians represent the Indians as people of greater size, and much more robust than those of other nations. He himself "seldom saw in India a person either lame, crooked, or otherwise deformed". Among many factors, climatic and cultural (like wholesome nourishment, cold bath, oil message etc.), which he recounts, he says that "temperance and education contribute, in an uncommon degree, to the bodily conformation, and to the increase of these people". Then he describes the method and practice of teaching and instruction as he found them in Malabar schools.

We may here also quote the testimony of Brigadier-General Alexander Walker who served In India between 1780 and 1810. He says that "no people probably appreciate more justly the importance of instruction than the Hindus". According to him, "they sacrifice all the feelings of wealth, family pride and caste that their children may have the advantage of good education". He also found that this love of learning was no exclusive characteristic of the Brahmins but "this desire is strongly impressed on the minds of all the Hindus. It is inculcated by their own system, which provided schools in every village." He adds that the "spirit of enquiry and of liberty has most probably been effected by the soodors [Shudras] who compose the great body of population, and who were in possession of the principal authority and property of the country".

Even during the early days of the British, when they had not entrenched themselves so well, indigenous education was thriving. Discussing the famous "Nuddeah School" of Bengal, an article (*Calcutta Monthly Register*, January 1791) has the following to say: "In the college of Nuddeah alone, there are at present 1,100 students and 150 masters. Their numbers, it is true fall very short of those in former days. In Rajah Roodre's time (Circa 1680) there were at Nuddeah, no less than 4,000 students and masters in proportion." All, the teachers as well as the pupils, were supported by the revenue of free land, the Rajah's treasury supplying any deficiency.

The fact of wide-spread education — a school in every village — was uniformly noticed by most early observers. Even writing as late as 1820, Abbe J.A. Dubois says that "there are very few villages in which one or many public schools are not to be found...that the students learn in them all that is necessary to their ranks and wants...namely, reading, writing, and accounts".

The Government Survey

For a hundred years, the hands of the British Government were full with the problems of military conquest and revenue system. But for the consolidation of their power, they had to turn to other more intangible aspects of the country's life. Education, so important an Institution, could not be left out of their vigilant attention. The Raj made a thorough study of the prevailing indigenous educational system before introducing its own. Surveys were made in the Bombay Presidency (1820-1830), and the Madras Presidency (1823-1826). A limited, semi-official survey was also made in the Presidency of

Bengal ten years later by W. Adam, an excommunicated Baptist missionary, and the findings were published in 1835 in *A Report on the State of Education in Bengal.* [His first Report was followed by two more, published in 1836 and 1838.] When Punjab was annexed in 1849, the British Government had already developed its Educational policy which it put into operation immediately in this region. G.W. Leitner, Principal of Government College, Lahore, and for some time also the Director of Public Instruction, Punjab, made his own investigations and published his Report in 1883.

Adam's Reports on Bengal became celebrated and saw several reprints, the last in 1983 with a scholarly introduction by Joseph Dibona, the Associate Professor of Education at the Duke University, Durham.[1] Leitner's Report on Punjab, which has been unavailable for decades, has also been reprinted in 1971 by the Languages Department, Punjab.[2] Madras data was the most comprehensive but it never came out in print though its conclusions were known and were referred to by several authorities in several occasions. Dharampal has collected this data on its fullness and published it for the first time. With a long, illuminating introduction, and with many appendices including long portion from Adam's Reports and Leitner's *History*, his *The Beautiful Tree* may be considered as the single, most comprehensive document in the subject.[3]

It turned out that what the Government undertook was not a sample survey but a veritable census. The Madras study and Adam's study of the Thana of the Nattore in the Rajashahy District of Bengal counted every school, scholar and teacher. These reports described the mode of instruction. They touched many points: curriculum, text-books, the hours of coaching,

---

[1]*One Teacher, One School: The Adam Reports on Indigenous Education in 19th Century India*, by Joseph DiBona, Biblia Impex Pvt. Ltd., New Delhi.

[2]*History of Indigenous Education in the Punjab since Annexation and in 1882*, by G.W. Leitner, 1883, Reprinted by Languages Department, Punjab, Patiala, 1971.

[3]*The Beautiful Tree: Indigenous Indian Education in the Eighteenth Century*, by Dharampal (Biblia Impex Pvt. Ltd., New Delhi).

the tuition fees, the financial support of the system. They also contained information regarding the state of the female education; they collected the caste-composition of the scholars and the teachers and also their religious and linguistic affiliations. In this way, these reports, besides throwing light on the educational state of the period, became a mine of information on many sociological facts.

The Mode of Instruction

There were certain characteristic features of the Hindu mode of instruction. Reading and writing were combined. As a pupil spoke aloud a letter, he also wrote it with his finger on the ground in sand. When he had acquired a little proficiency, he could use an iron style or reed or some other instrument to write on a palm-leaf or plantain-leaf. Wooden-boards and brazen-plates were also used. The writing could be effaced with a wet cloth, and boards and slates used again for writing upon. The method was economical.

The very first lessons which taught a knowledge of letters also provided moral and religious instruction. A letter was learnt by referring to a word beginning with that letter, then by a verse which was also a moral maxim, in order to impress it better in the memory. For example the letter 'k' stood for *kubrā* (hump-backed), and it was accompanied by the verse: *kakkā kar kartā kī pūjā, wahī nirañjan aur na dūjā* (worship the Creator; He is pure and He has no second). Again, the alphabet 'd' was accompanied by this verse; *dosh na dīje kāhū; dosh karam apne kā* (do not attribute your failure to others; attribute it to your own destiny). G.W. Leitner gives a whole list of these verses for all the letters. Thus the very first lessons which taught knowledge of the alphabets also provided moral and religious instruction.

There was also another feature of this mode of learning: the pupils learnt in groups of four or five, generally led by a more advanced student. Describing the method, A.D. Campbell, Collector of Bellary, says: "The economy with which children are taught to write in the native schools, and the system by which the more advanced scholars are caused to teach the less advanced, and at the same time to confirm their own knowledge is certainly admirable, and well deserves the imitation it has received in England." This refers to the well known fact that some of the features of the Indian indigenous education were borrowed by Europe.[4]

Grass-roots Schools-system

Even though already much decayed when the British undertook the survey, the remains indicated an immense edifice which had its foundations deep in the culture of the country and had penetrated every village. W.Adam's Report of 1835 showed that in the then states of Bengal and Bihar, there were 100,000 indigenous elementary schools, or one school for every 31 or 32 boys of school-going age, as the author calculated. The Madras Report which was the most comprehensive showed that there were 12,498 schools containing 188,650 scholars. During the same period, schools of a similar nature were found scattered throughout the Bombay Presidency too.

---

[4]The Indian system of education was so economical, so effective that some of its features were exported to England and Europe. The "monitor", the "slate", the "group-study" were directly borrowed from the old Indian practice. A short account of this practice is available from an eye-witness report of a European named Pietro Della Valle published in 1623. But 200 years later, around 1800, two Britons, Dr. Bell and Mr. Lancaster, who were servants of the East India Company, introduced in England a "New System of Schooling", embodying Indian practices of teaching. Both claimed originality for themselves. In the controversy that ensued, it was found that both had borrowed from India without acknowledgment, of course. In this connection we have the testimony of Brigadier-General Alexander Walker who served in the East India Company from 1780 to 1810. While reporting on teaching methods in Malabar, he says that the new British "system was borrowed from the Brahmans and brought from India to Europe. It has been made the foundation of the National Schools in every enlightened country. Some gratitude is due to a people from who we have learnt to diffuse among the lower ranks of society instructions by one of the most unerring and economical methods which has ever been invented". According to him, by this method, "the children are instructed without violence, and by a process peculiarly simple".

Leitner found that 8000 pupils still received their education in the indigenous schools of Punjab in spite or "the 26 years of repressive education of the Educational Department".

The data shows that the female education was very much neglected though it was not altogether absent. Certain regions like Malabar and Joypoor in Vizagapatam made a better showing then other areas. In these regions, we also find that the Shudras did better in the matter of female education than the upper class Hindus including the Brahmins. In the Punjab, according to Leitner, "female education is to be met in all parts". According to him, the Punjabi woman has not only been "always more or less educated herself, but she has been an educator of others". He tells us that even before the annexation of the Punjab, six public schools for girls in Delhi were kept by Punjabi women.

The Reports also show that besides the system of public education, there was also widespread private coaching. The Collector of Canara wrote, that whatever education was there in his district was "entirely private". In Madras, the number of pupils taught privately at home was considered to be "above five times greater than that taught in the schools", according to Sir Thomas Munro, Governor of Madras Presidency. In Malabar District, 1,094 Hindu students of advanced learning, were being coached privately, while only 75 attended the only one public institution financed by the impoverished Raja. The Collector narrates the pathetic story of this ancient institution, first destroyed by the Muslims in 966, and later on ruined by being denied its revenues by the British. According to Adam, in the Nattore Thana, while only 659 pupils were taught in any kind of public schools, 2,382 were taught at home.

Private coaching including self-education remained an important part of the Indian scene. Edward Thompson writing in the 1930's says: "There are in India poor folk who never went to any sort of school who have learnt to read. . . There must be more literacy in the sense of reading the vernaculars, than the numbers in schools indicate, or else how every

Bengal bazaar swarms with these frightfully printed (but cheap) texts of Ramprasad, Chandidas, Krittibas's Ramayana (before the War, according to Dinesh Sen, two hundred thousand sold every year). . . Sarat Chatterjee told me that in 1921 the twelve annas edition of his fiction had brought him in twelve thousand rupees in royalties, which I estimate to be on a sale of two hundred thousand."

Higher Education

There was also a well-developed system of specialized education and higher learning.

According to the *Survey of Indigenous Education in the Province of Bombay* (1820-30), there were 16 schools of higher learning in Ahmednagar; and in Poona there was as many 164 such schools out of a total of 222 educational institutions of all description.

Madras Presidency reported 1,101 schools (with 5431 students) of higher learning, Rajahmundry heading the list with 279 such schools. Trichnopoly had 173, Nellore 137 and Tanjore 109. These taught 5,431 scholars who learnt here, according to their specialization, the Vedas, or Law, or Astronomy, or Poetics, or Music, etc.

Hamilton said in 1801 that within the limits of the 24-Parganas, beyond the limits of Calcutta, there were 190 seminaries, all indigenously maintained where Hindu Law, Grammar and Metaphysics were taught. Ward, who wrote in 1818, enumerated 28 institutions of higher learning in the city of Calcutta alone where Nyāya and Smriti Shāstras were taught. There was well organized instruction in the Indian system of medicine and inoculation against small-pox was also taught.

Adam gives much data on the subject. According to his Report, in the Thana of Nattore in the District of Rajashahy alone, there were 38 higher schools of learning with 379 scholars, of whom 261 came from distant places. We have the same story from another corner in India, namely the Punjab.

Leitner's Report says: "The Vedas were, comparatively speaking, little taught in the Punjab in Ranjit Singh's time, the teachers chiefly coming from the Dekkan"; but, he adds that in Sanskrit and in Grammar, "Punjab Learning was proverbial throughout India, whilst Punjabi Pandits also excelled in Niaya (Logic), Mimansa, the Dharmshastras, Vedant and Sankhya (six Shastras), Patidhant and Siddhant (Astronomy)".

Subjects

The subjects taught in these schools of higher learning were the Vedas, Sāṁkhya (Philosophy), the Six Darśanas, Law, Logic, Poetics, Grammar, Astrology and Astronomy, and Medicine. Fra Paolino Da Bartolomeo, describing education in Malabar also mentions the following subjects: Chess (*ciudarangam*), fencing (*payatta*), Navigation (*naushantra*) and the use of the spear on foot (*hastiludiun*). Another interesting subject taught was silence or *mauna*. Yes, *mauna* too has to be taught and it is as important a subject as any other. We learn from Leitner's Report that Ranjit Singh also gave grants to architects and gun-makers. It is not clear whether the grants were personal or meant for teaching their arts to other deserving students.

The Pandits

Adam praises the teachers for their learning which was equalled only by their modesty. He found them "not only unpretending but also plain and simple". Though "adepts in the subtleties of the profoundest grammar" of a language "probably the most philosophical", and masters of logic, ethical philosophy and of their national laws, they were "discriminating and mild". He found in them "no abjectness to a supposed or official superior". They praised other Pandits for their learning, generally in their absence, rather than themselves. Let us salute their memory. What was said about the country's cotton-weavers could as justly be said about its teachers and Acharyas — their bones are bleaching the plains of the country.

Text-books

The Collector of Bellary District reports that "the three books which are most common in all the schools, and which are used indiscriminately by all the several castes, are the Ramayana Mahabharata, and Bhagvata". Thus contrary to the current notion, the highest ethical and spiritual literature of the Hindus was open to all irrespective of their caste. Very much unlike the West, where the Bible remained unread and even a prohibited reading for many, many centuries; and, in fact, many times its translators into vernacular were burned at the stake — till the triumph of Protestantism, which gave birth to an opposite movement called bibliolatry.

F.W. Robertson, Collector of Rajahmundry District, names 66 text books including the Ramayana, various Shutcums (Krishn Shutcum, Suryanarayan Shutcum, Jankeya Shutcum, Narayan Shutcum), and various Charitums (like Vamana Charitum, Mala Charitum, etc.). Some text-books, like the Visvakaram-Purana, were special to the manufacturing classes. Adam names 29 text-books taught in elementary schools in Bengal, and 120 books taught in higher Institutes. These related to such subjects as Grammar (20), General Literature (11), Law (17), Vedanta (4), Logic (31), Astronomy and Astrology (19), Medicine (4), etc.

In his Report on the Punjab, Leitner names hundreds of text-books — Sanskrit, Persian, Arabic and Gurmukhi — taught in Hindu and Muhammadan schools of different grades in the Punjab. For example, text-books taught to Sikh students of Gurmukhi schools are divided into two sections: those taught to the beginners and those taught to advanced students. To the first section belonged Balopdesha, Panj Granthi, Janam Sakhi, the tenth Guru's Panj Ekadash, Bhagvat, Tulsi Ramayana, Vishnu Purana, Pingal (10 parts), Ashwa Medha, Adhyatma

Ramayana, Vichara Sagar, Moksha Pantha, Surya Prakash, the sixth Guru's Guru Vilas, Vashishtha Purana, and Daswan Askandha.

This must be embarrassing to the new-style, collaborationist Sikh intellectuals.

Education Open to All

There is a popular notion that education in India was monopolized by the Brahmins; but the data destroys this myth completely. This interested lie was first spread by the missionaries and the British rulers and the colonized mind of many Indian intellectuals still continue to sing their tune. But the data reveals a different story. It tells us that out of the total number of 175,089 students, both male and female, elementary and advanced, only 42,502 were Brahmins (24.25%); 19,669 were Vaishya students (about 11%); but 85,400 were Shudras (about 48.8%); and still 27.516 more were "all other castes", meaning castes even lower than the Shudras including the pariahs (15.7%). Thus the higher castes were only about 35% and the Shudras and other castes were about 65% of the total Hindu students. If we also include the Muslims who were about 7% of the total Hindu and Muslim students, then the share of the Brahmins was even less.

We have a table showing the caste-wise division of all male school students, both in absolute numbers and in percentage, of all the 20 districts of Madras Presidency. The data shows that the share of the Brahmins in certain areas was indeed very low. For example, in Seringapatam, it was only 7.83% in Madura 8.67%; in North Arcot, Brahmin boys were 9.57%, while the Shudras and "other castes" were 84.46%.

Even in higher learning, non-Brahmins were not unrepresented. In Malabar, out of 1,588 scholars of Theology, Law, Astronomy, Metaphysics, Ethics and Medical Science, only 639 were Brahmins, 23 Vaishyas, 254 Shudras and 672 "other castes". Only in the Vedas and Theology did the Brahmins have a near-monopoly, as the Shudras and the "other castes" had in other branches of advanced learning like

Astro-nomy and Medical Science. In Astronomy, out of a total of 806 scholars, Brahmins were only 78, Vaishyas 23, Shudras 195, and other lower castes 510. In Medical Science, the share of the Brahmin scholars was only 31 out of a total of 190. The rest belonged to the Shudras and "other castes".

According to the *Survey of Indigenous Education in the Province of Bombay* (1820-1830), Brahmins constituted only 30% of the total scholars in that province.

Adam tells the same story about Bengal and Bihar. In the five districts he investigated, the total number of Hindu students was 22,957. Out of these 5,744 were Brahmins, or about 25%. Kayasthas were about 12%. Students belonging to 95 castes find representation in his Report. It includes 66 Chanḍals, 20 Muchis, 84 Doms, 102 Kahars, and 615 Kurmis.

In spite of the claims of the missionaries, they did no better for the Hindu *low-castes*. According to Adam's findings, Burdwan had 13 missionary schools, yet they had only 1 Chanḍal student while the native schools had 60. The former had only 3 Doms and no Muchis while the latter had 58 and 16 respectively. Of the 760 pupils belonging to the lowest 16 castes, "only 86 were found in the missionary schools, and the remaining number in native schools".

As teachers, the Brahmins were even less represented. Out of a total of 2,261 teachers in these districts, Brahmins were only 208, or about 11%. In this region Kayasthas were the teachers par excellence. They were 1,019 in number, or a little less than half the total. Other teachers belonged to other 32 castes. Chanḍals had six, Goalas had five, Telis had eleven; while Rajputs had only two, and Chhatri and Kshetriya taken together had only three.

Comparison

It will not be out of place here to compare the state of instruction in India at this period with the one prevalent in the West, and particularly in England, the country with which we have better acquaintance. The West was at this time acquiring monasteries and new-style universities which were gaining fame for teaching theology, but it still had no national system of elementary education for instructing its younger ones.

In England, the attempt to introduce any semblance of wider instruction was first made in mid-fifties in the nineteenth century under factory laws. But the legislation "provided nothing more than that the children shall on certain days of the week, and for a certain number of hours (three) in each day, be inclosed within the four walls of a place called a school, and that the employer of the child shall receive weekly a certificate to that effect signed by a person designated by the subscriber as a schoolmaster or schoolmistress" (*Report of the Inspector of Factories*, Parliamentary Papers, June 30, 1857).

The level of literacy of these teachers was such that many of them signed the certificate of attendance at school with a cross. As a result, an Act had to be passed in 1844 which required that the "figures in the school certificate must be filled up in the handwriting of the schoolmaster, who must also sign his Christian and surname in full". But that did not improve matters very much. Sir John Kincaid, Factory Inspector for Scotland, tells us how a school teacher, one Mrs. Ann Killin, spelled her name sometimes with letter C, sometimes with K and in various other ways. He also tells us of a "schoolroom 15 feet long, and 10 feet wide, and counted in this space 75 children, who were gabbling something unintelligible" (Parliamentary Papers, 31st October 1858) About the "cultural" acquirements of these scholars, one may read Karl Marx (*Das Capital*, Part III, Chapter 10, Section 4), who quotes extensively from the *Children's Employment Commission Report*.

Punishment in India under the indigenous system of education was mild. Even in the Punjab region where it was more common, it consisted in making a student stand in a corner, or making him pull his own ears by passing his hands through his knees; or making him sit down and stand up for a number of times; or disallowing him to leave the class-room during the meal time. There were no fines. On the other hand, teachers in England were sadists — at least, this is what the English accounts of the period tell us. For example, Charles Dickens in his *Nicholas Nickleby* (1838-39) describes these schools and their teachers, particularly in Yorkshire. He says that these "schoolmasters, as a race, were the blockheads and impostures"; that they "were the lowest and most rotten in the whole ladder"; that they were "ignorant, sordid, brutal men, to whom few considerate men would have entrusted the board and lodging of a horse or dog". He said that these schools were opened by "any man who had proved his unfitness for any other occupation in life".

Sanction in Hinduism

The Indian national education system was no freak. It was grounded in Hindu culture and its system of local self-government. *Ludlow's British India* says that "in every Hindu village which has retained anything of its form...the rudiments of knowledge are sought to be imparted; there is not a child... who is not able to read, to write, to cipher; in the last branch of learning they are confessedly most proficient". The same source says at another place that "where the village system has been swept away by us, as in Bengal, there the school system has equally disappeared". Leitner quotes a report of a British Inspector of Schools in the Punjab which too brings out the intimate link between indigenous educational system and it underlying system of ideas and polity. It says: "The indigenous education of India was founded on the sanction of the Shastras, which elevated into religious duties and conferred dignity on the commonest transactions of every-day life. The existence of village communities, which left not only their municipal, but also in part their revenue and judicial administrations, in the hands of the people themselves, greatly helped to spread education among all the different members of the community."

British Hostility

The new rulers were understandably hostile to the indigenous system. As soon as the British took over the Punjab, the Education Report of 1858 says: "A village school left to itself is not an institution which we have any great interest in maintaining."

This hostility arose partly from a lack of imagination. To the new rulers, brought up so differently, a school was no school if it did not teach English. To such preponderant elements among them, the answer of a rare and imaginative administrator like Leitner was this: "If a collegium held, according to Hindu tradition, in the teacher's own house, is not a school; if to read and write Gurmukhi and the *naharas* is not to know the three or any r's, then, of course, all discussion is at an end... When, however, by school is meant an indigenous school; by a knowledge of reading and writing that of the indigenous characters; by learning or science, oriental learning and science, then indeed was education far extended when we took the Punjab than it is at present." To these who despised an indigenous school because it taught a small number of students, he answered: "If the Lahore Government College could be called a college when it had only four students, there is no reason why an indigenous school should not be called a school when it has less than ten students."

Financial Support

The teacher of an indigenous school was an idealist, but the system itself was founded on realistic public financial support. Schools were supported by the grant of rent-free lands and monetary assignments. During the British rule, this support was withheld or drastically curtailed. The data for rent-free lands to support local needs like the police, the temples, the education has not been fully worked out but that this portion was very large is beyond doubt. Dharampal shows that it was sometimes as large as 35% of the total land, and sometimes even 50%. Leitner gives the names of many hundreds of scholars who were endowed with such lands but whose grants were terminated and as a result of which the institutions they ran so well died down within a generation. The Collector of Bellary District wrote: "There is no doubt that in former times especially under the Hindu Government very large grants both in money and in land were issued for the sake of learning."

When the British started studying indigenous education, they had already been in control of the territory for over fifty years; and during these years much harm had already been done. The land grants were already stopped or curtailed. There was a general breakdown in the economy at large. The old classes which supported local institutions were impoverished. These and other causes combined to bring about a fast deterioration is the educational condition. Adam mentions many specific villages in Nattore Thana which at the time of investigation had only two schools where there had been once ten or eleven schools in living memory. The decay was fast.

Increasing Illiteracy

No doubt, indigenous education decayed and illiteracy increased during the British period. According to Sir Henry Lawrence, there was one school for every 1783 inhabitants of the most backward division of the Punjab at the time of annexation. But thirty years later in 1881, "there is one school of whatever sort, to every 9,028 inhabitants", according the President of the Educational Commission.

Adam estimated that there was 11% literacy in the Thana of Nattore during 1830s. "A century later the British considered this an accomplishment in many parts of India," says Joseph DiBona, the author of *One Teacher, One School.* This is the charge which Mahatma Gandhi also brought against the British when he said in 1931 that "today India is more illiterate than it was fifty or a hundred years ago". He charged that the British destroyed "the Beautiful Tree", an epithet he used to describe old Indian indigenous education and which Dharampal has also borrowed from him to provide the title to his book on the subject.

Indigenous education served local needs, both economic and cultural and religious. Under the British, it was divorced from both. For example, one Government report says: "If a boy learns arithmetic in our schools, he is of little use for the shop, because he finds there a different system of accounts, and the meanest Banya can cast up the intricacies of the grain-trade accounts by a mental process far more rapidly than if he had taken honours in Mathematics at the Calcuttta University."

Under the indigenous system, primary education was imparted in the local language. But the British Government introduced Urdu as the medium of instruction over a large territory of North India. This "practically excluded from primary instruction" the whole Hindu priestly class, the artisans and the agricultural classes, according to the testimony of the Brahmo Samaj. The common men and women wanted to learn to read in order to be able to study the Ramayana and other religious books which were available in their own language. But Urdu which was foreign to them did not help them in that direction. It was meant to make students *munshis* which was not their aim.

Cultural Self-alienation

While teaching a boy three r's, indigenous education also familiarized him with the nation's epics, religion and literature. This did not suit the white rulers and missionaries. So they put forward the principles of "secularism" and 'religious neutrality' — principles which continue to be pleaded even today by our brown sahibs with equal duplicity and equal harm to the deeper life of the nation. Pleading these convenient principles, the then Inspector of a provincial schools reported: "I directed the disuse of all books of a religious character in the schools." The Ramayana and the other great indigenous literature still continue to be on the Index of the so-called indigenous Government thirty-six years after independence.

Thus the nation's accumulated riches were denied to the new generations and they grew in self-forgetfulness of their rich heritage. The nation's sciences, philosophies, religion and literature were taken out of the life of the growing generations and these merely became the topics or subjects of Indology.'

Under the indigenous system, the Hindu schools were closed on *Poornima* of every month and on other Hindu festivals. Under the new dispensation, Sunday became the new holiday. Thus we were cut off from our calendar too with which so much else in our history and religious discipline and observances is also connected. In due course, came into being a class of Macaulay's dream, a class oblivious of its roots, a class of cultural barbarians, a class Indian in blood and colour but European and missionary in its contempt of everything Indian in general and Hindu in particular.

Deep down, the issue was not English language, or higher learning of the West or modern sciences. Hindu culture had a rich tradition of secular learning and it could easily imbibe whatever the West had to offer. In fact, it could even make its own contribution to the pool and perhaps help in taming the aggressive urges of modern sciences. The problem was deeper. It had to do with a pattern of self-forgetfulness and self-alienation that was imposed on the country. And we were so thoroughly brainwashed that we now delight in it. The imperialist-missionary policies of the British have now become the political religion of our own neo-intellectuals and administrators. The attack still continues under the guise of "Tradition versus Modernity".

Chapter 8

India and Greece

The movement of men and ideas from the West to the East is a recent phenomenon. There was a time when the movement was in the opposite direction and the East had gone to the West in a big way.

At that time, India's cultural frontiers too were wider than her political frontiers and her ideas influenced lands and people far away from her physically. Vedic India shared many of her Gods with Iran and one of them, Mithra (*Mitra*), went on a long journey to the West. Mithraea, temples dedicated to Mithra, have been found all over Syria, Asia Minor, Spain and even in many Western ports. One Mithraeum was found in London in 1954. Many relics have been found in Germany too, as at Hedernheim, near Frankfurt-on-Main.

The great Manu makes a very interesting observation. He says that originally the Paundrakas, Andhras, Dravidas, Yavanas, Shakas, Paradas, Pahlvas, Chinas, Kiratas, Daradas and Khasas were Khsatriyas, but at some stage they lost the guidance of the Brahmins; as a result, they lapsed from their sacred sacraments (*kriyālopa*) and lost their caste (10.43-4). At what time and under what compulsions of history Brahmanic guidance ceased is an interesting question.

Greeks

Hindu thought also exerted a great influence on ancient Greek thought as M.E. Pococke shows in his *India in Greece*. It is believed that Pythagoras visited Indian and learnt the doctrine of transmigration and many ascetic practices from here. One meets many parallel ideas in the Upanishads and Plato. These similarities are not fortuitous but they emanated from a common deeper vision and life-philosophy. Apollonius the "wise man of Tyana", perhaps the greatest saint of the Hellenistic world, a contemporary of Jesus, visited the wise men of India and was highly satisfied. Later on, he also visited Ethiopia to meet her naked ascetics, who, he believed, had borrowed their spirituality from India. But, as he already suspected, he did not find them worthy pupils of India.

Pythagoras and Orphic mysteries stand very high in Greek religion and they have family likeness with Hinduism. Lecky in his *History of European Morals* quotes an old tradition in Greece that Pythagoras had himself come to India and learnt philosophy from the gymnosophists. It seems he believed in an "all-pervading soul" which is at least one important attribute of Hindu *ātman*. He believed in rebirth or transmigration; he taught and practised harmlessness or non-injury; chastity was the leading virtue of his school of thought; he taught silence; he taught that the end of man is to "become like God". Orphic mysteries taught release (*lysis*) from all material entanglements, which is close to *moksha* of the Hindus.

Pythagoras taught the doctrine of the witness, *drashṭā* of the Hindus. He said that life is like a gathering at the Olympic Games, where some come to buy and sell, others to play, but the best of them come to look on. This is just like the Upanishads' two birds on a tree, one eating its fruits and the other just looks on. It has reference to the witness self of the Upanishads, the *kūṭastha* of the Gita. In higher Greek religion the doctrine of the life of a spectator holds a high place.

When we come to the period of recorded history, we find that India had intimate contacts with Greece which at this time was more a part of Asia than of Europe. Greek religion, philosophy and literature show lively Indian influences. India even at this time was known for its wisdom and many Greek philosophers like Democritus, Anaxarchus and Pyrrho visited India and according to Lucianus, the Goddess of philosophy first descended upon "the Indians, the mightiest nation upon the earth".

Apollonius

Apollonius of Tyna (born c. 4 AD), the great saint of the Greek world, was a Pythogorian teacher, a great ascetic, a celebate, a vegetarian; he was against every form of cruetly to animals; he protested against gladiatorial shows. He was a great name throughout the Pagan world. Dio Casius tells us that that Caracalla (211-216) erected a chapel to his memory. Apuleius ranked him with Moses and Zoroaster. Lampridius tells us that Alexander Severus included Apollonius with Abraham, and Orpheus amongst his household Gods. For this very fact, he became a hated name among the Christians. In their struggle against Christianity, Pagan philosophers often invoked his name. Hierocles, proconsul of Bithynia under Diocletian (c. 305) cited Apollonius' miracles to show that miracles were not the peculiar property of Christianity. Eusebius and later on Lactantius (c. 315) attacked Hierocles for this. But orthodox Christians could not believe that there could be such a great ethical and divine character outside the Christian fold. Augustine did not speak ill of him but rebuked those who regarded him as equal of Jesus. Among the early Christians he acquired the name of Antichrist, and he continued to be berated by the Church. Even in the fifteenth century, he was denounced as a detestable magician.

***Ātma-vāda* and Advaita**

He visited India to meet its wise men. He met one Iarchus and was deeply satisfied. The latter asked him: "What knowledge do you think we have that you lack?" Apollonious replied: "It is my opinion that your ways are wiser and much more godly. But if I were to find among you nothing that I do not know, I would also have learned that there is nothing further for me to learn." Iarchus told him: "You, our visitor, have (already) a share of this wisdom, but yet not all of it." Then the teaching began but what it was and about its nature nothing is said. The biographer, however, relates many anecdotes and throws interesting sidelights. He tells us that in their very first meeting, Iarchus told Apollonius everything about him, his ancestry on his father's and mother's side, his journey and the people he met and talks he had with them. Apollonius was amazed. Iarchus also told him about Apollonius' nature and said: "We discern every kind of soul, and have countless clues to discover them." "Ask me whatever you like, since you have come among men who know everything," said the chief of the Indian wise men to his distinguished visitor. He in turn asked the Indians if they knew themselves, expecting them to be like the Greeks in thinking it is difficult to know oneslef. But to his surprise, Iarchus replied: "We know everything because we begin by knowing ourselves. None of us would approach our kind of philosophy without knowing himself first." Apollonius had no difficulty in accepting this statement for it was also his own belief. He asked Iarchus what they thought they were, and the latter replied: "Gods." And why? "Because we are good men," Iarchus said (p. 80). Later on in his life when he used this doctrine before the Emperor of Rome when he was being tried for instigating treason, he also told him that Iarchus and Phraotes, the two Indians, "are the only humans whom I consider Gods and worthy of being called so".

Apollonius discussed the Greek heroes with Iarchus, and he well knew them. Iarchus said: "Troy was destroyed by the Achaeans that sailed there then, and you Greeks have been destroyed by the tales about it. You think the only heroes are those that attacked Troy, and so you neglect a larger number of more godlike men produced by your own country, by Egypt, and by India." Discussing Achilles, the hero of the Trojan war, he remarked that Homer makes Achilles come to Troy for Helen, and says that on his way he had captured twelve cities by sea and eleven by land. Then he compares him with an old Indian hero — in fact, he himself in an old incarnation — who founded sixty cities, most esteemed in the country. And who could believe that "sacking cities is more glorious than building them?" he asks. He further observes that "to prove your courage defending the liberty of your own land is far better than bringing slavery on a city, especially when it is because of a woman who probably did not mind being carried off".

Earlier when he had met an Indian king at Taxila, the descendent of Porus, the meeting with him was as memorable. The king lived simply and wisely. Asked about his diet, the king replied: "Of wine I drink as much as I sacrifice to the sun. What I catch in the hunt others eat: the exercise is enough for me. My food is vegetables, the centre of date-palms and their fruit and everything that grows beside the river. I also eat many things that grow on trees: they are harvested by these hands of mine."

Not that the king neglected kingly duties and military arts. He practised javelin and discus even while he went out to bathe. Learning shooting and archery went on while the king's party ate. "Shooting through a sling, using a hair as a target, and drawing an outline of one's own son in arrows while he stands against a board are others of their convivial pursuits." These continued even while they dined and drank.

The Greek saint was highly satisfied with his Indian visit. When he left the Indian philosophers, he wrote to them that they had shown him "a path through heaven," and that "I will continue to enjoy your conversation as if still with you, if I have not drunk of the cup of Tantalus in vain". He said that "he would recall all this to the Greeks, and enjoy your conversations as if you were present". He often spoke of these wise men to his audience later on in his life. To the Egyptians, he said: "I saw the Indian Brahmans living on the earth and not on it, walled without walls, and with no possessions except the whole world."

Apollonius believed that Egypt and Ethiopia derived their

wisdom from India, and that the Naked Philosophers of Ethiopia were emigrants from India. He also believed that Pythagoras (about 500 BC) and his sect derived their philosophy from India.

Apollonius's idea of a spiritual life was the same as that of the Hindus. He believed that spirituality belongs to purified *buddhi* and it was native to man and he distrusted those who hawked revealed truths. He advised a Roman emperor, Euphrates, to "approve and pursue the kind that is in accordance with nature. But avoid the kind that claims to be inspired: people like that about tell lies about Gods, and urge us to do many foolish things" (p. 130).

Once when asked why he studied philosophy, he said that it was "to know the Gods and to understand men, since knowing oneself was less difficult than knowing another" (p. 106).

He visisted all the shrines and he could see his God in all the Gods. He said that "none of the Gods refuse me, but they let me share their roof". We are told by his biographer that Apollonius lived in different sactuaries, moving and changing from one to another. When criticized for this, he said, "Even the Gods do not live in heaven all the time. They travel to Ethiopia, to Olympia and to Athos. I think it illogical that the Gods travel around every country of mankind, while men do not visit all the Gods" (p. 103).

It seemed that while he was outside the Greek and Roman world visiting barbarian countries which included India, all shrines were open to him.

It seems that it was not the custom even in Rome, so hospitable to all the Gods, for Telesinus, a Roman consul commented: "The barbarians have anticipated the Romans in a very praiseworthy deed."

He spoke of two Zeuses: one the statue of Zeus made by Phidias at Olympia; it was seated since that was the decision of the artist. But there was also another Zeus, Homer's Zeus "whom the poet describes in many shapes, and who is a more marvellous creation than the Zeus of ivory; for this Zeus was visible on earth, while the other was supposed to be in everything in the universe"[1] (p. 90-91).

Apolonious was not only open to various Gods, he was open to worshipping them with different rites. Not to him one rite or creed. When he met the wise men of India, he wanted to participate in all their religious worships. "I would certainly be doing a wrong to the Caucasus and the Indus, which I passed coming here to see you, if I did not steep myself in all your rites," he told the chief of the wisemen of India.

He practised non-injury to living beings. On one occasion he refused even when invited even by a kinge to participate in the chase. He believed in non-injury to living beings. He made no blood sacrifice. Apollonious said that "men make virtuous requests when their sacrifices are pure"; he said that "he believed that the Gods shared these opinion about sacrifice". He was accused of being a magician, of being able to foresee. To this he answered that his food was different from other men; that it was light which "keeps my senses in a kind of mysterious clairty, and prevents cloudiness from affecting them; and causes me to discern everything that is and will be, as if it were reflected in a mirror... Gods are aware of things before they happen, men when they happen, and wise men when they are about to happen" (p. 218-9).

Apollonius explains why he and Pythagoras stayed away from meat and used linen in their dress: He said that Earth grows everything for mankind and those who are willing to

---

[1]It does not mean Apollonius was opposed to image-worship. We are told of an interesting dialogue he had on the subject with an Egyptian priest. Apollonius defended the Greek fashion of worshipping the Divinity under the form of human image, sculptured by Phidias and Praxiteles, this being the noblest form we can conceive and therefore the least inadequate to the Divine perfections. Speaking for the Egyptian fashion of worshipping the Deity in the form of animals, the Egyptian priest said that as it is blasphemous to attempt to conceive an image of the Deity, the Egyptians therefore concentrate the imagination of the worshipper on objects that are plainly allegorical or symbolical, and do not pretend to offer any such image (Philostraus, *Apollonius of Tyna*, vi.19).

live at peace with the animals need nothing. But some "disobey the earth and sharpen knives against the animals to gain clothing and food. The Indian Brahmans disapproved of this personally and taught the Naked Philosophers of Egypt to disapprove of it too. From there Pythagoras, who was the first Greek to associate with Egyptians, borrowed the principle. He let the earth keep living creatures, but held that what the earth grows is pure, and so lived off that because it was sufficient to feed body and soul. Clothing made from dead creatures, which most people wear, he considered impure; he dressed in linen and, for the same reason, made his shoes of plaited bark. He derived many advantages from this purity, above all that of perceiving his own soul" (p. 212).

He believed in rebirth. Pythogoras had many births. In one birth, he also fought at Troy, and then "passed into several bodies according to the law of *Adrasteia*, whereby souls migrte. (according to tradition, a name of Namesis derived from an altar erected to her by Adrastus. But could it be Hindu *adrishṭa* in the ultimate analysis?). Finally, he returned to human form and was born the son of Mensarchides of Samos, so that he became a wise man who had been a barbarian, an Ionian who had been a Trojan, and a man sɔ immortal that he did not even forget he had been Euphorbus" (p. 212). Apollonius also knew his past and future births though as he himself says, "I did not announce before the Greeks what my soul had changed into or changed from in the past, or what it will in future, even though I know" (p. 215). Apollonius believed in the the doctrine of the immortality of the soul but discourged his pupils from meddling too much in such questions:

"The soul's an immortal thing, not yours to own
But Providence's. When the body wastes,
Like a swift horse that breaks its bonds, the soul
Leaps nimbly out, and mingles with light air,
Shunning its hatred, dreary servitude.
But what is this to you, who when you've gone

Will know it well? And why among the living
Bother yourself with thinking on such things?"

Buddhism goes West

In later times, Buddhism followed the track left by the Upanishadic teachers. Emperor Ashoka facilitated but did not initiate the process. In fact, long before he came on the scene, there were contacts, commercial and cultural, between India and Egypt through Yemen for a thousand years. The celebrated Girnar inscription of King Ashoka says that Buddhism was followed even in the domain of Antiochus, the Greek king whose empire included Syria, Phoenicia, Babylonia, Persia, Medea and Abyssinia.

Later on, though Buddhism withdrew from this region, the memory of this contact lingered for a long time. Alberuni (997–1030 AD) tells us that "in former times, Khurasan, Persia, Irak, Mosul the country upto the frontiers of Syria, was Buddhistic". Later on it "had to emigrate to the countries east of Balkh" when King Gushtasp came under the influence of Zaruthusthra's religion and his son, Isfendiyar, persecuted the Buddhists. But though Buddhism withdrew, it kept exerting its influence. According to the same authority, when the prophet Mani (216–76 AD) was banished from Iranshahr, he went to India, the usual asylum for those who faced religious persecution at home. Here he learnt the doctrine of transmigration and incorporated it into his own system. Later, through Manichaeism and other parallel channels, it became part of early Christianity.

Darkness descends on the Mediterranean World

A new phenomenon was taking place all over the Mediteranean world. While Rome was expanding outwards, it was contracting internally and losing inwardness. Its deeper spirituality connected with the names of Pythagoras, Plato, Stoics, and Plotinus began to withdraw within. Whether there was something in the new social and political environment or there was a change in the psyche is difficult to say; but old spirituality was getting to be understood less and less. On the other hand, there was a demand for Saviours and there were Saviours all around. A spirituality of hell and heaven, and last day, apocalyptical and millenarian, occupied the stage. Dogmas were fashionable. The external mind was taking over and projecting its own religions and Gods. A spirituality, not of seekers, but useful and serviceable to the kings was in the forefront.

This new religious cast of mind was forging a new iron-curtain, a far more effective one than a physical one. The new mind that was taking over was incapable of understanding deeper things of the spirit; it undestood dogmas and creeds; it dropped the law of karma, the theory of the Self. Antoninus, a neo-Platonist of the 4th century predicted that "a fabulous and formless darkness is about to tyrannize over all that is beautiful on earth" (*Encyclopaedia of Religion and Ethics*, 9.317).

But Indian spirituality remained an attraction throughout even when Europe was getting confused and swept off its feet. Plotinus whose name shines even up to this day, wanted to visit India.

Hindu thought, however, continued to exert influence on Europe through various channels. One channel was the works of Dionysius the Arepogite.

His work were seen and translated by John Scotus Erigena of the 9th century. He questioned the presence of Christ in consecrated bread and wine. He exalted reason above Biblical and clerical authority. He said that while "all authority that is not approved by true reason seems weak, but true reason, since it rests on its own strength, needs no reinforce-ment by any authority". He said that "God is everything that truly is, since He makes all things and is made in all things"; he also said that there was no creation in time, that God was neither masculine nor faminine; that God as "Father" merely meant that he was the creative substance or essence of every thing, and "Son" merely meant the divine Wisdom according to which all things are made or governed, and "Spirit" merely meant life and vitality of creation. This was dissolvent of the whole Trinity. He also said that heaven and hell are not places, but conditions of the soul. He said that all things are immortal, that animals too, like men, have souls that pass back, after death, into God or creative spirit from whom they emanated, that all history is a vast outward flow of creation by emanation, and an irrestible inward tide that finally draws all things back into God. Pope Nicholas in 865 wrote to Charles the Bald either to send John to Rome for trial, or dismiss him from the Palace School, "that he may no longer give poison to those who seek for bread". We do not know what happened but we hear no more of him. William of Malmesbury relates that he "came to England and our monastery, as report says; was pierced with iron pens of the boys whom he instructed", and died from the results. He was later on forgotten but in the thirteenth century his book *De divisione naturae* was exhumed from oblivion; it was condemned by the Council of Sens (1225), and Pope Honorious III ordered that all copies should be sent to Rome and there be burned (Will Durant, *The Age of Faith*, pp. 477-79).

Index

Adam, W., published three reports on indigenous educational system in Bengal Presidency, 180-181; provided mine of information on many sociological facts, 181-182; on number of elementary schools in Bengal and Bihar, 184; on number of pupils taught at home in Nattore Thana (Bengal), 184; on indigenous institutions of higher learning in Nattore Thana, 185; on the learning and modesty of Pandits in Bengal, 187; on high percentage of low-caste students in schools in Bengal and Bihar, 189; on very few low-caste students in missionary schools, 189; on strength of low-caste teachers in indigenous schools, 189; on decline of number of village schools in Nattore Thana, 193.

Afro-Asian countries, being de-indigenized without being Europeanized in attempt to ape Europe, 122.

Āgamas, offering obeisance to, 22.

Alberuni, on why Hindu sciences retired far away, 178; on spread of Buddhism in West Asia, 204.

alien ideologies, India's youth being seduced by, 174; are combining again to annex what remains of India, 174.

Allah, avenging, mutton and beef and holy wars go together with, 154.

America, psychiatrist doing roaring business in, 169; machine replacing human mind in, 171; corruption prevails among professors in Multiversities in, 171.

Anand, Mulk Raj, Hindu by accident of birth but anti-Hindu by freely chosen role, 44.

ancient India, celebrated for its learning all over Asia and Europe, 177.

ancient Indian seers. See Hindu seers.

ancient sages, a vast internal life found by, 1; man's deceptive identities seen by, 1-2.

Animal World, difference between eternity-philosophies and time-philosophies in treatment of, 152-153.

Animals, made man's food by Biblical God, 10; in modern European and secular thought, 10.

anti-Hindu Hindus, created by foreign rule but very important in India today, 33, 89-90; have Missionary-Macaulayite-Marxist view of themselves, and their own culture, religion and history, 111.

Apollonius of Tyna, great sage of the Greek world, 97; his biography is witness to where India stood in estimation of Greek sages and philosophers, 97-98; contemporary of Jesus, 197; Pythagorean teacher admired throughout the Pagan world, 198; hated by Christians and named Anti-Christ, 198; visited India and was deeply satisfied after meeting its wise men, 198, 200; learnt *ātma-vāda* (Know Thyself) and Advaita from India's wise men who criticized Homer's heroes for their destructiveness, 198-200, 201; met an Indian king who practised great military arts but was a vegetarian, 200; spoke about India's wise men to Egyptian and Greek audiences, 200; believed that Egypt, Ethiopia and Pythagoras derived their wisdom from India, 200; distrusted those who hawked revealed truths, 201; visited all shrines and saw his God in all Gods, 201; defended worshipping Gods in human form, 201-202, 202n; participated in religious worship of India's wise men, 202; practised non-injury to all living beings and explained why he and Pythagoras were vegetarians, 202-203; believed in rebirth, 203; accepted immortality of the soul, 204.

Arab money, spells most ominous development, 49.

Arabia, to be taken into account while thinking of Indian "Muslims", 47.

Arnold, Sir Edwin, translations of Hindu Sanskrit texts won admiration of, 125.

Aryan invasion theory, birth of, 108; Indology with all its intellectual irresponsibility can be seen in, 115, 115n-116n.

Aryans, made to migrate from Europe to India as conquerors, 108.

ātma and *anātma*, Sanatana dharma on, 1-3.

Augustine (St.), rebuked those who equated Apollonius of Tyna with Jesus, 198.

Augustine and Martin Luther, greatest sadists in Christian history, 141.

Aurobindo, Sri, saw incomparable truth in Hinduism, 38, 43; "assimilative appropriation" taught by, 38-39; called synthesis of Vedānta as the highest or "Hindu synthesis", 39; trenchant exponent of both Hinduism and Indian nationalism, 45; called for an "aggressive defence", 52; on Nirvāṇa, 82-83.

Bangladesh, large-scale infiltration (planned invasion) from, 58.

Baroque art, fails to find adequate expression for mystic experience, 156; Catholic Christianity never recovered from orgy of emotionalism and sensationalism of, 156n.

Bates, Searle, finds tolerance foreign to Hinduism because Hindus did not practise persecution, 120.

Bayazid, does not represent mainstream Sufism, 198.

Bengal Presidency, surveys of indigenous educational system in, 180-181.

Bhakti in Hinduism, 78-79.

Bharatavarsha, ancient dimensions of, 34.

Bible, Neo-Hinduism finds Vedānt in,

112; the word "consciousness" unknown to, 118; has a wrathful, jealous and vindicative being as integrating principle of the universe, 151; folly and wickedness of its followers traced to, 151; prohibited reading for commoners and its translators burned at the stake for many centuries, 187.

Bible's Hebraic tradition, narrow-mindedness, intolerance, materialism and lack of mysticism in, 106.

Biblical Chronology, inherited by modern Europe, 19-20; many European thinkers argued for primacy of, 102.

Biblical God, animals under the curse of, 10.

Bombay Presidency, surveys of indigenous educational system in, 180; number of schools of higher learning in, 184; Brahmins in minority in indigenous schools in, 189.

Book, The, no good to anybody to have religions of, 152.

Bouchet, J., primacy of Biblical Chronology argued by, 102.

Brahmanic and Shramanic traditions, great science of man given by the two together, 2.

Brahmins, have been and remain the poorest caste, 30; prophets were unknown to, 101; "divine wrath" seen in decay and deprivation of, 103.

Brazil and Mexico, havested colossal debts, inflation, economic bankruptcy and great social upheaval by adopting Western pattern of industrialization, 122.

Brentano, acclaimed Indian culture with ecstasy, 105.

British Government, survey of indigenous educational system by, 180-181.

British rule, increasing illiteracy caused in India by, 193-194; cultural self-alienation brought about among Hindus due to adoption of Urdu as medium of education by, 194; Hindus excluded from primary schools due to principle of "secularism" and "religious neutrality" introduced by, 194-195.

Bruno, most moving character depicted by Aldous Huxley, 143.

Buddha, had healthy contempt for intellectual systems and rationalists of all ages, 62; silence on God and soul of, 63-68; nature of his experience of *nirvāṇa*, 68-71; follows the Upanishads, 70; sees Nothingness of the phenomenal world, 71-75; claimed no originality for his way, 87.

Buddhism, at a disadvantage vis-a-vis Christianity and Islam, 50; Hindu in origin and development, 60-61; seen as revolt against Hinduism by intellectuals of materialist-secularist persuasion, 61; should not be equated with moral discipline (*śīla*) alone, 62; existentialist rendering of, 62n; nihilist rendering of, 70; very different atmosphere or ethos from Hinduism created by literature of, 75; dryness and abstract approach of, 76-78; doctrine of *anātma* in, 80-83; Transitoriness and Painfulness of Existence in, 83-87; leaves an impression of emptiness and transience, 84; dry, ascetic and arduous *sādhanā* of, 85;

powerful developments in, 86; not cursed with a sacred book, 152; shaped educational system in Japan and Burma, 173; goes west, 204; Alberuni on West Asian spread of, 204.
Buddhist and Hindu education, no child-beating in, 141.
Burnouf, introduced Indian culture to Tolstoy and Wagner, 143.

Calvin, Christian thought carried to its logical conclusion by flagellation theology of, 141.
Cambodia, much of old India found in, 178.
Carey, William, complained that "India swarms with Deists", 101; saw Hindu Sanskrit texts "filled with nothing but pebbles and trash", 107, 125.
caste in India, different from caste in the West, 30; of modern persuasion is a Western-Christian construct, 31.
Castes and Communities, 27-31; were pluralist Hinduism in action, 27-28; shared in common deeper truth taught by Hindu dharma, 28-29; the world today needs the Hindu system of, 29; became depressed under foreign rule, 30.
Catholic Christianity, never recovered completely from orgy of emotionalism and sensationalism of baroque art, 156n.
Catholics, have a World-Centre in the Vatican, 51.
Chakravarty, Nikhil, Hindu by accident of birth but anti-Hindu by freely chosen role, 44.
Chamberlain, B.H., on all round education by Buddhism in Japan, 173.
child-beating, Christian habit of, 141 and n.
China, deep cultural and spiritual roots of, 89.
Christendom, adequate rendering of contemplative life never achieved by plastic arts of, 156.
Christian art, paints God the Father as Pope in Italy, Spain and monasteries of France, as Emperor in Germany, and as King in England France, 158; depiction of Jesus passed through many styles and followed many fashions in, 158-159; eventually settles for expressing suffering, cruelty, horror and loathsomeness, 158-159; has no equivalent of Far Eastern Buddhas and Bodhisattvas, 159; Virgin Mary's portrayal passed through many phases and various theological ideas in, 159n; narrating Biblical themes and propagating dogmas was the underlying idea of, 161.
Christian Church, dogmas of, 17; found texts in sacred books to justify abominations like religious wars, persecution of heretics and breaking of faith with unbelievers, 152.
Christian ethics, Aldous Huxley on iniquities of, 131n; found meaning in most abominable things, 132.
Christian Europe, destroyed completely the religion and culture of Classical Greece, 94-95; grew in complete ignorance of Greek learning, 95-96.
Christian God, magnified and flattering portrait of Tiberius and

Caligula, 140; a great sadist, 140-141; associated with wholesale slaughter of Pagans and retail torture and murder of heretics, 151.

Christian missionaries, train recruits in their Seminaries specifically for missionary work in native lands, 52; receive massive foreign funds for subverting Hindu culture and India's political set-up, 55; propose strategy of using Hinduism against Hinduism, 99; unintended effect on Europe of the reports of, 100; Oriental Movement opposed by, 107-108; a living monument of doctrinal and practical intolerance represented by the apparatus of, 120.

Christian philosophers, found no difficulty in justifying iniquities and tyrannies, 132n.

Christian theology, modern anthropology a development of, 21; social sciences, philosophies and ideologies of modern Europe carry forward the old bias of, 21.

Christian-Western vocabulary, Experience and Tolerance quite new concepts in, 118.

Christianity, has powerful international links, 49; not a religion but a political creed, 50; anthropomorphic and monolithic God of, 78; destruction of Pagan temples and suppression of Pagan rites all over Roman Empire by, 94n-96n; waged war against Greco-Roman approach to life of the spirit, 96-97; European scholars and philosophers propagate Indian origin of, 102; justified by Neo-Hinduism, 112; coming back under Hindu auspices after being rejected by Western Rationalism, 112; forced by Hindu influence to speak the language of "experience", "plurality" and "consciousness", 118; source of Original Sin in, 141; meat-eating and persecution of heretis go together with the angry God of, 154; frozen meat greatest enemy of, 154-155; has no idea of inner man or man's inner depths, 157-158; shares the iconoclastic passion of Islam, 162; borrowed transmigration from Buddhism through Manicheaism, 204.

Christianity and Islam, great and systematic attackers and persecutors of cultures in various parts of the world, 148; made violent and persecutory by their concept of a personal God, 150-151.

Christians, have a strong ecumenical movement, 50; maintain hundreds of Seminaries for training missionaries for working in native lands, 52; massive foreign funds received by, 55; were enthusiastic child-beaters in the Age of Faith, 141.

Colonial-Missionary forces, triumph of the narrowness and obscurantism of, 111; soldier-scholars of, 111.

Communism, has powerful international links, 49.

Communism and Liberal Democracy, complementary forces subserving the same psyche, 90-91.

Confucianism, receives warm reception in highly intellectual circles of Europe, 100.

consumerism and hedonism, subtle and insidious working of, 91.

Da Bartolomeo, Fra Paolino, on method of teaching and writing in India, 179; on subjects taught in Malabar, 186.
da Gama, Vasco, soldiers, missionaries and traders land together in Calicut with, 99.
Dacier, A., primacy of Biblical Chronology argued by, 102.
Das Kapital, Neo-Hinduism finds Vedānta in, 112.
Dayananda (Swami), saw an incomparable truth in Hinduism, 38, 43.
Della Valle, Pietro, on features of Hindu system of education borrowed by England and Europe, 183n.
"developing country", euphemism for "backward" or "underdeveloped" country, 174.
Dharampal, published unpublished survey of indigenous educational system in Madras Presidency, 181.
Dharma, ten-fold laws of, 12.
Dibona, Joseph, published Adam's Reports on indigenous education, 181.
Di Nobili, Robert, pretended to be Romanic Brahmin to promote Christianity, 99.
Dickens, Charles, on schools and teachers in 19th century England, 191.
Dionysius the Aeropagite, mistaken for Dionysius the first disciple of St. Paul and admitted into the tradition of Western Christianity, 147 and n.
dominant ideologies, common characteristics of, 90-91.
Dubois, Abbe J.A., on widespread education in India's villages, 180.
Dow, Indian texts translated by, 103.

East, the, had gone to the West at one time, 196.
East-West Dialogue, ambiguity about Indian contributions to, 93.
East-West encounter, presented as intellectual enterprise by the West in search of knowledge, 113; piracy, gun-boat diplomacy, political domination, religious arrogance, economic enslavement and cultural genocide main expressions of, 113; very little moral worth of the knowledge gained by the West in, 113-114.
Eckhart, saved from Inquisition by his death and never reckoned by the Church among her mystics, 146.
Ecological Ethics, teaching of Sanatana dharma on, 11-12.
education, a nation's definition of man decides its theory of, 166; is self-defeating if it deals only with secular concerns, 167.
Educational Planning in a Developing Country, a much talked subject, 174-175; may deepen problems of our deeper cultural life, 175; a vast and difficult subject, 175-176; exploring the past may provide some seed-ideas for, 176.
Egypt, Indian Brahmans taught doctrine of non-injury to Naked Philosophers of, 199; Pythagoras meets Naked Philosophers of, 203; a thousand years contact between (ancient) India and, 204.
elitist forces in India, have intimate intellectual, organizational and financial links with the West, 111.

Emerson, translations of Hindu Sanskrit texts won admiration of, 125.
Encyclopaedia of Religion and Ethics, hate-book and declaration of war against non-Christian cultures and peoples, 114; on female education in Japan, 174.
England, dismal state of education in middle of 19th century in, 190.
Enlightenment (European), eclipse of "natural light" seen in India by thinkers of, 103; Indian influence used in support of the forces of, 106.
Epics (Ramayana and Mahabharata), offering obeisance to, 22.
Erigena, John Scotus, persecuted and killed for introducing neo-Platonist approach in Christianity, 147 and n, 205-206.
eternity-philosophies, Hinduism and Buddhism are great, 153.
Ethiopia, their spirituality borrowed from India by naked ascetics of, 197, 201, 203.
Eurocentricity, natural result of European Imperialism, 107; Oriental Movement downgraded by, 107.
Europe, stupendous egocentricity in modern times of, 19-20; old bias of Christian theology carried forward by social sciences, philosophies and ideologies of, 21; Indian presence gives an edge to or even shapes internal controversies of, 92; did not know Classical Greece, 93-94; old affinity between regions and peoples distorted by the Christian interlude in, 97; systematic Semiticization dropped an ideological iron curtain on, 100-101; warm reception for Confucianism in highly intellectual circles of, 100; entered by India as a widening and deepening force, 111; Neo-Hinduism shaped by and during presence of, 111; divinely ordained mission of, 121; "philosophical reason" claimed as monopoly of, 121; made by God in His own image, 121; economic and political colonialism went hand in hand with intellectual colonialism of, 122; though confused by Christianity yet Indian influence remained attractive in, 205.
European colonialism, linguistic, spiritual and ethnic affinity between India, Greece, Rome and Europe resisted by, 97; Hegel justified historical necessity of, 110; Aldous Huxley on evils of, 131n; Oriental Movement opposed by, 108-110.
European intellect, profoundly inadequate for dealing with other people's cultures, 114; can be quite credulous and careless about facts, 114-115.
European thinkers, Indian thought satisfied many, 101; original home of all religions seen in India by many, 101-102.
European thought, context for exploration of all cultures provided by, 121.
European xenology, Indologists ignore the (abusive) language of, 116n-117n.
Europeanization of the Earth, Christian, Imperial and philosophical Europe has always believed in, 120-121; inevitable according to Merleau-Ponty, Hegel, Husserl, Heideggar and Francis

Fukuyama, 121-122; means intellectual colonialism and de-indigenization of all non-European countries, 122; has meant externalization and impoverishment of the Spirit, 123; started with Semiticization of Europe, 123; the earth needs a new philosophy instead of, 123.
Europeans, came to India as conquerors and adopted the view of Muslim invaders regarding Hinduism, 124-125.
Exclusive Gods, conceived in exclusive ideologies, 5; cults of exclusive prophets born of the cult of, 6.
Experience, quite new concept in Christian-Western vocabulary, 118-119; most significant and conspicuous word in Indo-European dialogue, 118; Dean W.R. Inge finds gravity in religion shifting from authority to, 118; H. Cox speaks slightingly of a "gluttony" of, 118; H. Gadamer finds the concept "most obscure" and "among the least clarified concepts", 118; William James found the word good and clear enough, 119; Religious Experience Research Unit (RERU) established at University of Oxford, 119.

Fa-hien, on India's monasteries as centres of teaching, 177.
Fichte, acclaimed Indian culture with ecstasy, 105.
Foreign Funds, received by Muslims and Christians, 54-55; Hindus should raise the question of, 55.
Francis, St., his attitude towards animal world was not unequivocal, 153 and n.
freedom struggle (India's), two approaches inherited from the immediate history of, 40-41.
Fukuyama, Dr. Francis, celebrates triumph of the West, 122.

Gandhi (Mahatma), saw an incomparable truth in Hinduism, 38, 43, 45; treated in the West as representative of Neo-Hinduism and not as one who contributed to the shaping of Neo-Christianity, 117.
Gāyatrī Mantra, formulated the aim of Hindu education, 168.
Geden, A.S., on Buddhist influence on education in Japan, 173.
German Oriental Renaissance, was erected on Bopp's linguistic (Sanskrit) foundation, 105.
Germans, restored their self-respect by identifying with ancient India, 106.
Germany, stir caused by Indian thought most conspicuous in, 103-104; called the India of the Occident, 105-106.
God, various ways of denying, 7-8; denied in women by theologies which lack Goddesses, 8; as conceived by Hinduism, 78.
Goddesses, character of theologies which lack, 8; Hinduism honours women as, 31.
Gods, 3-4; worship of many forms of in Sanatana dharma, 4-5; exclusive ideologies conceive exclusive, 5-6.
Goethe, acclaimed Indian culture with ecstasy, 105.

Government of independent India, so-called, "secularism" pleaded by brown sahibs of, 194; nation's cultural riches denied to new generations by, 194; class of Macaulay's dream created by, 195.

Greece, Classical, did not know Europe, 93-94; Christian Europe destroyed completely the religion and culture of, 94-95; discovery of Sanskrit links Europe to, 97; of Pythagoras, Plato and Plotinus had more in common with India than Christian Europe, 98; more a part of Asia than of Europe, 194; India visited by many philosophers of, 197-198.

Greek and Roman world, kindness towards animals practised and taught by great teachers of, 153n.

Greek learning, understood through their own categories of thought by modern Europeans, 96; accorded reception because it was totally misunderstood and misconceived, 97.

Greek thought, ancient Hindu thought exerted great influence on, 196.

Greeks, knew themselves as Hellenists, not as Europeans, 93.

Gujral, Inder, Hindu by accident of birth but anti-Hindu by freely chosen role, 44.

Hacker, Paul, sees tolerance of Hinduism as "inclusiveness", 119.

Haksar, P.N., Hindu by accident of birth but anti-Hindu by freely chosen role, 44.

Halbfass, Prof. Wilhelm, subject of 'India in Greek tradition' treated competently by, 97-98; discusses "tolerance" as a modern European idea not applicable to Hinduism, 119-20; says not a word about the vast (Christian) missionary apparatus, 120.

Hamilton, on indigenous institutions of higher learning in 24 Parganas (Bengal), 185.

Hardy, Sir Alister, Religious Experience Research Unit (RERU) established at Oxford by, 119.

Hegel, 92; admitted discovery of Sanskrit as great event in history, 105; saw Indian people as always vanquished, 107; deemed spread of Sanskrit as "dumb, deedless expansion", 107-108; excluded the Orient from history of philosophy, 109; attack on Oriental Renaissance led by, 109-110; justified historical necessity of European colonialism and praised the British as missionaries of civilization, 110; was soldier-scholar of colonial-missionary forces, 111; saw Europe moving towards an "absolute idea" beyond reach of other cultures, 121.

Heidegger, M., refers to complete Europeanization of the earth and mankind, 121-122.

Hellenistic world, greatest saint of, 197.

Herder, J.G., 92; found morality of Indians "pure and simple" and their God as "great and beautiful", 101; saw India as "lost paradise" of all religions and philosophies, 102; derived all peoples of Europe from Asia,

105; acclaimed Indian culture with ecstasy, 105.
Hess, Hermann, translation of Hindu Sanskrit texts won admiration of, 125.
Hindu *āchāryas*, have hardly any prestige left, 48.
Hindu architecture, incomparably more rich than Muslim architecture, 161-162.
Hindu art, described by epithets like 'barbarous' and 'ugly' by most Western critics, 155.
Hindu Backlash, vested interest in weak Hinduism makes Marxists and Muslim raise the cry of, 46-47.
Hindu-baiters, so-called "liberal" Hindu intellectuals are, 43-44.
Hindu-Buddhist culture of Asia, the West in need of learning from, 123.
Hindu centres of learning, destroyed by Muslims in the interior too, 178.
Hindu communalism, positive and negative, 44.
Hindu culture, was faced with grave problems while meeting the West and Islam on unequal military terms, 37; continues to be under attack by neo-intellectuals and administrators in independent India, 195.
Hindu dharma. See Hinduism.
Hindu (system of) education, indigenous, *Gāyatrī Mantra* formulated the aim of, 168; two organically linked aims of, 168; helped to conquer *vikshepas* of the mind, 169; complete rapport between teacher and taught emphasized by, 170; attributes of a student in, 170-171; was open to all irrespective of caste, creed and sex, 172, 188-189; our present educational system can benefit by old principles of, 173; carried to neighbouring countries by Indian monks, 173-174; eighteenth century European reports on excellence of, 179-180; surveyed by British Government of India, 180-181; characteristic features of mode of instruction in, 182-183; England and Europe borrowed many practices of, 183 and n; grass roots schools system of, 183-185; had its foundations deep in the country's culture, 183; widespread private coaching in, 184; higher learning in, 185-186; subjects of higher learning in, 186; not monopolized by Brahmins, 188; dismal state of education in eighteenth century Europe as compared to, 189-191; grounded in Hindu culture and its system of local self-government, 191-192; British hostility to, 192; public financial support for, 192-193; British rule caused fast decay of, 193.
Hindu elites, condemn Hinduism to prove their Indian nationalism, 44; becoming illiterate about their cultural heritage and history, 48; apologetic and ashamed of their (Hindu) identity, 52;
Hindu festivals, vulgarity creeping in celebration of, 55-56.
Hindu India, has more in common with Greece of Pythagoras, Plato and Plotinus than Christian Europe, 98; to be accused of lacking religious liberty if it questions Christian

"undertakings", 120; badly mauled by but survived the Muslim onslaught, 178-179.
Hindu intellectuals, false division into "liberal" and "communal" of, 43-44.
Hindu Pandits, excelled in learning as well as modesty, 186.
Hindu Passivity, 112-118; regarded by Halbfass as basic characteristic of Indo-European dialogue, 112-116; Hindu impact on Europe ignored by notion of, 117-118.
Hindu priests, have become indigent and illiterate, 54.
Hindu psyche, making claims for persecutors and their ideologies becomes part of, 148n-149n.
Hindu Psychology, role of man's mind and senses according to, 168.
Hindu Reawakening, teachings of the leaders of, 38-40.
Hindu *saṁskāras*, are deep and profound, 54.
Hindu Sanskrit texts, mischievous motives of British rulers and Christian missionaries in translating of, 125; admiration of many others in the West won by translations of, 125.
Hindu seers, purpose of education according to, 167; practical discipline for education evolved by, 167; sought fountainhead of all knowledge and sciences, 169; taught harmony with oneself, one's fellow-men and one's environment, 170.
Hindu society, election politics being used for dismemberment of, 48.
Hindu temples, most of them are in a state of destitution, 48; have been under unprecedented attack for a thousand years, 53; should now become more than places of worship, 53-54.
Hindu text-books, made highest ethical and spiritual literature open to all, 187-188.
Hindu thinking, vast time and space of, 19-20.
Hindu thought, exerted great influence on Greek thought, 196; continued to influence Europe through various channels, 197.
Hindu universality, has nothing to do with the universality of consumerism, or crusading religions, or Marxism, 40.
Hinduism, *jīva-dayā* expressed by widespread vegetarianism in, 11; views human history in great time cycle, 21; rejects ideologies which see the world as dead, inert and passive, 21-22; represents ancient wisdom of humanity and religious past of many countries, 22; went abroad and influenced cultures and religions of many lands, 24; raised fundamental questions and made profound answers, 24-25; made available its truths to the least of its members, 25; Reason and Religion reconciled by, 25; also described as *varṇa-āśrama dharma*, 26; right to self-defining lost in lean years of, 28; women honoured as Goddesses in, 31; its very virtues became weaknesses of, 32; became a dirty word under physical and ideological attack from monolatrous creeds, 32-33, 52; made India great, happy and creative while it flourished, 33; is

now being subverted from within, 33; has suffered much but also fought with great valour, 35; retains its humanist and universalist core, 35-36; should recover its unique civilizational principles, 36; leaders of Hindu Reawakening see a great truth in, 38; strengthened Aurobindo and Gandhi in their nationalism, 45; never crossed its borders to wage war, 46; some problems faced by, 48-49; India held together by, 49-50; the only adequate religion of the Spirit, 50; at a disadvantage vis-a-vis Christianity and Islam, 50; target of attack by well-equipped aggressors, 55; comprehensive spiritual values of, 56; regarded as unmitigated evil by Christian missionaries, 99; has concerned itself with all beings, animate and inanimate, past, present and future, on all planes, visible and invisible, 117; idea of tolerance seen by Christian missionary scholars as foreign to, 119-120; Krishna Consciousness and Saiva Siddhanta Church offer more than selected or edited ideas of, 125-126; noble life and noble death go together in, 139; has family likeness with Pythagoras and Orphic mysteries, 197. See also Sanatana dharma.

Hinduism and Buddhism, are great eternity-philosophies, 153.

Hinduism-Buddhism, making great impact on Western religious thinking, 124; European conquerors adopt Muslim invaders' view of, 124-125; difference in entreatment of animal world between Judaism-Christianity and, 152-154; defined as eternity-philosophies, 153 and n.

Hinduism Today (Hawaii), consolidating international Hinduism, 126.

Hindus, self-alienation of, 32-35; learn to look at themselves through eyes of alien rulers, 33; find an escape route in "synthesis" of all religions, all scriptures, all prophets, 34; become used to a shrinking and shrunken India, 34; under attack again from traditionally hostile forces, 34-35; are refugees and second grade citizen in their own country, 35; save their self-respect through self-alienation, 37; learn to look at themselved through borrowed eyes, 38-40; by accident of birth, 44; reason for lack of homogeneity among, 45-46; stupendous neglect of social dimension of corporate life by, 50; have no Centre, no common platform, 51; should have a Study-Centre, 52-53; should rejuvenate their temples, 53-54; should raise the question of foreign funds received by so-called minorities, 55; Social Evils of, 55-56; should look at Islam, Christianity and Communism from Hindu angle, 56-57; should beautify their land, 56; should undertake ideational, cultural and educational work, 56-57; not Muslims but Islam is the problem of, 57-58; popularise Semitic prophets as their own, 112; have no concept an *ummah* or a divinely ordained mission, 115-

116; can have no xenology because they have no concept of an *ummah* or a divinely ordained mission, 116; survived attack of Islam and Christianity by self-denial and self-repudiation, 148n; admit right of individuals to worship different conceptions or aspects of the divine, 152.

Hindus and Buddhists, total absence of bloody persecutions, religious wars and proselyting imperialism among, 152.

History of India, written from British-Christian point of view, 57.

History of Philosophy, exclusion of India from, 110.

Hiuen Tsang, on Buddhist monasteries, 177.

Holwell, Indian texts translated by, 103.

Hugo, Victor, hails Germany as India of the Occident, 105; translations of Hindu Sanskrit texts won admiration of, 125.

Humanism, replaced God by Nation, Class, Party, Culture and Art, 144.

Husserl, E., sees European culture as comprehending and cancelling all other cultures, 121; says "Europeanization of all foreign parts of the world" is the destiny of the earth, 121.

Huxley, Aldous, initial reaction to India of, 126; rejects Indian spirituality, 126-127; lived in and subscribed to a rational world, 127-128; initial influence of Indian spirituality and religion on, 128-129; explores fashions in love-making, 129-131; influenced by Hindu-Buddhist tradition of *brahmacharya*, 130; on evils of European colonialism, 131n; on philosophy of meaninglessness, 131-132, 131n-132n; on inequities of Christian ethics and reaction to it, 132n; finds the world supremely good and meaningful, 133; builds bridges between different dimensions of the universe before and after he came under Indian influence, 133-134; passionate life advocated by, 134; revolts against moralists and utopians around, 134-135; turns away from women, 135, 135n-136n; replaces doctrine of "multiple man" with that of "higher man" under Hindu-Buddhist influence, 135-137; follows the lead of Western Science on Spirit and Body, 137-138; learns art of dying from Hinduism, 138-140; adopts Hindu view of death and immortality, 140; always distrusted monotheism, 140; on Jews and Arabs of the desert, 140; on modern medicine, 140n; opposition to monotheism of, 140-141; sees a great sadist in Christian God, 140-141; traces Jehovah, Original Sin and Christian God to Hebrew enthusiasm for child-beating, 141; did not undergo sudden conversion to spiritual view, 141-143; his first reactions to *Bhagvadgītā*, 142 and n; maturing of Hindu-Buddhist influence on, 142-143; quotes Buddha's repeated instructions on Mindfulness, 143; teaches self-understanding, 143-144; re-establishes God and finds

Humanism not enough, 144; on Perennial Philosophy, 144-145; rejects revealed religions, their historical fatalities, privileged intermediaries, surrogates and authorised proxies, 145-148; finds Christianity and Islam difficult to reconcile with mysticism, 145; leaves out Popes, Church Fathers, Church Councils, Church theologians and Church dogmas while examining mysticism, 145; quotes (St.) Paul for opposing the claims of a historical Jesus, 145-146; quotes most from unrepresentative mystics like Eckhart or unrepresentative statements of St. John of the Cross, 146; finds mysticism not native to and incompatible with Christianity, 146-147; discovers that mysticism acquired place in Christianity by a pious fraud, 147-148; finds mysticism missing from the Quran and mainstream Sufism, 148; finds in Christianity and Islam a great deal opposed to perennial philosophy, 149; could not conclude that all religions are the same, 148-149; forced to refer many times to spirit of persecution in Christianity and Islam, 149; finds no persecution in Hinduism and Buddhism, 149; rejects the most cherished doctrines of Christianity, 149n; notices no blood in Buddhism, 149n; tells how Inquisition was instituted by time-worshipping Catholicism to perpetuate a creed, a ritual and eclesiastico-politico-financial organization, 149-150; tells how Bible-worshipping Protestant fought long and savage wars, 150; wishes that Catholicism knew Buddhism better than fairy tale *Barlaam and Josaphat*, 150; notices Islam's black record of holy wars and persecution, 150; cites Hiuen Tsang to record that India knew no persecution before advent of Mohammedans, 150n; finds the personal God of Christianity and Islam violent and persecutory, 150-151; says Muslims brought to India the idea of God as military general, 151; finds God of Christianity associated with wholesale slaughter of pagans and retail torture and murder of heretics, 151; traces to the Bible the folly and wickedness of its followers, 151; sees continuity between religions and secular crusades, 151n; finds a sole sacred book undesirable, 152; sees Old Testament as a treasure house of barbarous stupidity justifying every crime and folly, 152; finds Religions of the Book lacking a pluralist view of God, man and his nature, 152; notices difference between Hinduism-Buddhism and Judaism-Christianity in treatment of the animal world, 152-154; defines Hinduism-Buddhism as eternity-philosophies and Judaism-Christianity as time-philosophies, 153 and n; does not find St. Francis' attitude to animal world entirely unequivocal, 153 and n; finds correlation between religion and diet, and Semitic God and what his follower eat, 154-155;

develops a new eye for Hindu-Buddhist art, 155-156; finds transcendental dimension missing in European art tradition, 156 and n; concludes that plastic arts of Christendom never achieved adequate expression of contemplative life, 156; points out Taoist landscape painters of China as first to concern themselves with significance of nature, 157; notices that Christian art has no equivalent of Far Eastern Buddhas and Bodhisattvas, 159, 160; found Muslim architecture dry, empty, barren and monotonous, 161; disappointed by Taj at Agra, 161; finds Hindu architecture incomparably more rich than Muslim architecture, 161-162; refuses to revise his opinion about Taj, 162n; on experiments with chemical doors to mystic experience, 162-164; changes his negative view about meditation, 163n; opened up the West to influence of the East, 164-165; was profound student of Europe's religious, literary and artistic traditions, 164; wrote 26 articles on Vedānta, 165.

India, has preserved spiritual traditions lost by many countries, 22; is the land where Sanatana dharma flourished, 24; never tried to set up an empire, 24; had castes but no casteists in old days, 30; was great, happy and creative while Hindu dharma flourished, 31-32; anti-Hindu Hindus rule the roost in, 33; when cultural boundaries extended beyond physical boundaries of, 34,196; reawakening of, 38-40; Western-Missionary view of, 41-42; not a nation according to Marx, 42; Islam, Christianity and Communism combine in subversion of, 57; anti-Hindu state and ruling class of, 89-90; old affinity between regions and peoples best represented by, 97; many European thinkers see original home of all religions in, 101-102; entered Europe as a widening and deepening force, 111; has no xenology of European fancy, 115; should have brilliant Occidentalists like European Orientalists, 117n; knew no religious persecution before coming of Mohammedans, 150n; education becoming increasingly costly in, 172-173; should give up the barren path of imitation in education, 173; alien ideologies of materialism, hedonism, nihilism, communism, disunity and division running riot in, 174; promoted from backward or "underdeveloped" country to "developing" one, 174-175; was never backward in philosophies concerning deeper aspects of man's education, 175; celebrated all over Asia and Europe for its learning in ancient days, 177; entered a dark period under Muslim onslaught, 178-179; had intimate contacts with ancient Greece, 197; was visited by many Greek philosophers, 197-198; usual asylum for those who faced religious persecution at home, 204.

India and China, tremendous psychological pressure for acceptance of European word-view exerted on highly developed cultures of, 122.
India, China and Egypt, were masters of many sciences, 122.
Indian art-tradition, rendering of Gods in visual art-forms in, 157-158.
Indian culture, placed on lofty pedestal by the entire Romantic movement in the West, 105.
Indian influence, importance of, 106; remains unacknowledged and unnamed by Western intellectuals, 117-118; forces Christianity to speak the language of "experience", "plurality", and "consciousness", 118.
Indian intellectuals, tune of (Christian) missionaries and British rulers continues to be sung by the colonized minds of, 188.
Indian Marxists, prefer Turkish conquest to British conquest of India, 42-43.
Indian "Muslims", Islamic theology, Arabia and Pakistan to be taken into account while thinking of, 47; have many Madrasas, 50; receive massive foreign funds, 55; should be told about their predatory imperialism, 58.
Indian nationalism, remained rooted in Hindu vision of human and cosmic unity, 39-40; deeper internationalism in harmony with deeper (strain of), 41; condemned *a priori* if with Hindu orientation, 44; retains full imprint of Hindu universalism, 117n.
Indians seers, see Hindu seers.
Indian spirituality, Europe always attracted by, 205.
Indian thought, missionary approach to, 99; many European thinkers satisfied by, 101; idiom of Neo-Christianity and Neo-Europe modified by, 117.
Indians, Goddess of philosophy first descended on, 197.
India's education, see Hindu (system of) education.
India's elite, have shown no appreciation of India's intellectual and creative contribution, 110; learn to look at their country and people through European eyes, 111.
Indo-European encounter (dialogue), a new phase in, 103-104; the word "experience" becomes most significant and conspicuous in, 118.
"Indo-European roots", invented in place of Sanskrit roots, 108-109.
Indology, intellectual irresponsibility at work in, 115, 115n-116n.
Inge, Dean W.R., finds gravity in religion shifting from authority to experience, 118.
Iran, old affinity between regions and peoples distorted by Muslim interlude in, 97; many Gods shared with Vedic India by, 196.
Islam, Sri Aurobindo on its role in India, 45; unassimilable identities created in India by advent of, 47; has powerful international links, 49; not a religion but a political creed, 50; teaches constant *jihad* against *kafirs*, 51; anthropomorphic and monolithic God of, 78; spiritual impediment between India and Europe reinforced by triumph of, 98; justified by Neo-Hinduism, 112; difficult to reconcile with mysticism, 145; has a great deal

opposed to perennial philosophy, 148-149; black record of holy wars and persecutions by, 150; found religious and artistic self-expression in demolition of shrines of "other Gods", 162; Christianity shares iconoclastic passion of, 162.

Islam, Christianity and Communism, all unite in subverting India, 57.

Islamic and Christian ideologies, local religions under systematic attack of, 90.

Islamic Sufism, no element of perennial philosophy in mainstream of, 148.

Islamic theology, to be taken into account while thinking of Indian "Muslims", 47.

I-tsing, on Nalanda university, 177.

Jacolliot, L., propagates Indian origin of Christianity, 102.

James, William, the word "experience" was good and clear enough for, 119.

Japan, Buddhist monks developed system of education in, 173.

Jehovah, indignant, God of enthusiastic child-beaters, 141; kosher and persecution of heretics go together with, 154.

Jesus, held as incarnation of Rishi by Neo-Hinduism, 112.

Jews and Arabs, produced nothing valuable until they absorbed cultures of polytheistic races, 140.

Joad, C.E.M., sees counter-attack from the East in influence of Hinduism-Buddhism on the West's religious thinking, 124.

John of the Cross, St., last great representative of Dionysian mysticism but stood for orthodox Christianity, 146n, 148.

Jones, William, saw relation between Sanskrit and European classical languages, 104; offerd hypothesis of a *third unknown* source for both East and West, 108.

Judaism-Christianity, defined as time-philosophies, 153.

Jung, Carl, translations of Hindu Sanskrit texts won admiration of, 125.

Kant, saw Hindus as gentle and tolerant after reading translations of Hindu Sanskrit texts, 125.

Khilji, Bakhtiyar, *vihāra* at Odantapuri destroyed and Buddhist monks slaughtered by, 178.

Kothari, Rajani, Hindu by accident of birth but anti-Hindu by freely chosen role, 44.

Krishna Consciousness, offers more than selected or edited ideas of Hinduism, 125-126.

La Grue, primacy of Biblical Chronology argued by, 102.

Law of Karma, hundreds of thousands of Westerners believe in, 117.

Leibnitz, wanted Chinese (Confucian) missionaries to visit Europe, 100.

Leitner, G.W., published report on indigenous educational system in Punjab, 181; on number of pupils in indigenous schools in Punjab, 183-184; on female education in Punjab, 184; on indigenous institutions of higher learning in Punjab, 186; on text-books in indigenous institutions in Punjab, 187-188; on sanction of Shastras for indigenous system of

education, 191; supported indigenous educational system against official hostility, 192.
Lillie, A., propagates Indian origin of Christianity, 102.
Linguistics and history, discovery of Sanskrit revolutionised basic concepts of, 104.
Lucianus, says Goddess of philosophy first descended upon Indians, 197.

Macaulay (T.B.), soldier-scholar of colonial-missionary forces, 111.
Madras Presidency, publication of unpublished survey reports on indigenous educational system in, 181; number of schools and scholars in, 181; number of pupils privately coached in, 184; number of schools of higher learning in, 185; text-books in indigenous schools in, 187; proportion of Brahmins low in indigenous schools of, 188; high non-Brahmin representation in institutions of higher learning in, 188-189.
Mahmud (Ghaznavi), India ruined and Hindus turned into atoms of dust by, 178.
Majer, F., felt drawn to banks of Ganges and Indus, 102.
man, prophetic ideologies neglect discussion of, 24; Hindu definition of, 166-167.
Manu, on loss of caste by some Kshatriyas due to loss on guidance by Brahmins, 196.
Many Lives, Many Planes, *Moksha*, as taught by Sanatana dharma, 13-15.
Market, the new Moloch-God, 19.
Marx, Karl, India not a nation according to, 42; combines Macaulay, Mill and Bishop Heber in most uninhibited form in regarding British conquest as a blessing for India, 42; subordination of non-European cultures to Europe touched new heights in, 109; soldier-scholar of colonial-missionary forces, 111; held as incarnation of Rishi by Neo-Hinduism, 112; on "cultural" acquirements of scholars in 19th century England, 190.
Marx and Engels, great civilization of China not mentioned even once in *Selected Works* of, 42.
Marxism, old Western imperialism under new slogans, 42; represents sustained attack on deeper India, 43; converges completely with Imperialism in works of M.N. Roy, 43-44.
materialism and hedonism, destructive culture of, 19.
Mediterranean world, darkness descends in form of apocalyptical and millenarian spirituality on, 204-205.
Megasthenese, struck by depth of India's learning, 177.
Merleau-Ponty, M., sees Europe as authorised to understand other cultures, 121.
Mill, J.S., soldier-scholar of colonial-missionary forces, 111.
Mindfulness, instruction of Buddha and Gita on, 143.
missionary apparatus, a living monument of doctrinal and practical intolerance, 120.
Missionary Seminaries, train recruits specifically for missionary work in native lands, 52.

Mithra (*Mitra*), Vedic God, many lands in West Asia and Europe had temples dedicated to, 196.
modern anthropology, a development of Christian theology, 21.
modern culture, sick at heart and sick in mind, 168.
modern education, wants to achieve an aim which eludes it, 169; based on a vision of man in conflict with himself, his fellow-men and his environment, 170.
modern Europe, stupendous ego-centricity of, 19-20; old bias of Christian theology carried forward by social sciences, philosophies and ideologies of, 21.
modern materialist thinking, everything for man's use in, 11.
modern schools, educate for competition and conflict, 170; deeper minds remain unprepared in, 171.
modern society, based on maximum consumption and maximum exploitation of men, animals, earth and elements of Nature, 170.
Modern Western Thought, 16-20; has one agreement with Sanatana dharma in allowing reason freedom to question and inquire, 16-17; derives the higher from the lower, 17; explains world and man in physical terms, 17-18; inadequate ethics of, 18.
Monotheism, sadist theology and God of, 140-141.
Moral Code, 8-9; derived from what men have thought of their deity, of themselves, and of their neighbour, 8.
More, Thomas, speaks of "rational religion" and "natural theology", 100.
Mosaic-Christian Revelation, furious arguments for primacy of, 102.
Moses, Jesus, Muhammad, described as impostors in a pamphlet published in Europe in 1598, 100.
mosques (in India), millions of them given face-lift and equipped with public address system, 55.
Muhammad, held as incarnation of Rishi by Neo-Hinduism, 112.
Mukherjee, Prof. Radhakumud, on ancient Indian education, 172.
Muslim art, funerary, dry, empty, barren and monotonous character of, 161.
Muslim "self-consciousness", greater aims and historical dynamics of, 47.
Muslims, super-positive nationalism of Hindus on behalf of, 45; have a powerful pan-Islamic movement, 50; have a World-Centre in *R'abitah al-'alam al-Islam*, 51; massive foreign funds received (in India) by, 55; should be told about their predatory imperialism, 58; great centres of learning destroyed and Buddhist monks slaughtered by, 178.
mysticism, difficult to reconcile with Christianity and Islam, 145; not native to and incompatible with Christianity, 146-147; acquired a place in Christianity by a pious fraud, 147-148.

Nalanda University, destroyed by Muslims after glorious existence for a thousand years, 178.

Nayar, Kuldip, Hindu by accident of birth but anti-Hindu by freely chosen role, 44.
Nazism, a typical time philosophy like Judaism-Christianity, 154.
Nehru (Pandit Jawaharlal), represented response of a defeated nation trying to restore its self-respect through self-repudiation, 41; the only "nationalist-Muslim", 44.
Neighbour, 9-10; prophetic religions exclude non-believers in their definition of, 9.
Neo-Christianity, Gandhi's contribution to shaping of, 117.
Neo-Christianity and Neo-Europe, influence of Indian thought modiefies idiom of, 117.
Neo-Hinduism, 93; a Hinduism shaped by and during presence of Europe, 111; defends Hinduism in borrowed idiom of Europe, 111-112; justifies Christianity and Islam and many non-Indian cults, 112; uses traditional Indian categories to promote Semitic religions, 112; finds Vedānta in Bible, Quran and *Das Capital* and holds Jesus, Muhammad and Marx as incarnations of Rishis, 112.
neo-intellectuals of India, imperialist-missionary policies have become political religion of, 195.
Newton, argued for primacy of Biblical Chronology, 102.
Nietzche, sees Reformation as "reaction of backward minds" and "protest of antiquated spirits", 96.
Nork, F., propagates Indian origin of Christianity, 102.
Novalis, acclaims Indian culture with ecstasy, 105.
Nuddeah School (Bengal), 179; report on students and teachers in, 180.

Odantapuri, Muslims destroyed a great centre of learning and slaughtered Buddhist monks at, 178.
Old Testament, ancient ignorance sanctified as revelation in, 152; treasure house of barbarous stupidity justifying every crime and folly, 152.
One Life, One Judgement, Hell, Heaven, 15-16; man's life an interlude between two blanks in the perspective of, 15; reward and punishment as conceived by ideologies of, 16.
Oriental Movement (Renaissance), erected on foundation of Sanskrit in Germany, 104; used against Classical Renaissance in Germany, 106; invited opposition from Christian missionaries and European Imperialism, 106-111; downgraded by Eurocentricity, 107.
Orientalists, ignore (abusive) language which conveys European xenology, 116n-117n.
Original Sin, derives from Christian enthusiasm for child-beating, 141.
Orphic mysteries, family likeness with Hinduism of, 197.

Pagan rites, suppressed all over Roman Empire by Christianity, 95n-96n.
Pagan society, easy prey of crusading fraternities, 46.

Pagan temples, destroyed all over Roman Empire by Christianity, 94n-95n.
Pakistan, to be taken into account while thinking of Indian "Muslims", 47.
patriots, so-called "communal" Hindus are, 43.
Planning Commission (of India), is West-oriented, 175.
Plato, on purpose of education, 168; many parallel ideas in Upanishads and, 197.
Plotinus, wanted to visit India, 205.
Pococke, M.E., on influence of Hindu thought on ancient Greek thought, 196-197.
prophetic ideologies, saints of, 7; life, heaven and hell in, 16; neglect discussion of man, 24.
Prophets and Saviours, cults of exclusive gods gave birth to cults of, 6.
Protestantism, gave birth to bibliolatry, 187.
Protestants, have a World-Centre in World Council of Churches, 51.
Punjab, survey of indigenous educational system in, 181, 183-184, 186, 187-188, 191-192; state of female education in, 184; decay of education and increasing illiteracy under British rule in, 193.
Puranas, offering obeisance to, 22.
purgatory, a sort of detention camp, 16.
Pythagoras, visited India and learnt doctrine of transmigration, 196; family likeness with Hinduism of, 197; came to India to learn philosophy, 197; taught doctrine of the witness (*drashṭā*), 197; first Greek to associate with Egyptians and their Naked Philosophers, 203.

Quran, Neo-Hinduism finds Vedānta in, 112; no element of perennial philosophy in, 148.

Rabiah, does not represent mainstream Sufism, 148.
R'abitah al-'alam al-Islam, Muslim Vatican (Word-Centre), 51.
Radhakrishnan, saw a rationalist in Buddha, 61n.
Rajagopalachari, C., comment on *Hinduism vis-a-vis Buddhism* by, 60n.
Ramayana and Mahabharata, embodied spirituality represented by, 165.
Rational World, ideas, ideals and *avant-gardists* of, 127-128.
Reason and Religion, reconciled in Hindu dharma, 25.
Red Indians, astonished to see white people beating their children, 141n.
Reformation, revolt against Renaissance, 96; Nietzche's comment upon, 96.
religious ideologies, poor, 3; conceive their God in image of human passions, 4-5.
Religious Renewal of the World, depends on world-wide renewal of Sanatana dharma, 21-22.
religious terrorism, ideologies of one life, one judgement, heaven and hell give birth to ideology of, 16.
Revelations, share quality of their source, 7.
Riencourt, Amaury, on European philosophers, poets and

historians acclaiming Indian culture with cries of ecstasy, 105.
Rishi and Muni traditions, see Brahmanic and Shramanic traditions.
Roger, Indian texts translated by, 103.
Rollan, Romain, translations of Hindu Sanskrit texts won admiration of, 125.
Roman and Protestant orthodoxy, Christian enthusiasm for child-beating has its source in the infinitely offended Father of, 141.
Rome (ancient), expanding outwardly and losing inwardness, 204; spirituality of Saviours, heaven and hell and last day spreading in, 204-205.
Rosicrucians, propagate Indian origin of Christianity, 102.
Roy, M.N., on blessings brought by Islamic conquest to India, 42-43 and 43n; Marxism converges completely with Imperialism in works of, 43-44.
Rumi, does not represent mainstreme Sufism, 148.

Saiva Siddhanta Church, offers more than selected or edited ideas of Hinduism, 125-126.
Sāmkhya, 68, 74-75, 76, 78.
Sampradāya, vow of a Hindu when joining a particular, 38.
Sanatana dharma, has a spiritual anthropology different from anthropology based on psycho-physical definition of man, 2; anthrosophy (*ātma-vāda*) of, 3; teaches that truth triumphs, 3; worships Gods under many symbols, 3-4; conception of God in, 5-6; preaches neither exclusive gods nor exclusive prophets, 6; cannot become a proxy religion, 6-7; teaches purification of mind, 7; believes man to be spiritual and moral in essence, 8, 12; *daṇḍa-nīti* held in high esteem by, 9; all orders of beings included in the definition of neighbour by, 10, 20; sees Gods in animals, 10-11, elements (of Nature) cherished by, 11; larger view of man taught by, 11-12; makes allowance for different capacities, talents, starting points and needs (of *sādhakas*), 12; meaning of true conversion in, 13; many lives and planes of existence in, 13-14; also teaches *moksha*, 14-15; lot of thinking on life and death in, 15; views of modern thought about world, man, and his conduct rejected by, 18-19; egocentricity of modern Europe rejected by, 19-20; is a universal religion, 20-21; relates one's world to one's consciousness, 21-22, was known in many lands under many names, 22; is a Great Refuge which protects those who protect it, 22-23; well explained and confirmed in their lives by a succession of great sages, 36; represents the soul of India according to Sri Aurobindo and Vivekananda, 45; not a one-book one-prophet religion but repository of spiritual knowledge of countless sages and seers, 88; old name for Hinduism, 89. See also Hinduism.
Sanskrit, modern Europe linked to old Greece by discovery of, 97; basic concepts of linguistics and

history revolutionised by discovery of, 104; German Oriental Renaissance erected on foundation of, 105.
Sanskrit roots, "Indo-European roots" invented in place of, 108-109.
Sasseti, F., relation between Sanskrit and Europe's classical languages seen in second half of sixteenth century by, 104.
Satellite Ideology, developed by intellectual comparadores of dominant imperialist ideology, 41-43.
Saviours and Mediators, ideologies of one life, one judgement, hell and heaven encourage the cult of, 16.
Schelling, thoughts about India of, 92; acclaimed Indian culture with ecstasy, 105; looked upon India with respect and admiration, 110.
Schillar, acclaimed Indian culture with ecstasy, 105.
Schlegle, F., saw India as source of everything without exception, 103, acclaimed Indian culture with ecstasy, 105.
Schleismacher, acclaimed Indian culture with ecstasy, 105.
Schweitzer, Albert, finds no good in the universe yet asks man to be good by self-will, 135n.
Schaupenhauer, 92; not disappointed by India in his search for a philosophy which is at once metaphysics and ethics, 101; deeply moved by reading translations of the Upanishads, 104; introduced Indian culture to Tolstoy and Wagner, 105; on "confused empty verbiage" of Hegel about India, 109; looked upon India with respect and admiration, 111; finds solace in translations of Hindu Sanskrit texts, 125.
Self-Alienation, 32-35; caused by foreign rule, 32-33; leads to loss of millions of members of Hindu society, 34; cultural surrender gives rise to politics of, 37; forces which sustain politics of, 41-47; increasing forces of, 49.
Semitic personal God, ordains meat-eating and violence towards fellow human beings by Jews, Christians, and Muslims, 154.
Semitic prophets, popular among Hindus as their own, 112.
Semitic religions, traditional Indian categories used by Neo-Hinduism to promote, 112; poor understanding of man and divinity in, 157-158.
Shudras, did better than upper castes in matters of female education under indigenous educational system, 184; indigenous educational institutions had high percentage of, 188-189.
Siam, see Thailand.
Student movement today, dissipation and deterioration in, 174.

Tagore, Rabindra Nath, poet of the soul's Godward aspiration, 89-90.
Taj at Agra, disappointed Alduons Huxley, 161; Huxley refused to revise his opinion after a second visit to, 161n.
Tamil Nadu, old account of a school in, 172.
Taoism, at a disadvantage vis-a-vis Christianity and Islam, 50.
Taoist landscape painters, first to concern themselves with significance of Nature, 157.

Taxila, drew students from all over India, 172.
Thailand (Siam), Buddhist monasteries provided location for schools of, 174; much of old India found in, 178.
Thapar, Romila, Hindu by accident of birth but anti-Hindu by freely chosen role, 44.
Theologies, undeveloped, have been great source of imperialist wars, domination and oppression, 8.
Theory of Aryan invasion, see Aryan invasion theory.
Theosophy, propagated Indian origin of Christianity, 102; Indian influence became popular through, 125.
Thieme, P., contradictions in tracing the tradition of Indian xenology by, 116n-117n.
Thomas, Apostle, myth of visit to India by, 114.
Thompson, Edward, on widespread literacy through self-education in Bengal in 1930s, 184-185.
Thoreau, translations of Hindu Sanskrit texts won admiration of, 125.
Tibet, India's learning preserved by, 178.
Tieck, acclaimed Indian culture with ecstasy, 105.
time-philosophies, Judaism, Christianity and Nazism are, 153-154.
Tolerance, quite new concept in Christian-Western vocabulary, 118, 119-120; called "inclusivism" by Paul Hacker and "inclusivism" paraphrased as "non-violent fanaticism" by H. Von Glasenapp, 119; discussed by Halbfass as a modern European idea inapplicable to traditional Hinduism, 119.
Tolstoy, most striking among those who sought cure for European spirit in India, 105; translations of Hindu Sanskrit texts won admiration of, 125.
Toynbee, translations of Hindu Sanskrit texts won admiration of, 125.
Transcendental Experience, Ineffability of, 66-68.
Transcendental Meditation (TM), hundreds of thousands in the West visit camps of, 125.
tribals, many Rajput gotras found among, 30.

unassimilable identities, Indian society faces problem of, 48.
unity of all religions, spiritual infirmity of Hindu mind, 148n-149n.
Universality, 20-21, not found in tribal god of a particular *ummah*, 20.
Upanishads, 49, 64, 66, 67, 68, 69, 70, 71-72-73, 76, 82, 84, 85, 87, 132, 138, 144, 15n, 168, 170, 197; offering obeisance to, 22; seen by Schopenhauer as documents of "almost superhuman conception", 104.

Vanavasis and Harijans, mischievous elements are active among, 57.
Varṇa-aśrama Dharma (Hindu social system), 26-27; very different from caste-system, 26; knew no slavery or serfdom or imperialism or feudalism, 27.
Vatican, the, Catholics have their World-Centre in, 51.
Vedānta, 67, 68, 69, 70, 74, 82, 83-84; leaves an impression of joy and freedom, 84; Ramayana and

Mahabharata give us life-creations of, 165.
Vedic India, many Gods shared with Iran by, 196.
Vedic seers, concentrate on Atmic truth, 2 3.
Vegetarian Diet, high place in Indian spirituality found by, 154.
Vegetarianism, practical expression of *jīva-dayā* in Hinduism, 11.
Vivekananda (Swami), saw an incomparable truth in Hinduism, 38, 43.
Voltaire, thoughts about India of, 92; saw India as home of all religions, 101-102; looked upon India with respect and admiration, 111.
Von Glasenapp, "inclusivism" of Hinduism paraphrased as "non-violent fanaticism" by, 119.

Wagner, Indian culture introduced to, 105.
Walker, Brigadier-General Alexander, on importance attached to education by Hindus, 179; Shudras found in possession of principal authority and prosperity in India by, 180; said "new system of schooling" in England borrowed from India, 183n.
Ward, on indigenous institutions of higher learning in Calcutta, 185.
Weithrecht, H.U., held foreign invaders as India's main contact with outer world, 113.
West, concentrates its archaeological labours on Palestine as first site of civilization, 22; India placed on lofty pedestal by entire Romantic movement in, 105-106; elitist forces in India have intimate intellectual, organizational and financial links with, 111; can learn from Hindu-Buddhist culture in its spiritual crisis, 123; new awareness of spiritual wealth of non-European and non-Christian cultures in, 124; deeper Indian concepts very much current in religious thinking of, 124; Bible reading by commoners prohibited and punished for many centuries in, 187; movement of ideas from East to, 196.
West to East, movement of men and ideas from, 196.
Western art tradition, simplistic portrayal of Jesus or Pope as God the Creator in, 158.
Western-Christian horizon, inability to rise above, 119-120.
Western critics, Hindu art has been incomprehensible to, 155.
Western imperialism, many parts of the world destroyed economically and culturally by, 90.
Western intellectuals, Indian influence on the West remains unacknowledged and unnamed by, 117-118.
Western schools and colleges, emptiness and revolt of modern youth in, 167; degenerating into sanctuaries of all kinds of excesses, 171; atmosphere of learning declining in, 171.
Whitman, Walt, translations of Hindu Sanskrit texts won admiration of, 125.
Wilkins, Indian texts translated by, 103.
Wilson, H.H., on objects of Indian studies, 106-107.
women, in Hindu dharma, 31.
World-Centres of totalitarian forces, work through local plans, 51-52.

World Council of Churches, Protestants have a World-Centre in, 51.

Xavier, Francis, wanted to be where there were no Muslims or Jews, 46; advocated destruction of Brahmins, 99; looked for out and out pagans after having failed to convert Muslims, 117n.
Xenology, India misses European fancy for, 115; Orientalists ignore language used by European, 116n-117n.

Yeats (W.B.), translations of Hindu Sanskrit texts won admiration of, 125.
Yoga, 68; Pātañjala, 78; utter stupefaction and insensibility according to Hegel, 110; teaches practical method of going within and exploring larger life and worlds, 167; not suppression of life and mind and body but expression of the higher self true aim of, 167-168.
Yogic Gods, true spiritual transcendence and immanence belong only to, 3.

Ziegenbalg, B., says Hindus lost their original monotheism when seduced by devil, 99-100.
Zimmer, Henrich, translations of Hindu Sanskrit texts won admiration of, 125.